Praise for GAME CHANGER

"For over 50 years, Harold Hamm has been in the middle of America's energy story. His journey is, in a word, 'unconventional.' The thirteenth child of an Oklahoma sharecropper, Hamm permanently altered the energy world by embracing Horizontal Drilling and propelling the U.S. shale revolution. He helped take his country from energy scarcity to energy abundance and turned us into a global energy superpower.

"He has advised presidents, heads of state, policymakers, politicians, and the so-called energy experts whose decisions impact our daily lives. Hamm is unsparing in his critiques of energy policy here and across the globe. Now he wants to share his journey—and what a sensible energy future looks like—with everyone who cares about our shared future."

—MIKE ROWE, *TV Host,*
Writer, and Spokesman

"Nothing changes the global game as much as oil and natural gas. There's no one better than Harold to tell the story and offer real solutions."

—MIKE POMPEO, *70th U.S.*
Secretary of State

"I'm a huge fan of Harold and I have witnessed up close his leadership, not just in the industry, but in helping to shape better energy policy to increase America's security."

—STEVE SCALISE, *Majority Leader of*
the U.S. House of Representatives

"With ingenuity, determination, and pure grit, Harold Hamm's risk-taking and entrepreneurship transformed America's energy landscape and made possible U.S. energy security and independence. From pioneering the Horizontal Drilling revolution that unlocked vast shale oil reserves in North Dakota and beyond, to leading the charge to lift America's forty-year-old ban on crude exports, Harold's global impact has been immeasurable and is an inspiring story worthy of sharing."

—GOVERNOR DOUG BURGUM, *North Dakota*

"Harold Hamm personifies the true heroic entrepreneur. He solved America's dependence on the fuel of other countries, creating our energy independence through innovation that revolutionized energy production in our country. Harold's book is an inspiration for every hopeful innovator."

— CHARLES SCHWAB, *Founder and CEO,*
The Charles Schwab Corporation

"Harold Hamm's story is one of fortitude, against all odds. From his humble Oklahoma roots to his ability to go to Washington and lift the export ban on American crude, Harold has lived his life with purpose. His commitment to pioneering Horizontal Drilling has impacted all of our lives for the better."

—BARRY SWITZER, *Former Head Coach*
of the University of Oklahoma
Sooners and the Dallas Cowboys

" 'Played out'; that's what 'they' said about the oil fields in North Dakota. 'Opportunity of a lifetime' is what Harold Hamm envisioned. A sharecropper's son. A self-made American original. Harold Hamm has led the country to energy independence. And does he have a story to tell."

—HARRY SMITH, *Award-winning*
NBC News Correspondent

"The tale of how Harold Hamm mobilized innovation and marched it into battle to secure American energy independence is inspiring and historic – a story of world-changing impact that deserves to be told as an inspiration for generations to come. However, it's Harold's capacity for quiet encouragement, and his commitment to supporting leaders behind the scenes, that I find so compelling. The things Harold touches become better — and that's certainly true for Oklahoma State University. But I'm personally a better leader because of Harold's influence and vision."

—DR. KAYSE SHRUM, *President,*
Oklahoma State University

"Harold Hamm's contribution to society is arguably one of the most significant of our lifetimes. One would be hard pressed to find someone who has had a greater impact on mankind's quality of life anywhere else in the world. Through tenacity, perseverance, passion, hard work, and raw talent, Harold envisioned and commercialized horizontal drilling in previously inaccessible tight oil reservoirs. Experts educated in petroleum engineering and energy executives like me were taught that what he was trying to accomplish was impossible. Fortunately, Harold didn't read those books.

"This technological feat enabled American energy independence and a benefit of a trillion dollars per year to consumers around the world through lower oil prices. Without the shale revolution that Harold started, consumers would have to pay over one trillion dollars more every year just for energy. How did he do it and what did this accomplish? Read his book and find out. It's a delightfully entertaining book (a Horatio Alger-type tale) about the shale revolution's contribution to global security and quality of life of every single person on the planet. His writing style is so genuine and entertaining that you feel as if you're having a fireside chat with Harold. Full of wit, stories, and humility. Enjoy."

—**BILL BERRY,** *Former CEO,*
Continental Resources

(Something Better)

Oil

By Harold Hamm

Little did I know as a young boy, I was setting forth my life's destiny in a high school paper I titled "Oil (Something Better)." That journey unfolded over a lifetime that you'll discover through the pages of this book.

GAME CHANGER

GAME CHANGER

Our 50-Year Mission to Secure
America's Energy Independence

America's Oil and Gas Champion
Harold Hamm

Foreword by Mike Pompeo

Forefront
BOOKS

Game Changer: Our 50-Year Mission to Secure America's Energy Independence

Copyright © 2023 by Harold Hamm

Published by Forefront Books.
Distributed by Simon & Schuster.

Library of Congress Control Number: 2023907082

Print ISBN: 978-1-63763-185-0
E-book ISBN: 978-1-63763-186-7

Cover Design by Bruce Gore, Gore Studio, Inc.
Interior Design by Bill Kersey, KerseyGraphics

Dedication

AS USUAL, THE WORLD SEEMS TO BE LONG ON DEMAND AND short on credit.

I would like to dedicate this book to the people who deserve the credit, the same people to whom I have dedicated my life: the thousands of hardworking folks who keep our lights on and our country moving. Every day, they do the jobs many take for granted. They are the tool pushers, roughnecks and roustabouts on drilling rigs, pumpers, welders, truck drivers, heavy equipment operators, field geologists, and engineers. These are the men and women, thousands strong, who are on the front lines of Continental Resources, the company I founded, and all the other companies driving America's Energy Renaissance, serving our country 24/7.

You'll find them producing American energy on the frozen plains of North Dakota and the searing-hot prairies of Oklahoma. We owe them so much. This is their story as much as it is mine. Because without them, without their skills and commitment, our modern life would not be possible. The next time you flip your bedroom light switch, push to turn the ignition key of your car, or board an airplane on the way to visit Grandma, remember America's energy workers made it possible.

Thank them for making American energy abundant, affordable, and—most importantly—reliable. Thank them for showing up and doing their jobs more responsibly than anyone in the world. They deserve your undying admiration and respect. They have mine.

I have done my best to work side by side with them and to help advocate for them, to represent them and their work ethic, and to celebrate the many benefits of the oil and gas we produce for people around the world.

And we are just getting started. We are working to inspire the next generation of energy leaders who will continue to meet the growing energy demand around the world from America's abundant natural resources.

Finally, to my children and my grandchildren—who are the ultimate delight in my life—I am proud of who you are and who you are still becoming.

To Deana, I will always admire your creativity and your kindness. As the oldest, you have set the standard for being a mother, daughter, and friend. You've put up with me the longest.

To Shelly, I'm so proud of the interest you've taken in the company and industry. You are the pulse keeper of our culture, and your contributions have earned you the recognition as one of the 25 Influential Women in Energy. You have a heart of gold.

To Tom, my only son, you're a better man than I ever was or will be. I am proud of the person you are today.

To Jane, I admire the empathy you have for others and your drive to be an advocate for those without a voice. You have found your passion in criminal justice reform, and I take great pride in watching you lead the way in this arena.

To Hilary, you're a world changer. You're an independent thinker and always looking out for other people. I've enjoyed working together on the important progress we're making at the Hamm Institute for American Energy.

Contents

Foreword

By the Honorable Mike Pompeo, Seventieth Secretary
of State of the United States of America

A NATION'S POWER CAN BE MEASURED IN MANY DIFFERENT
ways. One can measure the size of its population or the
manpower of its army; count the number of guns, missiles, and
tanks it has at its disposal; measure its total gross domestic
product; or quantify its cultural impact on the world.

All these paint convincing pictures, but there is only one
resource that runs through all of them: energy. Without energy,
a nation's economy cannot be powered onward. Tanks and
missiles prove powerful tools, but you must have the energy
to develop and produce them and the energy resources to fuel
them. Even culture cannot be broadcast around the world
without the required energy to do so at home. Everything in our
world today—*everything*—runs through energy. Nations that
are reliant on foreign producers for their domestic energy needs
are thus put at high risk of being forced to show deference to

their suppliers in other matters of policy. Nations that are energy independent, in turn, are masters of their destiny.

This is a book about America's energy story and one man, Harold Hamm, who has been at the center of it for over fifty years. Throughout his career, Hamm has been the innovative, bold, tough, and unconventional visionary who, more than any other individual, has charted America's path toward energy independence and historic prosperity.

Harold Hamm is the embodiment of the American dream. Born to humble beginnings in Oklahoma, Harold changed the energy world forever by embracing Horizontal Drilling and, in doing so, propelled the U.S. shale revolution. He helped take America from energy scarcity to energy abundance. His personal energy, creativity, and willingness to challenge conventional wisdom have changed the world.

I saw this firsthand when I was leading a Wichita, Kansas–based energy equipment company. But I did not meet Harold until I reentered public service as a congressman from south central Kansas. My engagement with him was based on the truth that America needed greater abundance of affordable energy, not less, and that we—the United States—had the ability to deliver it from within, making America not only more secure and more prosperous but also more risk-averse to its environment and that of the entire world.

This shift in American energy was most visible during the Trump administration, when, thanks in part to Harold's wisdom and guidance, America became energy independent. Gone were the days when U.S. leaders were forced to approach oil cartels in the Middle East with hat in hand or watch helplessly while Russia used its energy supply to hold European nations hostage to its whims. America was instead a global energy superpower on which our allies could depend for their energy needs and whose energy abundance gave us much-needed leverage over our adversaries. Harold Hamm's work driving the adoption of Horizontal Drilling and his counsel to America's leaders were vital in effecting this seismic change.

As Secretary of State, I came to trust Harold both as an experienced and invaluable adviser on energy matters and as a friend. Energy was a vital part of our diplomatic work, and Harold's wisdom helped us achieve truly historic outcomes for the American people.

On February 1, 2020, I traveled to the Republic of Belarus and met with its president, Victor Lukashenko. Belarus was in a bit of an oil spat with its patron, Russian President Vladimir Putin. So at a press conference with Belarusian Foreign Minister Vladimir Makei, I said, "We're the biggest energy producer in the world, and all you have to do is call us." This was the first American administration in decades in which the Secretary of State could say that. Those words had consequences. This was possible only because of people like Harold Hamm.

This is not only a book about history, though. It is a book about America's future. The energy independence achieved under the Trump administration was done away with by those who followed us. This happened because the objectives of too many policymakers today no longer revolve around the prosperity of the American people; rather, they sacrifice American prosperity in pursuit of vague, lofty, and ever-changing goals related to climate change and green energy. That is why I hope readers will appreciate Harold's exceptional life and understand the truth that lies at the center of it. As we look toward the future, understanding the true advantage that American oil and natural gas provide is essential to our economic well-being and national security.

Nothing changes the global game as much as oil and natural gas. There's no one better than Harold to tell this story and offer real solutions.

A Note about Research

YOU'LL READ PLENTY OF MY OPINIONS AND RECOMMENDA-tions in these pages, but this book is rooted in science and history. I believe facts, documentation, and objective numbers are necessary to create a strategy for any endeavor. You can see a complete list of research cited at the end of this book.

Introduction

I KNOW THAT PEOPLE DO, IN FACT, JUDGE BOOKS BY their covers, and some will assume this is a political book. So be it. But this is also a personal book. It's impossible to be in this business for decades, making it a passion, and not wind up in the political arena. Where there are laws and regulations, there will be politics. The oil and natural gas sector is not a mess; it's our nation's policies that have been and continue to be a mess. Human history has always been about *power*—some people search for energy to power our lives, while others are searching for political power to control our lives.

Whether or not your elected officials and their appointees care about how energy affects your future, I hope *you* care. I wrote this book for you.

Why is oil and natural gas such a big deal? Because the modern world runs on the stuff and so does *your* world. You might not be as interested in the industry as I am, but we all should pay close attention to energy-related policy decisions. They impact our finances and our future as well as our national security.

The current "energy crisis" is unnecessary and self-inflicted, and so was every other so-called energy crisis of the past century.

In these pages, you'll discover how we got in this situation—the good and the bad—and I'll present proven solutions for every challenge ahead.

"Dire" Predictions

Petroleum has been used for less than 50 years, and it is estimated that the supply will last about 25 or 30 years longer.

— July 19, 1909, *Titusville Herald,* Titusville, Pennsylvania

Starting as early as 1909 and continuing to today, many of the narratives from a cast of dubious characters—from Jimmy Carter to Al Gore to Alexandria Ocasio-Cortez (AOC) to Joe Biden to Gavin Newsom—have predicted dire, cataclysmic consequences for humankind related to fossil fuels. These are from "respected" news sources, scientists, and government agencies from the past century. Time and again, they have been proven wrong. If we believed everything we were told by the so-called experts, we'd be living in a constant state of "FUD"—fear, uncertainty, and doubt. There's just no good reason to use untrue, doomsday predictions to frighten the public, other than to drive someone's personal or political agendas.

Take Al Gore, for example. In 2006, he told Katie Couric in an interview on NBC's *TODAY* show that Manhattan would be underwater within decades if nothing changed. In 2009, he warned that scientists believed the Arctic could be "completely ice-free" during the summer within five to seven years.

Obviously, Mr. Gore's predictions were wrong, and one can only guess his motivations. Did he wish to further his speaking engagements, book sales, or Academy Award–winning documentary? I don't know, but the inconvenient truth is that he is still flying around the world using jet fuel.

And then there is AOC. In 2019, she predicted the world would end in twelve years.

For a few chuckles, you might enjoy Myron Ebell's article with Steven Molloy titled "Wrong Again: Fifty Years of Failed Eco-Pocalyptic Predictions" highlighting the ice ages, cooling catastrophes, and other events that never materialized.

The reason we've enjoyed such a great quality of life in America is because of affordable, abundant energy. For people who believe oil and natural gas producers don't care about our environment, I look forward to proving them wrong. I've been in the business for over five decades and have been concerned enough to take positive actions to counter our industry's environmental and social impact each and every day. Producing more energy with less impact is a key driver for my company and me.

America can return to and maintain energy independence. We can replace today's artificial energy scarcity with abundance. We can make energy more affordable for hardworking Americans—and for people all around the world.

To this day, I still see these possibilities and think, *Wow. This is what I was meant to do.*

The Greatest Story Never Told

There are so many myths—which is a nicer word than *lies*—about the oil and natural gas industry. There are those who have inflicted narrative damage intentionally on us. One example is the way in which folks refer to the renewal or renaissance in American oil and gas exploration. They've labeled it *fracking*. They're either demonstrating their ignorance of drilling and how this all came about, or they're intentionally disparaging it. You'll be surprised—and even shocked—by many of the facts I document in these pages. This is the first book to tell the true story of Horizontal Drilling and the American Energy Renaissance. It's long overdue.

While it's easy to gripe and complain about the detractors of our industry and the millions (if not billions) being spent against us, I believe we must put our focus on reversing that damage and changing the narrative for the better. I have always said that this is one of the most powerful industries in existence—particularly when we come together to solve a problem. I saw firsthand an example of this occurring just recently as I had the opportunity to attend a joint trades summit where I gave a short presentation. This is a group of trade associations and companies from across the country that represent the oil and gas industry. I shared with them that the facts are on our side and that we can repair the harm that has been done against us. It's not about a story for story's sake but about the fact that what we are doing is good for the world. If everyone pulls on the same rope, we can't help but correct this narrative.

I am reminded of something Billy Graham said once: "Courage is contagious. When a brave man takes a stand, the spines of others are often stiffened."

I chose to do that fifteen years ago, and while I may have gotten some barbs in my back, has it helped? Absolutely. I've seen a lot of people standing up for this industry, willing to tell the good stories about American energy. They are plentiful. Telling those stories is just as important as drilling the wells.

There has been consolidation in the industry. We are down to the real players. They want to make a difference and are in it for the long haul. And they're in it for the right reasons.

I may be just an optimistic geologist, but this is what I believe. I believe we can be successful in changing the narrative by working together.

CHAPTER 1

Opportunity

" *Opportunity is missed by most people because it is dressed in overalls and looks like work."*

—THOMAS EDISON

I'LL NEVER FORGET IT. IT WAS MAY 2007. I WAS WITH MY executive team in Portland, Oregon. We were nearing the end of a grueling, two-week cross-country investor road show for the initial public offering (IPO) that would take Continental Resources public. Our eyes were on a *huge* opportunity—the Bakken. From coast to coast, we were meeting with potential investors, sharing our plans to develop the Bakken resources of North Dakota into the largest U.S. oil discovery of the twenty-first century; at least that's what I thought. Our team's job was to convince Wall Street.

We had already enjoyed great success in the Montana Bakken, but I knew there was something even more special about what remained to be found in North Dakota. We had drilled a few successful wells there and knew we were very close to cracking the code to make the North Dakota Bakken produce commercially on a very large scale. It hadn't been as cooperative up to this point as I would've liked, but I knew it had a great amount of potential. A successful IPO could provide the needed capital to allow our company to make it work.

Going public was a monumental decision for me. I knew I would miss the freedom of being private that I had enjoyed for the past forty years. But I knew this was for the greater good —of my family, the company, the industry, and even our country—if we could break the code on this huge resource.

As we were about to round out the West Coast swing of our national road show, news broke that St. Mary Land & Exploration Company (now SM Energy) had a well on the western side of the Nesson Anticline in the Bakken that didn't work. Three days later, Bill Barrett Corporation had another well nearby that also failed to produce in commercial quantities. Bill Barrett was a very well-respected and credible explorationist. These results cast a pall on our prospects for a positive IPO. Much of the acreage we owned lay west of the Nesson Anticline.

The news and its timing were a gut punch, to say the least. Here you have a bunch of optimistic oil and gas producers from Oklahoma pitching our next great discovery, only to have two well-respected companies publicly saying their well results had failed.

When Barrett suddenly didn't believe in the Bakken, the investors on our road show didn't either. So instead of our stock pricing at the top of our expected range above $17, we ended up at the bottom at $15, netting us only $14.10 after fees. That was about a $100 million difference, which was a huge swing for us at the time.

I gathered our team and financial advisers in a meeting room at our hotel in Portland to discuss and hear one another's thoughts and perspectives. Should we take the IPO funds or remain private?

I listened intently and then recall stepping away from the group to do some soul-searching of my own. We had poured so much time, money, and expertise into seeing this through up to this point. We needed the additional funds to hold the leases we currently had, buy additional leases we needed, and fund the drilling and development of the Bakken. This was a highly competitive game and we wanted to keep our advantage. We were out of time—it was go or no go.

I had an enormous decision to make. It remains vividly clear in my memory to this day.

I returned to the others in the group with my mind made up: let's get to work and unlock the Bakken.

Having come to this decision, I thought to myself, *Was I the unluckiest guy in the world to have this news break at this particular time, or would this decision pay off as I had hoped?*

Lucky 13

I've been lucky in my life. As a youngster, I was lucky to have my family. Lucky thirteen to be exact. Being the youngest child of the brood, I had a dozen siblings. My six sisters loved me and helped take care of me. It was almost like having six additional moms. I needed them all while growing up.

My dad was a tenant farmer. He didn't even own the land where we lived. Every autumn, our family would pile into the back of our pickup truck and drive to West Texas to pull cotton to make extra money. The whole family participated. I was five years old picking cotton bolls and piling them up in the middle of the row for my dad to swoop up into the cotton sack. We were paid by weight—a whopping two cents per pound. Have you ever thought about how many fluffy bolls of cotton you'd have to pick to bag one pound? I sure have. My back still aches when I think of it. The more we bagged and loaded on trucks or trailers, the more money my family would have come winter.

No, I wasn't born two hundred years ago. But in mid-twentieth century rural Oklahoma, most farms in the region were not mechanized so human power was often employed. Our cotton-pickin' jobs would end around Christmastime or when the first snow fell. That was the signal to return to school. Since my brothers, sisters, and I had to forgo school for most of the fall to help support our family, I always started the school year a little behind my fellow students when it came to the curriculum. I had a burning desire to learn, and I wanted to be first in the class (and never last), so I always managed to quickly catch up. By my teens, I realized I had no idea what specifically I was interested in learning—until a school assembly in 1963 when I was seventeen years old.

Never Work?

I was lucky that a potter showed up at my school. Our guest speaker that morning was John Frank, the successful founder of Frankoma Pottery. I learned that Mr. Frank taught pottery and art at the University of Oklahoma while also working with the geological survey that discovered Oklahoma's rich deposits of clay.

I didn't care about pottery or art, and I was fighting sleep deprivation. But John awakened something in me that day. On the stage at his potter's wheel, he transformed an ugly lump of clay into a beautiful object; then he casually knocked it back down and created a new one. But it was his message that captivated me most.

He beamed as he shared how much he loved his craft and the business he'd built. "Life is better when you have a passion. Find yours and learn all you can," he said with a smile. "If you enjoy your profession, you'll never work a day in your life."

I'd never heard anything like those words and never imagined that work could be that much fun. His challenge hit me like a ton of bricks: "You need to figure out right now what you have a passion for and go for it!"

That sounded amazing. And impossible. Later that day at the truck stop where I worked, I wondered, *What the hell am I passionate about? I'm just trying to get through school each week, and all the while pumping gas and fixing flats at work!* I started paying more attention to my community of Enid, Oklahoma, and to what—and who—sparked my interest.

I was lucky there was an oil boom happening around Enid. And somewhat different than the people I had grown up with in Lexington, the folks in the oil business seemed larger than life—optimistic, charismatic, and generous. After hearing Mr. Frank's challenge, all that new excitement suddenly appealed to me. And it didn't hurt that all those oil guys were making dang good money.

Coincidentally, a school project was assigned by my distributive education (DE) class instructor that same month, requiring us to write a paper about any business or career we found interesting. I chose the topic of oil. It must have been destiny. (I've always considered my DE instructor, Jewel Ridge, to be an inspiration. In addition to being a veteran, he was one of the developers of Oklahoma's vocational technology educational system, known as "vo-tech," the best of its kind in the country.)

I began by researching the petroleum industry and its early pioneers in the field such as Sinclair, Getty, Phillips, and Skelly. Their stories, personalities, and legacies were so fascinating that

I surprised myself and thought, *Wow. That's what I want to do.* I began to imagine myself as an oil and gas explorer—a person who could unlock ancient wealth and find hidden value where no one else could. I started to see myself as one of those "wildcatters" of the early oil boom in Oklahoma—the brash explorationists who changed the world for the better and gave away huge parts of their fortunes to charity. I not only decided to be in the business for myself, I also wanted to be, like them, a leader and steward of the industry.

My paper bore the straightforward title of "Oil (Something Better)." To say this endeavor was a turning point for me would be an understatement. Little did I know, I was setting forth my life's destiny in a high school paper. Here is an excerpt from the paper I wrote over sixty years ago as a junior in high school. It is still helpful today, if I do say so myself, as a primer on the history of the oil industry:

Excerpt from My High School Term Paper, "Oil (Something Better)"

Oil is the decayed remains of prehistoric creatures that has changed form through time, pressure, heat, and other extreme conditions. The magic of oil was probably discovered thousands of years ago. Ancient Greeks used it as a preservative in mummification. Roman charioteers used it to make the wheels of the chariot roll easier. The Romans contributed its name petroleum, petro *meaning "rock" and* oleum *meaning "oil."*

For years people in the U.S. called petroleum "rock oil" since it was found in shale rock. Oil was prized in early times for medicinal purposes. Even drugstores have sold bottled oil. Indians skimmed oil from the water of certain springs and used to treat their ailments. Until the middle 1800s, however, very few people wanted or needed oil. It was a nuisance to the salt makers because it polluted the salt deposits.

The first need for oil was to light homes and lubricate machines. With the scarcity of whale oil, something needed to fill its place. People found that Indian medicine, when purified, would burn in a lamp, giving off a much brighter light than whale oil. Besides this fact, it was also cheaper. It was also found that when crude oil was separated, a part of the oil was very heavy and slick. This would make an excellent lubricant for the new machines. Before long, promoters began to lease lands with oil springs on them. The first method of collecting oil was by skimming. This was done by running the water of oil producing springs through wooden troughs lined with baffles. This method was slow and expensive.

The Pennsylvania Rock Oil Co. of New Haven, Connecticut, began to look for a more successful way to secure oil. They hired Edwin L. Drake to go down to Titusville, Pennsylvania, to inspect operations and find a way to increase production. He knew nothing of the oil business. He was an intelligent man who liked to solve problems. Drake soon realized that the current method must be replaced by something faster and more efficient. He knew that oil had been found in salt wells, so he decided to dig a well in search of oil.

Amid the jeers of bystanders, he organized a crew of well diggers and set them to digging. Soon, after they had dug about fifteen feet, a sticky black pool began to form in one corner of the hole. Oil had been discovered. Drake's well might have been highly successful, if a rock hadn't been dislodged and the well flooded with water. Drake then tried the newest method of salt drilling, which was by using a drill screw on a length of steel pipe. Operations went well until the hole was flooded with water again. Drake solved this problem by using a length of pipe that he set into the hole to serve as a casing. Mud was bailed out by men. This was the first form of casing in an oil well.

Drilling on this well had begun in the early months of 1859. On August 29, 1859, oil was struck at 69 feet. Soon the oil boom had been spread, and production rose from 200 barrels in 1859 to 3,057,000 in 1862.

Of course, the bottom fell out of the market. Transportation was the first problem to arise in the new industry. With the drop in the market, there was a great need for cheap transportation to the cities and towns. Skinners transported the oil to Oil Creek, where it was sent down the Ohio River in barges. The skinners, who were a ruthless lot, demanded high freight prices, and the trip down the river was very risky. Pipelines were the answer to this first problem. The pipelines and teamsters became natural enemies and many battles resulted.

Railroads were then built to help distribute the black gold. Soon the teamsters and barges were things of the past. Sam Kier, a medicine-oil peddler, decided that his product would sell better if it was purified. He got a whisky still with a tight lid and began to boil a batch of petroleum. His neighbors protested against the horrid smell, so he decided to move his still out of town. He used a bigger still and a hotter fire. After the gas escaped, a pale liquid began to drip from the spout. He had discovered kerosene, the first product to be unlocked from crude oil.

Refineries sprang up everywhere. A boom had started in the business. The new by-product of crude oil gave off a bright light in lamps. The demand for the new product was great. The only drawback in the new discovery was that sometimes kerosene would explode very easily. People disregarded this hazard and bought the kerosene anyway.

> *This discovery was very important to the social life of the public. Instead of going to bed shortly after dark, people could now enjoy a full social life or take care of business matters with plenty of light. Chemists and oil technicians have constantly been working to find new uses for oil, different products, and a more efficient way to process oil. Gasoline, the product that caused kerosene to explode, was the greatest of all. With this important discovery came a new way of life for the people of the world. New discoveries have ranged from a better type of lubricant for machines to the making of petrochemicals such as plastic and medicine.*

Hopefully I've improved as a writer—and I certainly have as an oilman. The idea of oil exploration was exciting to me as a young man, and it still is. With all due respect to Mr. John Frank, the potter who first challenged me to find a career I loved, I've worked many long days in my life, but I've sure enjoyed it.

Thinking Deeper

When I decided to write this book, my challenge was where to start. I'd accumulated a few dozen cardboard boxes of papers, files full of newspaper clippings, hundreds of articles that seemed important at the time, and rooms full of books, plaques, photos, and the mementos one tends to collect over a successful career. Next to a photo of me with former Israeli Prime Minister Benjamin Netanyahu was a framed tie with little *H*'s all over it. Khalid A. Al-Falih gave me that tie when he was Saudi Arabia's energy minister—symbolic of the geopolitical journey one can take in the oil and gas business.

I had my team cover the walls of our conference room with papers, pictures, memorabilia, and a timeline that measured approximately thirty feet long by eight feet high. Maybe everyone should consider building their own timelines in their garage, attic, or basement because it forces us to remember and rethink what we've lived through. In my case, the process triggered a few epiphanies.

First was the fact that nearly every energy-policy decision in this country was driven by the fear of scarcity. Beginning in the 1950s, the "experts" predicted an America that would run out of oil and natural gas. The only disagreement was how soon.

Second, over the past several decades, people (who were seeking to gain the market share it enjoyed) cast the oil and gas sector as the enemy and the cause for nearly all of earth's ills, past, present, and future. And as a bonus, those employed in this industry were also labeled as enemies.

Third, bad energy policy led to bad laws, regulations, and decisions that you and I are still living with today. Bad energy policy is bad for you, bad for the economy, and bad for the environment. There's a better way.

None of these obstacles was evident when I started Harold Hamm Truck Service back in 1966 as my on-ramp to the oil and gas industry. At that point in my life, my big dream came with a big question: *Could I afford the monthly truck payment and make it in the industry I'd fallen in love with?*

CHAPTER 2

Trucking and Trusting

I APPRECIATE TRUCK DRIVERS. HOW ABOUT YOU? I HAVE A deep understanding of how they drive our economy. Literally. And despite what some may assume, I take no pleasure in the fact that over the past few years, truckers paid record-high prices for diesel—the remaining primary driver for inflation today, as all goods require transport. This will continue as long as our government restricts oil and gas exploration and production. It's all so unnecessary, and it hurts not only drivers and their companies but also every American family.

Another reason I appreciate truck drivers is because I began my career as one. I put a million miles on my truck before I could afford to step out and risk everything on oil and gas exploration.

In 1964, my first job after high school was driving for Johnny Geer Tank Truck in Enid, Oklahoma, which was a small company with only three trucks when I was hired. I started out at the bottom of the oil and gas industry, cleaning the sludge out of oilfield stock tanks. I've always said the only direction you can go from there is up.

We soon found ourselves hurting for business within our original work area around Enid. I convinced the owner, Johnny Geer, to let me take his new bobtail truck to Ringwood, Oklahoma, where an oilfield boom was underway only twenty miles west.

Within a few days of driving, shaking hands, and talking about the business, I landed some new accounts. In a few months, we had several trucks operating out of Ringwood. This enabled a whole new area of work for us, so I established a truck yard there.

We grew this trucking business to more than ten trucks in just a couple of years, and Johnny gradually trusted most of the management to me. But some of his personal challenges started to create more turnover and problems at the company. I had to make the painful decision to quit. I took pride in what I had helped build, but I knew I couldn't compromise high standards for customer service and still be successful.

Three weeks later, I was hired to work in the refinery of Champlin Petroleum, a major oil company headquartered in Enid. It was the best job in the area for blue collar folks like me at the time. But there was a problem. More specifically, *I* was the problem.

In my previous job, I'd enjoyed the freedom of the oil patch and had grown to love it. I missed the people and the excitement of exploration and production of oil and natural gas. Big company limitations, union rules, and being confined at a refinery complex felt like someone had taken me out of the wild and put me into a cage at the zoo.

I started looking around for opportunities, and one soon presented itself that would allow me to be in business for myself. A man I knew from my time in Ringwood was behind on his truck payments and offered to give me his water truck if I'd take over the payments and buy his extra equipment. I worked out a deal with the financing company to catch up on his late payments, but I still needed a $1,000 loan to purchase operating permits, hoses, and tools. (That was $10,000 in today's money.) Since I was under twenty-one years old, the bank required a cosigner for the loan, so I asked Charles Potter, the owner of the truck stop where I worked in high school, to cosign. He took the risk, and I'm still grateful for him. Everybody thought I was crazy for leaving my job. But I knew it was the right thing for me to do.

I was in debt—but I was in business!

Most oil and gas companies today got their start as service operators or drillers. I started my company in the transportation sector as a one-truck operation.

At the age of twenty in 1966, I moved my wife and our two little kids from a small house we owned on the east side of Enid to a rental house in Ringwood. Looking back, I realize how stressful all those changes were on my wife and young family. At the time, I saw only possibilities.

I somehow knew that I could be successful where others had failed. I had a simple business philosophy: *a day's work for a day's pay.* So that's what I did—and it worked. Over time, I took on a business partner, Les Phillips, to help me as my business grew past the point I could keep up by myself. In 1968, we started to expand our trucking business as Hamm & Phillips Service Company. Les and I remained partners in business for the balance of his life. By 2004, Hamm & Phillips was the largest oilfield fluid service company in Oklahoma and had expanded its area of operation into five surrounding states with several operating divisions.

We had several other notable companies within our service sector. Ron Boyd was executive director of some of these companies, including a well-servicing company and rental tool company. When our companies combined with John Schmitz and L. E. Simmons, who also had similar oilfield services, these turned into Complete Energy Services. A consolidation of management and equipment proceeded a successful IPO that took advantage of increasing commodity prices from growing consumer demand. This occurred in 2007, or the beginning of a period we like to refer to as the "Cinderella years" for market investors and the entire service sector as it grew from Horizontal Drilling development. Although I remained on the board of directors for many years afterward, this consolidation freed up my primary focus from oilfield services to running Continental Resources, my exciting, demanding, fast-growing exploration company. Without this experience in the services sector, I wouldn't be the explorationist I am today. So let's get back to those early days of my career.

Lower Education: Boots on the Ground

My first experience being in business for myself was certainly an education, but I wanted to learn more about the industry I loved—and learn fast.

Even though I couldn't afford college, I was set on the idea of becoming a professional geologist. I continued to ask customers, associates, and fellow field workers across the spectrum as many questions as they'd allow. We didn't yet have any wells or oil and gas production, but I was determined to be in the oil and gas business.

In November 1967, I incorporated my first exploration and production company, the Shelly Dean Oil Company, named after my daughters, Shelly and Deana. That same business would eventually become Continental Resources.

At night, I'd study well logs, searching for hidden opportunities that might've been overlooked by bigger oil companies that had drilled these wells before. When a well is drilled, detailed records are kept about which conditions and minerals are found at depth. This industry practice allows engineers and geologists to understand what rock types, bottom hole pressures, and oil and gas exist within a wellbore. Samples of rock removed during drilling are also studied under a microscope to uncover the geologic makeup of the formations cut up by the drilling bit.

Reviewing this data is like trying to decipher ancient writings, and I found it quite fascinating. Still do. One evening, a pattern emerged that caught my attention. There was something about a particular well that had been drilled about thirty-five years earlier and had blown out and burned the drilling rig down. I had a hunch that a much larger oil reservoir existed. The replacement well hadn't proven to be that productive initially but had accumulated over one hundred thousand barrels of oil over its life.

When these wells were originally drilled in the 1940s, operators were basically drilling blind, doing the best they could with the logging technology they had. On some wells drilled nearby, I noticed that a cake of mud had built up on the inside of the wellbore at a certain depth, even though the well density logs showed nothing. The data indicated a consistent pattern, but no one else had picked up on it. I saw porous rock, and I "smelled" oil (not literally this time, but figuratively) in the Oswego Formation near McWillie, Oklahoma, in Alfalfa County.

I bought open leases where I could, obtained other leases from farm-ins (agreements to drill for a shared interest) with other companies, and bought a few wells from Getty Oil Company on a trend line that I had superimposed between other dry holes with similar mud cake characteristics in the general area. I reworked those existing wells I had bought from Getty opening up the Oswego Formation, and in 1969, I set about drilling a new grassroots well. The re-works proved to be "commercial" (profitable) and the newly drilled well came in nicely at about five hundred barrels of oil a day.

The second well in that field, a step-out wildcat, or unknown exploratory well, was five miles away from production of any other wells and flowed seventy-five barrels *an hour*. The third well nearby gauged one hundred barrels of oil *an hour*. All from six thousand feet deep! Heck of a way to begin an exploration company. This wasn't a giant field. It contained about six million barrels of recoverable oil, and I didn't own all of it. But it was definitely a giant find for our fledgling company and me.

Although oil prices were still pretty low at the time, I believed they were about to go up. So I trusted my hunch and took a risk. Within a few months, I had the resources to expand both my business and my education. I was exhilarated I could *finally* begin college. I could also buy a drilling rig to protect my reserves in the Oswego and drill my own leases. Rigs were in very short supply in 1974.

In this moment, I was struck by the fact that some well-informed risk-taking changed *my* world. I began to believe I could change the *whole* world if I could only incorporate the help of other like-minded people in this wonderful, exciting industry.

Industry mentors in this initial period of my career meant so much to my success. Professionals who were kind enough to answer my endless questions—such as local geologists Jack Ferchau and Jack Cutbirth; Paul McRil, a Schlumberger engineer, who took time to teach me how to read electric well logs; J. R. (Curley) Pearson, who taught me the basics of drilling and down-hole techniques; Floyd Harrington, who taught me well-servicing skills; and Don Longdon, the best well-stimulation expert in the business—all taught me how to complete wells to achieve the best results. Without their help, I couldn't have climbed the learning curve as quickly as I needed to. Their helpfulness is one more example of the generosity of this industry. Each of them and countless others took it on themselves to help a determined young man who wanted desperately to learn and earn his way in his chosen devotion.

When I bought those first leases from Getty, I bet they high-fived one another thinking they had gotten the better end of that deal. Boy, were they wrong. Maybe they thought I was lucky, but I knew it wasn't luck; it was science. The potential of that field was hidden only to those who hadn't studied the data closely enough. Its success was a turning point for the company and me, and it would fuel countless other opportunities.

Higher Education

What did Malcolm Gladwell say? The world-class experts in any given field have practiced for ten thousand hours. Well, in my early career years, I got really good at driving my red truck. So it was time to start a new ten-thousand-hour journey.

In 1974, right before my thirtieth birthday, I enrolled at Phillips University in Enid, Oklahoma, which had a great geology department. I didn't really care about earning a degree; I simply wanted to learn everything I could about petroleum geology, mineralogy, earth sciences, and the business of oil and gas. But to take all the petroleum geology courses I needed, I also had to take on a full course load of business, literature, history, chemistry—the works.

While those wells meant my finances took a huge turn for the better, I was realistic in my self-assessment: *I knew just enough to be dangerous*. I needed as much of a technical education as I could possibly get, as fast as I could get it. At that point, I was running multiple businesses, and I became a full-time student as well. And I loved it. Between work, classes, and my growing family, it was a very busy time. It grew busier as I began to see opportunity in other nearby oilfields in the Mid-Continent area of the U.S.

One of my first oilfield prospects was a lease position in a natural gas unit known as the Fox Unit in Blaine County, Oklahoma. It became a nice producer and was the first of a long line of successes in Blaine County. Blaine County is still a large part of the oil and natural gas production in Oklahoma, and our company is still involved there. Expanding our activities, we began to explore and develop a play in Major County, Oklahoma, in the Sooner Trend field. My exploration career was proving to be fun and exciting—and profitable.

College Career Curtailed

When I enrolled in college in 1974, Les and I agreed that he would take over operation of the day-to-day trucking enterprise so I could focus on the exploration and production side of the business as well as my studies. But in 1977, he was unable to access insurance on the trucking business, and eventually the policies were slated to be canceled. I had no choice but to involve myself again to guarantee the insurance policies and the success of the company. Later I bought the entire interest in the company and helped Les set up a Mack Trucks dealership we could utilize.

It took a great deal of time and effort to run the trucking company along with the exploration and production company. Unfortunately, something had to go, and that was the balance of my college education. I had been able to learn all the basics of geology from my courses at Phillips University. What I learned there has served me well. While that was the end of my college career, it was not the end of my learning. I am a lifelong learner.

Growing a Company

I'd always known that a company was only as good as the folks you work with. Because of the success of these new wells, I had the opportunity to hire talented petroleum engineers, geologists, and financial experts—the best and brightest in all aspects of the business. At this point in my career, I began building the structure of the corporate framework necessary to grow and prosper in the face of adversity. Eventually it became a dream team that would go on to change the world.

Over the next dozen years, Oklahoma's exploration expanded to practically every basin in the state and almost every producing horizon. It was exhilarating to grow the company and our oil and gas production at the same time. From the very beginning, we did it differently. Some oil and gas companies would stop exploring during the low end of the cycles and lay off their exploration teams: geologists, geophysicists, and engineers. We decided against that at Continental. A company's best assets are its people. In fact, some of our biggest discoveries came during downturns and in basins that were out of favor.

I learned early the value of honoring the basic science of geology and applying it to everything we did in the business and in every basin. It always gave us a leg up on competition as we worked with geologic concept after geologic concept, one after the other. For the most part, our growth has been organic—through the drill-bit. We are a self-generating shop for exploration prospects. Our bold, adventuresome passion for exploration and technical expertise has allowed us to expand our successes from Oklahoma to the major producing areas of the continental U.S., including the Williston Basin of Montana, North and South Dakota, and into Canada; the Illinois Basin of Kentucky, Indiana, and Michigan; the Texas/Louisiana Gulf Coast; the Texas Permian Basin; and the Powder River and Washakie Basins in Wyoming.

Our dedication to our people allowed us to retain the industry's greatest professionals and is something we still hold on to today. We are unique in our commitment to keeping our teams together during times of volatility and severe downturns.

Trusting the Future

I've had a few premonitions in my time. From 1974 to 1982, I had invested heavily in building a drilling rig fleet. They are capital intensive, and you make money only when they're fully deployed.

In April 1982, things were going a little *too* well. Prices for our services were going up and up—and people were paying in full, months in advance for future drilling services. *This is too good to be true*, I thought. Something didn't feel right about the state of the market. So I decided to get out of the rig business and sold all eleven rigs to a group of investors for $32 million. Yet again, people were scratching their heads about me and whispering, "He's leaving money on the table in the middle of a boom. Has he lost his nerve?"

Nope. I was changing my game. I wanted to *find* the oil, not continue to provide oilfield and drilling services for it for my entire career. I also felt that a downturn was imminent.

It was.

On July 5, 1982, Penn Square Bank, Oklahoma's largest oilfield lender, failed. The boom ended, and a decade of bad times engulfed the industry. I learned later that a market over-supply of an overly regulated wedge of interstate natural gas had filled much quicker than anyone believed it could, after having reached $9 per mcf (the volume of one thousand cubic feet) in 1980 and 1981. As this gas supply was replenished, prices normalized at about $3 per mcf, erasing much of the drilling activity associated with the prior high price period and setting the stage for the collapse.

Oklahoma City became a national news story with the collapse of Penn Square Bank. It rattled the U.S. financial system, and several banks fell like dominoes, including Continental Illinois National Bank & Trust Company. This signaled the end of an oil boom.

Was I lucky or prescient? I had just trusted my gut, and now we were suddenly in the catbird seat. With cash from the sale of the drilling rigs, I could buy oil and gas properties from distressed companies finding themselves short of cash as commodity prices for oil and gas fell.

We were ahead of the acquisition curve and found that "cash is king." We used the money to buy wells and production from debt-laden companies across the full spectrum of the industry, from independents to majors who were selling off their properties because they couldn't afford to keep them or were entering bankruptcy. We purchased six hundred wells from Denver-based Petro Lewis. They needed cash, and I just happened to have some. They weren't optimists anymore, but I was looking toward the future.

I suppose that's something else I've learned about business: too many companies lose their courage when they reach a certain size, and no matter what their motto is, all get to the point of just preserving the status quo.

In 1985, President Reagan entered into a partnership with the Saudis to provide the monarchy protection in exchange for a flood of cheap oil with which he would try to drown the Soviet economy. (I recommend Peter Schweizer's excellent book on the subject, *Victory: The Reagan Administration's Secret Strategy That Hastened the Collapse of the Soviet Union.*) The price of oil dove from about $30 to less than $10 per barrel. That's like a gallon of gasoline going for thirty cents today. As you can imagine, that hit the entire industry hard. Our government overlooked its impact on domestic oil producers and chose to play geopolitical chess instead. Countless businesses in the oil patch were crushed. But as always, there were new opportunities. Remember those eleven drilling rigs I had sold before the bust? I repurchased them for ten cents on the dollar and prepared for the next uptick in oil prices.

In addition to buying other companies' producing properties, I started exploring high-potential prospects in search of large fields. As an explorer, I wanted to find some *giant* fields, and I focused my hunt on oil. Over time, I became convinced oil would prove to have a better intrinsic value than natural gas in the coming years. There were very few explorationists or companies whose leaders shared this view at this particular time (1983).

CHAPTER 3

Whale Tales and Industrial Evolution

Total U.S. consumption of oil in 2021: 7.26 billion barrels
Recoverable U.S. reserves of oil in 2020: 373 billion barrels

(A very conservative fifty-one-year supply, but I
believe we'll have abundant oil and natural gas
for at least the next one hundred years.)

AMERICAN SOCIETY HAS ALWAYS BEEN DEEPLY ROOTED IN agronomy, the science of soil management and crop production. As a people, we find it hard to believe in or count on anything other than what's stored in the grain bin because a drought or bad luck might prevent us from, replacing those commodities in the future. So it is easy to fall into the camp of those who believe we are, always "running out" of oil and natural gas, gauged only by our consumption of found reserves.

This has been the case since oil was first discovered, and it still is the case today. For the past century, the so-called experts who have told us we would run out of oil seem to have difficulty

Global Petroleum and Other Liquids

	2020	2021	2022	2023
SUPPLY & CONSUMPTION	(MILLION BARRELS PER DAY)			
Non-OPEC Production	63.12	63.89	66.56	68.31
OPEC Production	30.75	31.66	34.44	34.66
OPEC Crude Oil Portion	25.59	26.23	28.95	29.18
Total World Production	93.87	95.55	101.00	102.97
OECD Commercial Inventory (end-of-year)	3,025	2,677	2,781	2,863
Total OPEC Surplus Crude Oil Production Capacity	5.38	5.44	3.31	3.63
OECD Consumption	42.03	44.60	46.03	46.31
Non-OECD Consumption	49.95	52.88	54.57	56.24
Total World Consumption	91.98	97.48	100.61	102.55
PRIMARY ASSUMPTIONS	(PERCENT CHANGE FROM PRIOR YEAR)			
World Real Gross Domestic Product	-3.3	5.9	4.3	4.0
Real U.S. Dollar Exchange Rate*	1.7	-3.9	2.2	-1.2

*Foreign currency per U.S. dollar.

Source: "Short-Term Energy Outlook," U.S. Energy Information Administration, March 3, 2022, https://www.eia.gov/outlooks/steo/report/global_oil.php

The point of this chart? No surprise, except to many in government and media, the world is producing and using a huge amount of oil. A good chunk of that is produced right here in America.

trusting the energy industry to do what it's done for over one hundred years—innovate and discover ways to fuel growth through continuous, ongoing exploration and development.

The more you know about any topic, the more accurate and valuable your opinions can be. Well, let's apply this notion to the oil and natural gas industry. The biggest enemy to sound energy policy is ignorance. And it doesn't take a geologist to point out that there are rich deposits of ignorance about our industry.

So in this chapter, I'm offering a Hydrocarbons 101 course for you to better understand how the industry works, why it matters to you, and why it matters to every living thing—from plants to horses to giant ocean-dwelling mammals. *Especially* the giant ocean-dwelling mammals.

What Saved the Whales?

Do you know what saved the whales from extinction? An oil well in Titusville, Pennsylvania. (Yes, the same town where the local paper would later declare that oil would run out by 1939.)

Prior to the Civil War, America and other parts of the world were rapidly industrializing. Energy demand was growing, and whale oil was the fuel of choice for lighting. Huge fleets of whalers prowled the oceans slaughtering the behemoths and then boiling their carcasses for their precious oil—all to meet the needs of the growing number of city dwellers.

By 1846, there were over seven hundred registered vessels in our nation's whaling fleet, operating out of seacoast towns such as New Bedford, Nantucket, and New London. The business was global, with some of the sailings lasting two years or more. Whaling captains were the heroes of their day, braving the seas and monster whales to bring the oil home. Remember *Moby-Dick*? At the time, it was one of hundreds of popular pieces of literature depicting whalers as courageous heroes.

(Fast-forward to today's reality TV shows such as *Deadliest Catch* and you'll get the idea.) But just as hunters did to beaver and bison, the whaling industry pushed the whale population to the brink of extinction.

In 1846, a Nova Scotian physician and geologist, puttering around with crude oil in his lab, created a solution for whale extinction—kerosene. Kerosene burned cleaner and brighter than whale oil and smelled considerably better. The only problem was finding a reliable, affordable source to make more of it.

A decade later in the summer of 1859, the whales finally caught a break. A fellow named Colonel Edwin Drake and a salt well driller named William Smith figured out a way to tap into the oil reservoir beneath the ground in the far eastern corner of Pennsylvania. Their revolutionary idea was to drive an iron pipe into the ground, drill down inside the tube, prevent the hole from collapsing, and keep mud and groundwater from getting inside the well. We're still drilling inside pipes today, albeit in a far more sophisticated way.

America's very first well produced twenty-five barrels a day, and its discovery quickly led to others. America's domestic oil industry was off and running, or at least on pace for a fast walk.

Energy evolution occurred from human ingenuity, moving the world forward to a more-efficient fuel that is also less cruel to produce. That evolution continues, and will continue, unless we sabotage it by policies that force transition before we're ready with a feasible backup plan. Simply put, banning whale oil before a better alternative was available would have left us in the dark and without the energy to innovate.

Quite suddenly, the world changed as we began the shift to an affordable, reliable, and easily transportable source of energy that also created much less impact on our ecosystems. Not only were the whales getting a reprieve but so were our forests as we shifted away from burning wood. Hydrocarbons provided the energy needed to propel us into an electrified, more prosperous, and healthier world.

Supply, Demand, and Oklahoma Oil Sand

The rush was on to find more of this game-changing mineral. Oil prospectors looked for oil seeps, mineral springs, paraffin dirt, salt domes, and formations of sedimentary rock. They talked to locals and listened for stories and even sometimes tracked down a hissing vent in the earth, striking a match to see if they could ignite a flame. The science and technology were rudimentary, and the prospectors were mostly fortune hunters, but some started finding oil.

In the Oklahoma Territory in 1897, the Nellie Johnstone No. 1 well was drilled by George B. Keeler and William Johnstone. This attracted the interest of many explorers, which in short order ushered in one of the largest finds on the planet at that time. In the subsequent ten years before statehood, Oklahoma became the largest oil-producing entity in the world. Visionaries and risk-takers started to make their way to Tulsa, Oklahoma, which quickly became the global oil capital. Some speculated Tulsa would create more millionaires in one generation than New England did in a century.

Without modern equipment such as 3D seismic sensors or computers to help, the early explorationists were said to have an "extra sense" that helped them locate oil. Some claimed they could "sniff" where the oil was. This might have been true, given that the natural geologic seeps leaked oil and gas out of the ground.

An aptly named fellow, Tom Slick, was a "sniffer" (I prefer the term *wildcatter*) who was fond of telling everyone he was going to find a lot of oil. He was right. In March 1912, he discovered the Cushing field that would yield millions of barrels of oil and flood Tulsa with billions of dollars over the coming decades. For a long time, Cushing would average over 200,000 barrels a day. At its peak, it produced over 300,000 barrels per day. By the late 1920s, Slick would become the largest independent oil operator in America, known thereafter as the earliest "King of the Wildcatters." The oilfields of Cushing ultimately produced 450 million barrels. Today it has a major tank farm and is known as "The Pipeline Crossroads of America."

And then there was Frank Phillips, an Iowa barber who came to Bartlesville, Oklahoma, with little money, but a lot of confidence. He missed on his first two wells but hit on the next eighty-one. Not bad. He and his brother would go on to form Phillips Petroleum Company, which would soon become one of the largest oil and gas companies in the world. The company found and developed the prolific Burbank Field near Bartlesville in northeastern Oklahoma. Frank started out like me, as an entrepreneur. But he learned on the go, intent on stewarding a sustainable, world-class organization. His quote from later in life has always stuck with me: "But it is a strange thing about money—regardless of how much you have, you can only wear one suit of clothes, sleep in one bed, and eat one meal at a time."

I wear fewer suits these days, preferring jeans and boots. But his wisdom still applies.

How Do You Find the Stuff?

Simple explanations are always the best. In fact, even as a young student writing my high school paper, I was able to grasp the concept and communicate in an easy-to-understand way. Here's another excerpt:

The operation of finding and developing oil is the most exciting and demanding part of the oil industry. The suspense before the strike is a thrill for every oilman in the business. Locating oilfields is still a gamble, although seasoned oil finders, research, and technology certainly eliminated much of the uncertainty. The picking of a suitable and probable place for finding oil is a very complex ordeal.

Geologists and geophysicists are prominent in this field. Through research they have found where oil is most likely to be found. Most oil is found in porous rocks such as limestone. Early oilfields were simplistic. It is trapped there by nonporous rock in the shape of an anticline. An anticline is an upheaval of rock or a meeting of different layers to result in the resemblance of an inverted V. The oil is held there by water pressure from below. Vaulted domes also may trap oil. This is simply where the rock is formed in the shape of a dome. The geologist's job is to find a place where the above conditions exist. Topography is studied to find ancient shorelines, sand edges, and sand bars which might give a clue to oil traps.

Let's pretend that we are observing the different stages of a producer being brought into production. The geologist has found signs of an anticline from observations of the topography. A seismograph crew has been called in and has found that there is a limestone layer of rock about 6,000 feet deep covered by a layer of impervious rock. Our firm has decided to secure drilling rights from the owner of the property, Mr. Carter. A lease man now comes into the picture to lease these rights. Without any difficulty, an agreement is made before any decision can be made about drilling. The seismic tests that were made also indicates an anticline. A considerable time is needed now for the final decision. In early days, drilling an oil well might cost

$100,000 to $2,000,000 so the oil company wanted to make the proper decision. Today's wells are more complex and expensive.

Finally, the decision is made to begin work on Champlin Petroleum's Carter No. 1, as we will name it from established practice. There were two main methods of drilling, rotary and cable tool in the early 1940s, but rotary rigs for these depths were best. At this time, the well will be drilled by a rotary outfit that is portable. The location of the rig is selected and the setting up begins. Land is excavated by a large dozer, and a pond is made close by to circulate mud to the bit during drilling. The rig, derrick, and tools are set up. Pipe stem, casing pipe, fuel, tools, and other necessities are hauled in. Last-minute adjustments are made, plans studied, and another "wildcat" is "spud" or begun.

The term wildcat *is an expression that means an unproven well in an unproductive area. It isn't proven until oil is found. Geologists collect and examine sample from the rock cuttings taken at five- to ten-foot intervals. A "show" with the samples showing fluorescence under a black light of ultraviolet rays, or a streaming cut, might call for a drill stem test to help determine the pressure and flow characteristics—to determine if it's worthy of setting production casing and attempting a well completion.*

The show was determined by the well site geologist to be worthy of a drill stem test, and a contractor was called in to furnish equipment to isolate the portion of the wellbore that gave the "show samples" from the rest of the wellbore and gave the zone an unhindered flow path to the surface upon opening the DST (drill stem test tool). Excitement builds as the test is conducted and a quantity deemed to be commercial flows to the test tank and is gauged at 40 barrels per hour. A good well indeed! And an unusual find as only three of ten wildcats found oil and gas in paying quantities in 1940. Those far-flung tests which found new fields were lucky indeed!

Clearly, I was intrigued with the business but still had a lot to learn. Heck, sixty years later, I'm still learning.

Over geologic time (millions of years), oil and natural gas often find their way to the surface, because they expand as they mature. Molecular expansion during maturation can double its volume over time, and that's why it seeps to the surface occasionally if it isn't trapped below. The expanding hydrocarbon exerts so much pressure that it actually *fractures* the surrounding rock. (Yes, nature technically likes to frack. But more on this later.) When a well hits a pressurized reserve, a "gusher" appears, just as you'd see in old movie footage. Those spectacles were mostly for public relations purposes in the early days since they created quite a mess and didn't reflect standard operations.

Exploration

Have you ever wondered how we find oil and natural gas thousands of feet underground? Do me a favor: if you figure out a sure-fire method, would you tell me?

We've come a long way from drilling into seeps or using our sniffers. The geological science of oil and gas exploration has evolved by leaps and bounds over the past century. In the late 1800s, a survey team traversed the entire state of Oklahoma via horse and buggy to map the topography, noting changes in the terrain and rock outcroppings. They weren't thinking about oil exploration, but those maps would later become indispensable tools in the search for oil. Surface topography provided clues to what could be found thousands of feet below.

In the 1920s, explorers experimented with sound waves, and then seismic waves, looking for geologic features that were likely to hold oil and gas. This was known as *single-fold* data originally and later was advanced to *two-dimensional* (2D) seismic. This 2D seismic was developed around 1935, and E. W. Marland's company, Continental Oil Company (now ConocoPhillips), was one of the originators of 2D seismic imaging. U.S. oil production enjoyed a noticeable increase as new fields were found with this early technology. Now we have more advanced "*3D*" and "*4D seismic*," which provide a much better underground graphic of the underlying formations, resulting in many new oil and gas discoveries. (It is also quite useful for wellbore control when drilling horizontally.)

What always intrigued me about exploration—from the time I researched my high school paper to today—was the belief that if you knew more about the science than your competitors knew, you'd find more oil and natural gas. I believed it then, and I still believe it now. Even though when I began drilling, there was no "right way" to find oil, my team and I believed we could learn to "read the cards," so to speak. And we did.

What Do We Do with All This Stuff?

Oil that's pumped up can be stored in tanks for later transport by truck to refineries. Bigger, established fields can have pipelines transport oil to local or regional networks to refineries. After refining, the oil becomes gasoline, diesel, jet fuel, and other products that can serve local markets or be shipped abroad.

Natural gas is an entirely different material. Because it's a gas and not a liquid—and will literally vanish into thin air—natural gas needs to be piped to a gathering point. Once it's gathered and pressurized, it goes through processing, where the liquids are stripped out of it. Two of these liquids are propane and butane.

Other materials such as moisture and oil are also removed. The resulting product is called dry gas, which is primarily methane. Methane is transported for heating homes, cooking, making fertilizer and plastic, and a thousand other uses.

Fun fact: natural gas does have a slight odor, but a foul-smelling chemical called mercaptan is added as a safety feature. This is so that leaks can be detected by anyone, even those who are not professional sniffers.

Horse Hockey

We are only a little over one hundred and fifty years into the hydrocarbon era of human history. For untold centuries, most humans lived in energy poverty, before we started exploring the potential in oil and natural gas. Our predecessors cut down a lot of forests, raised up some windmills, and built some rudimentary water wheels, yet we always struggled to develop any kind of sustainable and reliable energy infrastructure.

In 1820, an estimated 89 percent of the world's population lived in extreme poverty. By 1910, the figure was 74 percent. In 2018, it was 8.6 percent.

What was the game changer? I'd argue that the main catalyst for this progress was the availability of cheap, reliable hydrocarbon energy. In a geological blink of an eye, inventors transformed the world and raised the standard of living for the vast majority of Americans—and the world evolved.

Oil isn't just an energy source; it's a key ingredient in medicines, plastics, clothing, sanitation equipment, and virtually every modern convenience. Almost everything we depend on for our well-being is of hydrocarbon origin in one form or another. Prior to the nineteenth century, cities were petri dishes of disease. Pandemics swept through on a regular basis. Infrastructure was almost nonexistent; clean water distribution and waste disposal were problematic. Horses and mules ruled the roads and left a trail of *emissions* from their "tailpipes." Imagine for a moment a hot August day in New York, where tens of thousands of animals carpet-bombed the streets with secondhand hay.

Unless you're reading this book by the flickering light of a whale oil lamp, I bet we can agree that oil has made a positive difference in this world. And yet some energy adversaries and politicians want to go backward.

I happily admit I am an oil and gas enthusiast. I also see myself as an earth scientist with the bent of an explorer, going on journeys of discovery ten to fifteen thousand feet down. Topside, I'm an avid outdoorsman, forever appreciative of the bounties of the land and committed to its protection.

My story is uniquely American. I'm proud of what independent explorers and producers like myself and others have achieved, both here in America and around the world.

It might have taken the Hamm family a couple of generations to overcome poverty, but I'm eternally grateful for the lessons it taught me. My only advantage was my early disadvantage—growing up in poverty, in a very large family with something of a hardscrabble existence. And my greatest privilege was to be born in the United States of America, which gave me the opportunity to overcome seemingly insurmountable obstacles and find success.

CHAPTER 4

Setting the Stage for Terminal Oil Decline

 The oil and natural gas we rely on for 75 percent of our energy are simply running out. In spite of increased effort, domestic production has been dropping steadily at about 6 percent a year. Imports have doubled in the last five years. And our nation's economic and political independence is becoming increasingly vulnerable. Unless profound changes are made to lower oil consumption, we now believe that early in the 1980s the world will be demanding more oil than it can produce."

—PRESIDENT JIMMY CARTER, APRIL 18, 1977

59

POLITICIANS, FOR THE MOST PART, LIKE TO THINK OF THEM-selves as *moral* leaders. And their handlers are always spinning ways to make sure they occupy the perceived blameless high ground. Such was the case in the spring of 1977.

President Carter was having a rough time of it, and most of his political pain was self-inflicted. We were in the midst of our second "energy crisis." Inflation was ticking up. Do you remember the good, old days of double-digit inflation? I sure do. Imagine a young couple today applying for an 11 percent mortgage. How about a car

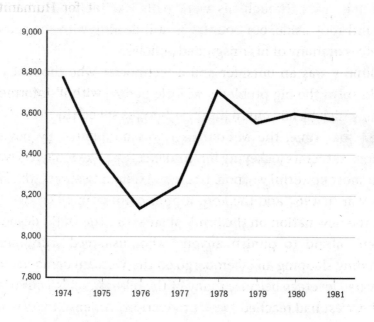

U.S. Field Production of Crude Oil
(Thousand Barrels per Day)

Source: "U.S. Field Production of Crude Oil," U.S. Energy Information Administration, accessed December 21, 2022, https://www.eia.gov/dnav/pet/hist/LeafHandler.ashx?n=PET&s=MCRFPUS2&f=A

Here's U.S. oil production just before and during the Carter years.
The conventional wisdom at that time, which his administration shared, was that we were running out of fossil fuels.

loan at 12 percent? That was the reality in late-seventies America. Carter's energy policy model was the original plan, supported and passed by a young senator from Delaware, Joseph Biden, among others. That plan consisted of ways to regulate, tax, and employ methods to eliminate and limit oil and gas-producing companies' ability to produce. Unfortunately for the president and fellow citizens, the natural results of those policies were diminishing supplies of domestically produced crude oil and natural gas, spiraling fuel prices, and runaway inflation coupled with growing dependence on the Middle East for crude oil—much as we have today.

President Carter's philanthropic leadership should be commended, and I greatly admire the impact he has made over the years through his work with Habitat for Humanity. Philanthropy aside, our country is still dealing with the consequences of many of his misguided policies.

Jimmy was an outsider and a technocrat who thought he could solve the big problems of little people with ill-informed ideas, which he laid out in his most famous speech in 1977.

At that time, the Middle East was dominated by power-hungry autocrats jockeying for influence, just like today. Oil was their most powerful weapon. Israel had fought two wars (the Six-Day War in 1967 and the Yom Kippur conflict in 1973), which had the new nation on the brink of survival. The OPEC despots weren't afraid to punish anyone who disagreed with them, including slapping an oil embargo on the Western democracies. They had leverage because many of the oil-producing countries in the West had reached "peak production." At least, that's what the experts told us. Truth was, that peak in production was due to very low prices for oil—less than $4 per barrel paid by the refiners to smaller producers in the oilfield. The refiners believed it to be in their best interest to keep prices low as they bought and processed more than they produced as a general rule. This practice worked out for them for more than two decades. Much of the oil came from the Middle East; of course, this was all disrupted in 1973 and came to an abrupt end.

The "oil embargo" of 1973 led to higher oil prices and a fraying of our relationships with Europe and Japan, which were incredibly dependent on oil from the Middle East and sought to distance themselves from the U.S.'s friendship with Israel. The rapid rise in oil prices contributed to one of America's longest recessions in history, in which unemployment peaked at 9 percent.

Previously, Republican President Richard Nixon inflicted wage and price controls. He instigated these controls on oil when it increased from the low of $4.00 per barrel to $4.25 per barrel in 1973. Laughingly now, he thought oil prices were getting "plumb out of hand." His administration's actions led to the first wave of mandates for automobile fuel economy standards, which, by the way, gave the Japanese the opportunity to flood the U.S. with small, lightweight cars and establish market shares that have only grown with time, nearly killing off domestic automobile production. As we well know, these weren't the only damaging ideas from Nixon.

Congress enacted a ban on oil exports in 1975 that took forty years to reverse. In 2015, we worked to remove the ban, and I pointed out to folks that the U.S. had banned the export of only two other commodities in our history—wood from the Western cedar tree and live horses shipped overseas for slaughter. I kid you not.

The move to hoard available supply only made matters worse. President Ford established the U.S. Strategic Petroleum Reserve (SPR) in 1975. The reserve is essentially a big lake of oil pumped into the salt domes underneath Louisiana and Texas that costs tens of billions of dollars in the mistaken belief there wasn't much oil left. There are currently three quarters of a billion barrels capacity with only a few hundreds of millions sloshing around down there. As the U.S. Energy Department likes to point out on its web page, the reserve is the largest of its kind in the world. So like all programs based on a fallacy of need, the reserve lives on and is more often drained for political purposes, as is happening as I am writing this book, than it is for national emergencies.

Not much has changed over the past fifty years. In the first quarter of 2022, the Biden administration decided its remedy to high prices was to draw down the reserve to the tune of a million barrels a day for six months. Of course, the whole idea of the reserve was to have it in times of national emergency directly threatening our national security. Tapping the reserve was merely a PR and political stunt. The price at the pump just kept going up, driven by demand outpacing supply, primarily due to Biden's policy of banning leasing on federal lands.

These political decisions have led to stagnant economic growth and inflation as oil prices tripled and quadrupled. Today we are again experiencing an era of "stagflation." Economic growth slows while prices go up. Not an easy trick to pull off, but the geniuses in Washington, D.C., have had lots of practice. Here we go again.

The Moral Equivalent of War

In April 1977, President Carter took to the airwaves and scared the bejeebers out of the country. He proclaimed that the oil crisis was likely to worsen and result in a "national catastrophe." It seemed, through the president's view, we were at war with ourselves.

He proclaimed, "Our decision about energy will test the character of the American people and the ability of the president and the Congress to govern this nation. This difficult effort will be 'the moral equivalent of war,' except that we will be uniting our efforts to build and not to destroy."

Our oil consumption was going up every year. Carter predicted that by 1985, America would be importing gobs of oil at a cost of $550 billion a year, up from $36 billion in 1976.

You didn't have to be an economist to realize that's some serious dough, and it would all be flowing *out* of our country, not in.

The president was a Baptist preacher to the core. We must repent—our cars were too large, too inefficient, and we often liked to drive by ourselves. (I always wondered what he thinks of the big, beautiful SUVs and pickups that grace our highways today.) He laid out a litany of remedies, beginning with my favorite word in times of trouble: *sacrifice*. Instead of finding new sources of oil and natural gas and removing the burdensome regulations that got us there, the president took the road more traveled and shamed consumption. Instead of looking to American companies, which have always led the world in exploration, he imagined conservation programs that would create a surplus of high-paying jobs. (This is political speak for a blossoming bureaucracy that takes money out of consumers' pockets and sends it to Washington, D.C.)

The speech also birthed the U.S. Department of Energy and a secretary to run it. James Schlesinger, a serious man with serious D.C. credentials, was the first. He was sent off to Paris to sign a bunch of international energy agreements. It seems the playbook progressives use today was printed way back in 1977.

Plentiful *Coal?*

The next part of Carter's speech contained the largest blunder of all time in energy policy. We are still feeling the effects of it in the world today. Buried in the speech was a call to action that still chokes the world:

"We need to shift to plentiful coal."

You heard that right. *Coal.* The stated goal was to increase coal production by two-thirds to more than 1 billion tons a year.

By 1975, U.S. coal usage had declined to just 18 percent of the energy mix post-World War II, and the country had moved to oil and gas to meet its energy needs. Oil and gas could be moved efficiently and reliably by pipeline and was more environmentally friendly. But when you're coal-rich, *think* you're running out of domestic liquid hydrocarbons, and want to give a big middle finger to the Middle East, I suppose coal starts to look pretty good to the uninformed experts—or those who want to eliminate oil and gas companies.

The logic was fractured: *We're running out of oil and gas. Only our adversaries have a lot of it. We can't keep spending money with people who hate us.* Right? Let's try coal again.

The speech spawned another initiative that warped everything it touched for decades to come. Allow me to introduce you to the 1978 Powerplant and Industrial Fuel Use Act, which barred new power plants from burning natural gas or oil to generate electricity. Interestingly, Al Gore, then a newly elected congressman from Tennessee, sat and listened to testimony on the environmental impact of Carter's plan to boost coal production. President Biden, serving as a U.S. senator from Delaware at the time, voted in favor of Carter's plan to shift to coal.

Here's part of what President Carter had to say: "The world now uses about 60 million barrels of oil a day and demand increases each year about 5 percent. This means that just to stay even, we need the production of a new Texas every year, an Alaskan North Slope every nine months, or a new Saudi Arabia every three years. Obviously, this cannot continue."

As soon as the speech was over, the red flags started waving. The president was basically asking the coal industry to go on a near wartime footing. Doubling production was going to stress the mining, processing, and transportation infrastructure to the limit.

At the same time, the early environmental movement became apoplectic. Coal was a huge contributor to air pollution, producing 1.75 times as much CO_2 per unit of energy as the natural gas it was to replace. And the president was now suggesting that the way forward was coal, without any new pollution controls or technology to mitigate the effects.

The potential pollutants were—and still are—a witches' brew of bad stuff: sulfur dioxide, nitrogen oxide, mercury, carbon black soot, and carbon dioxide. The smokestacks threw tons of particulate matter into the air every minute. And it gets worse.

The most efficient way to extract coal is through strip mining. This practice leaves terrible scars where it occurs and has devastating effects on surrounding water supply and wildlife. What's more, scientists were beginning to notice another nasty side effect of coal: acid rain. Air pollution reacted with water vapor in the atmosphere to create corrosive rain that noticeably damaged agriculture, buildings, and infrastructure such as bridges.

The new Carter-appointed deputy energy secretary, John O'Leary, brushed off the concerns. "The environmental constraints are no problem for 80 percent of the country, with 85 percent of the population. There are some areas you won't be able to site a coal-fired plant, such as in the Los Angeles Basin, or perhaps around Houston, but that leaves a lot of room."

O'Leary was convinced we could afford a decade of increased pollution from coal until scrubbing technology could catch up and make it more environmentally acceptable. Everyone knew coal was going to pollute. The only debate was for how long and how much. Thus began the rapid U.S. transition to electricity generated by coal, despite all the warnings.

While the right hand of the government was digging for coal, the left hand was slapping the oil and natural gas sector with price controls, ensuring no one would look for more. And just to hammer the coffin shut, they enacted a windfall profits tax on oil and gas companies. Here are some consequences of President Carter's speech, the legislation, and the resulting layers of regulation.

- Domestic pollution dramatically increased thanks to all the new coal-fired plants.
- The U.S. government pushed to sell coal to new markets in Asia. Along with the raw materials, we exported our coal-burning technology to the rest of the world so that thousands more coal-fired plants were built worldwide, spiking pollution across the globe. All the while, they labeled it "clean coal," an oxymoron designed to smoke-screen a flawed strategy. Incidentally, hundreds of coal plants are still being built in China and India today, primarily by Chinese firms that immediately copied the U.S. technology for coal plant construction.
- We became even more dependent on unreliable parts of the world for our oil and gas.
- We instituted an export ban on oil to preserve what we believed was a shrinking supply.
- U.S. manufacturing was hampered because of the increasing cost of energy. Major manufacturing sectors such as automobiles moved overseas.
- The Windfall Profits Tax and other harmful legislation and regulations pushed by Carter added more crushing burdens to the industry and ultimately hurt consumers.

- Radical environmentalism was born, injecting activists into the debate at the local, state, and national level.
- The U.S. EPA and Department of Energy became super powerful, enacting regulation after regulation and distorting the energy markets even more.

All this happened because of myths and misunderstanding surrounding domestic oil and natural gas—and pitiful legislation. Only recently have people begun to realize almost everything they thought was true was not. And the real loser was the American consumer. All these actions plunged America—the leader in oil and natural gas production—further into an "era of scarcity" and took our country into a phase known as *terminal decline* in the oil industry. The experts said it was irreversible. I knew they were wrong, and I set my sights to new fields and discoveries to disprove their peak-oil theory.

Somewhere along the way, I began to realize that America could be energy independent if given the unhindered ability to produce both oil and natural gas when freed completely of artificial price controls, regulatory burdens, and government production hindrances, thereby ending the "undeclared" war on our industry.

I even saved this political cartoon from 1977. It still applies quite accurately today with the current administration. Ironically, with the Biden White House, we are once again doubling down on a failed energy policy, much like that of the Jimmy Carter era: squeeze down on domestic oil companies and their production in favor of inadequate alternatives, which in effect increase our foreign dependence on the unstable Middle East and increase our use of environmentally harmful coal production globally.

CHAPTER 5

The Explorationist: Fifty Years on a Journey of Discovery

IN 1956, A GENTLEMAN NAMED M. KING HUBBERT BECAME famous for his prediction that oil and gas production would soon reach its peak and we were in a period of slow and perhaps precipitous decline. It became popular to call this *terminal decline*, indicating the belief there was not much that could be done to avoid it. *Hubbert's Peak* was a scary book and a scary idea. Our entire civilization depended on reliable and affordable energy.

Just about everyone could quote chapter and verse from the book. The idea of "peak oil" became the conventional wisdom. The evidence and math were compelling. The experts were convinced we faced an epic challenge and believed that time was not our friend. Like so many intellectual panics, millions of words were written, thousands of speeches made, and Lord knows how many congressional meetings were held.

The downturn deepened in the early 1980s as quiet panic grew in the energy industry, and competitors and "Big Oil" alike invested overseas. (The term "Big Oil" generally refers to the largest publicly traded oil companies.) My team bet it all on the lower forty-eight states. I had more unconventional ideas to test.

Potential Energy

People are a lot like oil and natural gas in at least one respect: we all have great potential that is ready to be unlocked with the right mix of circumstance, catalyst, and a little luck.

Although my entry into the industry was through the service sector, my life's work has been to find oil and natural gas. If you'll permit the comparison, the story has similarities to Indiana Jones— looking for treasure in places others passed over, ignored, or thought impossible.

Exploration is both art and science. At the beginning of civilization, humans read the heavens, navigating by the sun and stars. Trial and error led to leaps of progress. It's no coincidence that much of early recorded human history is about epic exploration. Fast-forward to the nineteenth century in Oklahoma. The "explorers" had pretty much passed over the state on the way to somewhere else.

As a young man, I pored over their stories. They were "explorationists" at heart, driven to find something new. A few succeeded on dumb luck. But the good ones—the geologists and engineers—mapped Oklahoma's sedimentary basins with amazing accuracy and found the oil and natural gas that changed the world. Oklahoma, for a time, was *the* global epicenter of energy exploration and production. In fact, Tulsa became known as the oil capital of the world.

What most people (and even some in my industry) didn't realize is that we had only tapped into an estimated 15 percent of the available hydrocarbons through conventional drilling. In other words, we had found most of the *easy* stuff—the hydrocarbons that oozed out of the rich source beds into underground pools, anticlines, and fault traps.

The remaining 85 percent was what I was after, the immobile portion. I knew there was much to learn, to find, and to explore. It became my vocation, a life's passion that is now half a century old. And God willing, I will keep at it.

What I was looking for wasn't over the next mountain range or across an ocean but under my feet, in geological formations hundreds of millions of years old. As technology evolved, the old maps and logs began to reveal their secrets. Repeatedly, I realized some really smart people had overlooked the obvious. Maybe they were focused on offshore reserves.

Once again, when the herd moved one way, we at Continental looked for opportunity in the opposite direction. We turned our backs on the conventional bread-and-butter plays the company had been built on and began searching for the high-risk and elusive deposits—first in Oklahoma and then throughout the Mid-Continent region of the U.S. This pursuit and change of direction shattered our reputation for very few "dry holes and uncommercial tests" by leading us to seventeen failures in a row in 1979! At this stage of my career, I voluntarily chose high-financial-risk, high-reward, and high-potential prospects versus run-of-the-mill, lower-potential, lower-return-rate deposits. I was in search of "elephants"—very large fields. Nobody else was hunting elephants onshore here in America, and certainly no one else expected any to be found.

Out of This World

No matter how good your drilling rig and crew are, you still have to drill in the right spot. Using 2D swath and 3D seismic technology (as it became available), we found a number of fair-sized fields including the Mosier Farms Field in Garfield County, Oklahoma. This leads me to my most unique and rare oil find to date.

There are many reasons the Ames Hole geological feature in Oklahoma was—and remains—significant. One is that this was an astrobleme: a large crater formed due to a meteorite impact. This was one of only six producing astroblemes in all of North America. Another reason the Ames Hole site was significant is that, to my knowledge, this was the first time that large areas of computer modeling were used in exploration in Oklahoma. This site had been completely buried and invisible from the earth's surface for approximately four hundred and fifty million years. By looking at all the data, our team of geologists and geotechs painted the virtual picture of the area. It took two full years.

Craig Roberts, a geologist from Ames, Oklahoma, oversaw the project along with our exploration manager, Rex Olsen. One day, I asked Craig how the computer maps were coming along, and he said he was almost ready but couldn't fix a glitch in the data that was making a large "cowtrack-looking thing" near Ames, Oklahoma.

Rex and I stopped by his office to take a closer look at the mapping and the image. After a few minutes, Rex, a remarkable UC Berkeley-trained geologist, looked at the eight-mile-wide "cowtrack" feature and said, "Wow, that sort of looks like an astrobleme."

For a moment, I considered nodding my head in agreement but decided to ask, "OK, what's an astrobleme?"

Long story short, this late-1980s exploration made national news and spurred us to increase the number of leases in certain points on the feature. Turns out, craters make pretty good receptacles for oil since they are depressions up to several miles deep that fill over time with the rich organic material we call crater shale. An early test well in this feature produced two hundred barrels of oil an hour, equivalent to almost five thousand barrels a day. And this was a vertical well—an *out of this world* well, indeed. All wells associated with this feature are still going today and will go on to produce twenty-five million barrels of oil.

I immediately started studying as much as I could learn about astroblemes. Not only did the Ames Hole contain a lot of oil, but scientists believe cosmic collisions like this killed off most of life on earth and eliminated the dinosaurs. I also encouraged my team to write and publish articles on our findings, as Rex and I had. Our geologic interpretation was met with initial skepticism, but it was ultimately celebrated.

Ames Hole was a first in many ways. One of only six producing astrobleme features in North America, it was first in high-yield production rates, first to be found by computer mapping over a township area, and first to be confirmed as a result of an asteroid's impact using core samples. All in all, this discovery was unparalleled geologically and established Continental, the little company from Enid, as a technologically advanced enterprise the world should pay attention to. It also allowed Rex Olsen, a remarkable explorationist, to ride off into the sunset with a great success under his belt. I'm grateful to him for these fond memories.

Should your travels take you to Enid or Ames, stop by the Ames Hole Museum for a quick geologic and technological journey through an otherworldly experience.

CHAPTER 6

Horizontal Drilling: The Game Changer

ON THE WALL OF MY LIBRARY, I KEEP A PAGE FROM *TULSA World* newspaper published in the Energy section in April 1991.

The article was written by Dr. Daniel Yergin, one of the foremost authors of our time, talking about the perpetual decline of oil and gas in America and across the globe, which was caused by overregulation. The history of American oil and gas was thought to be in the rearview mirror due to these burdensome regulations. I agree they were a huge obstacle to overcome; regulations have always been in the way and have grown only worse with more red tape being added every day by bureaucracy.

Coincidentally, on the same page of that newspaper, there was a two-column story with the headline "Enid Company Drilling Long Horizontal Well" (which referred to a project we were involved in with my good friend, Don Crawford with Oasis Petroleum of Texas).

The accompanying photo, provided by us, was of the oil rig with the caption "The Holtzen number 1-9 began drilling near Enid last week."

They didn't know it, but we were about to change the world using Horizontal Drilling.

The two articles were on the same page, but the worldviews could not have been further apart. My view, gleaned from over thirty years of field work, and some very recent breakthroughs in drilling technology our company was deploying, caused me to believe America had a century or more of untapped supply—even when you factored in growing global demand. I began making the point, first quietly and then loudly, that we could achieve energy independence if we unleashed our industry to innovate and produce free of governmental controls and regulations.

I have the utmost respect for Dr. Daniel Yergin, who at the time had just completed his book *The Prize: The Epic Quest for*

Oil, Money, and Power. The book would be awarded the Pulitzer Prize for nonfiction. I still have my original copy given to me and signed by Ed Long, a dear friend and Oklahoma's former secretary of education. Fortune shined on Daniel in a bizarre way—and the book's timing couldn't have been better. It came out just months after Saddam Hussein invaded the oil-rich kingdom of Kuwait and one month before the U.S.-led coalition began the first Gulf War to remove Iraqi troops from that country. Just about every policymaker in the world grabbed a copy or had their aides prepare a synopsis. To say the book was influential would be underselling it.

He got many things right. Petroleum did indeed drive the rise of capitalism and modern life. Oil became a "prized" commodity and changed the fortunes and trajectories of countries and continents. He dubbed the twentieth century the "hydrocarbon age" but implied that "The Prize" had been garnered by a few mostly large companies, the majors. Yergin's view was a great historical account of the oil and gas industry. But it did not allow for the great element of American ingenuity that was about to change the landscape.

Let me set the stage for what has become the game-changing technology that transformed American energy forever and describe the drivers that brought this revolution about. Many people believe Horizontal Drilling began in the 2000s. There's much more to that story.

Out of the Ashes

The term *out of the ashes* is a fitting picture of the world in which our Horizontal Drilling practices made their debut. As always, necessity is the biggest mother of invention and certainly something that was needed at this time. From the early 1900s to the mid-seventies and eighties, all the experts (like the aforementioned Hubbert) were predicting "terminal decline" of U.S. oil and natural gas production, including Yergin. And to make matters worse, the government was helping make it a self-fulfilling prophecy.

I saw something different.

Jimmy Carter's four years of punitive energy policy plunged the U.S. into severe energy scarcity. President Reagan emerged and began to lift some of those regulations as part of his deregulation strategy to help the economy recover; these included the Carter-era Windfall Profits Tax and other onerous regulations that were holding the industry back. However, the market distortion continued to send economic ripples through the oil patch.

For decades, government pricing schemes for natural gas had created artificially low prices. As you would expect, when the price of something goes way down, businesses are not clamoring to invest in that market. Finally, in 1979, the government was forced to decontrol pricing on certain categories of natural gas, including "deep gas" below 15,000 feet, to help fill the void. However, once this void was filled, a collapse of natural gas prices occurred by 1982. This triggered a series of events that caused a recession in the oilfield that lasted for the next decade.

Government policies crushed America's natural gas production, then took a toll on oil production. All of this happened in just a few years with a devastating effect.

Staying Alive

The industry's cries of "stay alive til '85" became haunting shouts of desperation by many operators pleading for prices to go back to prior sustainable levels. The number of oil and gas operators in the U.S. diminished by almost half as foreclosures and bankruptcies became the order of the day. A large number of oil patch banks and financial institutions were also crushed.

President Reagan's well-intentioned plan involving the Saudis was threefold:

1. Break the Soviets by starving their oily cash cow.
2. Deny Russia the Western technology it needed for its proposed natural gas pipelines to connect to European market.
3. Begin a space race known as Star Wars to further deplete Russia's capital.

All this was envisioned to bring an end to the lingering Cold War by the world's foremost nuclear powers, the U.S. and the Soviet Union. Reagan's plan worked, and the Soviet Union fell apart under the extreme economic pressure that he applied. Its breakup became one of the world's most significant events of the twentieth century.

In my world, oil prices were falling dramatically. Soon after, President Reagan let the other shoe drop. He moved to decontrol the natural gas market entirely by removing long-standing price regulations, thereby dumping all the nation's natural gas reserves on the market at once. Yes, it needed to be deregulated at some point, but it should have been done over a longer period to forgo a shock to the market and the resulting 50 percent decline in price. The natural gas oversupply hit and lasted for the next dozen years until the end of 1999.

In the summer of 1989, Congress passed legislation ending all controls on the wellhead price of natural gas by January 1993.

In the oilfield service sector, the active rig count plummeted from forty-five hundred in 1981 to under seven hundred in 1986. Many rigs went to the salvage yard as drilling contractors went broke, had to sell, or filed for bankruptcy. Many rigs were cut up for scrap iron.

Times were desperate. Get the picture?

Devastation spread across the industry. For many, the economic challenges appeared insurmountable. The Organization of the Petroleum Exporting Countries (OPEC) was producing literal boatloads of oil and had plenty of untapped capacity. Saudi Arabia was producing ten million barrels of oil every day from only five hundred and fifty wells. Various oil "experts" hypothesized the Saudis' production could ramp up as high as twenty-five million barrels per day for the next forty years. (Interestingly, it's about forty years later, and they seem to be close to being maxed out at twelve million barrels per day, no matter how much President Biden grovels and fist bumps.)

A mindset of terminal decline became entrenched in the U.S. as our nation's production fell to less than five million barrels a day. The voice of the herd was clear: "OPEC has oil, and we don't. It's time to panic." (I must have missed that policy class in college. And I'm glad.)

Meanwhile, on the natural gas front, there were concerns for future supply due to capital constraints, even though the market was still oversupplied as a result of deregulation. In plain English, few were exploring, so few were finding. Things were so bad (in the limited imaginations of big government) that preparations were made to construct receipt points for natural gas *imports* to this country. Yes, imports.

As an optimist, what do you do when everything around you collapses in the industry you love? Simple. You look for opportunity.

A thesis by Michael Ray, from Bartlesville, Oklahoma, caught my attention. He estimated the ratio of "mobile" vs. "immobile" oil to be incorrectly skewed. Again, in plain terms, for every barrel we extracted, there were two more we left in the ground that he termed "immobile oil." That seemed like a big prize for those who could figure out a way to unlock it. *There must be something better.*

From Exploration to Drilling

My deep and abiding passion in this industry has always been exploration. But I mentioned at the beginning of this chapter that Continental was experiencing certain large breakthroughs in well-drilling technology. Due to the role it played in future development, I believe it is worthwhile to read how this happened.

I wasn't especially enamored with drilling rigs—until 1973, that is, when I couldn't hire enough rigs to drill my leases. So I bought one. I partnered with an experienced drilling and production individual I knew, and together we started a drilling company with one rig in 1974. When the rig was available during slack times, we also contracted drilling for other parties, and as our business and reputation grew, so did our rig fleet.

Soon, we had built a half dozen rigs, then a dozen. We were doing some specialized drilling, including turnkey drilling projects, natural gas storage wells, and deep and high-pressure wells in the Anadarko Basin of Oklahoma.

Little did I know that the drilling expertise I gained, combined with my love for exploration, would help pioneer the technology for Horizontal Drilling that unlocked the American Energy Renaissance.

Thinking Sideways

Most people understand basic drilling, whether it's for water or oil: point the drill bit straight down and drill, the straighter the better. This is known as vertical drilling, and the entire oil and gas exploration industry—and the evolution of its equipment—was based on this simple approach.

By the 1970s, we were deploying some groundbreaking exploration techniques as well as accomplishing several drilling milestones. For example, the industry had drilled some wells that reached 31,000 feet deep. That's *six miles*. We at Continental, however, began to experiment with directional drilling with our rigs to exploit stranded oil and gas reserves under cities and other geographic locations. The industry had been doing deviated drilling onshore and offshore, but the fact we could "bend" a drill string to travel straight-down led me to believe we could take the concept even further. So we drilled down and gradually changed the angle over a few hundred feet. Highly deviated thinking led to highly deviated wells.

For instance, there was a lot of oil and gas in Enid, Oklahoma— *under* the city, to be more precise. As you might imagine, setting up a drilling rig downtown or in a park is not an option. *But what if you could drill outside a city, deviate the well, and then drill horizontally toward the reservoir?* That's exactly what we did. In the early eighties, we drilled sixteen wells in Enid. Fifteen of them—all but one—were horizontal, or highly deviated, directional wells under the city. We were also drilling wells beneath Oklahoma City, Chickasha, and numerous other municipalities. Our drilling personnel gained in experience and, consequently, reputation as we progressed.

We used the tools we had at the time and improvised the rest—whipstocks (curved steel shafts that started the deviated path), bent subs (short, strong, treated steel pipes with a slight bend), belly assemblies (more heavyweight steel rigging that pushed the bent sub along), single-shot surveys or wireline directional tools, and everything we had in the toolbox to guide the drill string (the entire assembly, all the way to the drill bit). It's fair to say our early equipment was *clunky* at best when compared to the technology of today. But hey, it worked.

Here's another example of our team's ingenuity regarding well placement in and around cities. We started drilling four wells from single locations utilizing intersecting rail yards. We called the drilling locations Eco-Pads®. Some members of our team wanted to trademark our techniques, but I was reluctant. I thought they would be impossible to trademark, and I really didn't want to limit the industry's advancement in efficiency and reduction of environmental impact. I eventually agreed. Turned out, it was possible, and the industry embraced it. Now the entire industry uses Eco-Pads® to drill anywhere from two to thirty-six wells on a pad size of about five acres.

Being able to access hard-to-reach reserves of oil and natural gas was only the beginning. For reasons we'd fully understand later, angled wells produced far more than vertical wells in the same reservoir. The lights went on.

Very soon, I knew Horizontal Drilling was a game changer. It's been a game changer for the American consumer ever since, and it will continue as such long into the future.

Imagine a typical vertical well intersecting with sixty square feet of a reservoir. Think of it like the bottom of a big straw. A horizontal well two miles long has eighty thousand square feet of wellbore exposure compared to sixty square feet of a vertical. Modern techniques using water and sand stimulate natural fractures in the rock—effectively increasing the exposure to two hundred thousand square feet and creating *twelve million* square feet of wellbore exposure. Imagine a straw with a lot of holes in it. Then turn the straw on its side. This straw effectively enables us to unlock reservoirs we could not produce vertically.

Finally, the key to accessing the remaining 85 percent of untapped oil and gas in the U.S. was at my fingertips. Suddenly I realized that many reservoirs I had vertically drilled earlier in

Bakken Well Schematic

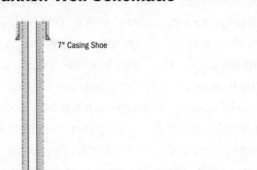

7" Casing Shoe

4 1/2" production liner to TD

Plug and Perf 30 stages: 1,000#/ft : 20 bbls/ft

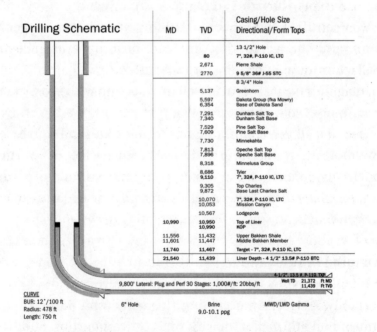

Drilling Schematic	MD	TVD	Casing/Hole Size Directional/Form Tops
			13 1/2" Hole
		80	7", 32#, P-110 IC, LTC
		2,671	Pierre Shale
		2770	9 5/8" 36# J-55 STC
			8 3/4" Hole
		5,137	Greenhorn
		5,597	Dakota Group (fka Mowry)
		6,354	Base of Dakota Sand
		7,291	Dunham Salt Top
		7,340	Dunham Salt Base
		7,529	Pine Salt Top
		7,609	Pine Salt Base
		7,730	Minnekahta
		7,813	Opeche Salt Top
		7,896	Opeche Salt Base
		8,318	Minnelusa Group
		8,686	Tyler
		9,110	7", 32#, P-110 IC, LTC
		9,305	Top Charles
		9,872	Base Last Charles Salt
		10,070	7", 32#, P-110 IC, LTC
		10,053	Mission Canyon
		10,567	Lodgepole
	10,990	10,950	Top of Liner
		10,990	KOP
	11,556	11,432	Upper Bakken Shale
	11,601	11,447	Middle Bakken Member
	11,740	11,467	Target - 7", 32#, P-110 IC, LTC
	21,540	11,439	Liner Depth - 4 1/2" 13.5# P-110 BTC

CURVE
BUR: 12°/100 ft
Radius: 478 ft
Length: 750 ft

9,800' Lateral: Plug and Perf 30 Stages: 1,000#/ft: 20bbs/ft

6" Hole

Brine
9.0-10.1 ppg

MWD/LWD Gamma

4-1/2", 13.5 #, P-110, TXP

Well TD   21,372   Ft MD
          11,439   Ft TVD

There's a lot going on 10,000 to 15,000 feet below your feet. Thanks to advances in technology, we have a far clearer picture of the subsurface of the earth.

my life could become commercial when drilled horizontally. I could hardly contain my excitement.

Testing Techniques

An opportunity to further test the magnitude of the potential of Horizontal Drilling presented itself in 1993 with a project to drill a short horizontal well on a turnkey bid, requiring us to assume all the risk. The project was in a natural gas storage field—a reservoir used to store extra gas for use in the winter. The existing wells were limited in their rates to fill and extract natural gas, and the goal was to change that for the better.

This was our first *real* attempt at Horizontal Drilling within a natural gas storage field. It was risky but could pay very well since there weren't many who could even attempt it—and fewer who had the guts to try. Our team took it on and devised a plan. We would drill a 2,500-foot lateral (horizontal well) to the storage formation that was only fifty feet thick. Talk about a needle in a haystack. Although drilling practices for horizontal work were practically nonexistent, we believed it was possible. Long story short, we proved it was possible.

Our well allowed natural gas to be injected or withdrawn *five times faster* than a conventional vertical well through the same size tubulars. The bells went off in my head. *This same result could be repeated over and over in an oil and gas reservoir. Game changer time!*

Changing Impossible to Profitable

Please allow me to put on my geologist hard hat and explain another way Horizontal Drilling changed the game. Across many of the sedimentary basins of the U.S., there are large areas of low-permeability rock that contain hydrocarbons that have migrated from shale source beds over many millions of years.

(Translation: there's lots of oil and gas saturating those rocks, but conventional drilling couldn't pull much out.) By connecting several thousand feet of a reservoir within a single wellbore, the recovery can be ten or more times greater. From a business standpoint, a well that was losing half its initial investment could double or triple its invested capital in as little as three years from a 5x multiple of increased oil and gas production—and become one of a thousand like it in an oil or gas field!

The Silo Field in Laramie County, Wyoming, near Cheyenne, was chosen to test the Niobrara Formation with horizontal laterals. This was a thin zone, therefore making it tougher to land in or stay in the zone for long distances. As I recall, we were stuck or sidetracking more time than we were drilling. (Sidetracking means to divert the wellbore to go around an obstacle, get back into the desired formation by going a different direction, or position the drill bit at another angle.)

The formation proved to be productive but not as profitable as we hoped. We sold our interest and continued searching for a better candidate to apply the technology.

Cedar Hills

Cedar Hills is a field on top of the Cedar Creek Anticline—a feature along a fault that extends one hundred and fifty miles from near Glendive, Montana, into Bowman, North Dakota, and down into Buffalo, South Dakota. Yes, it's a big field with plenty of wide-open spaces to ponder. At least, that's how it looks today. But in the beginning, it had been plagued with challenges. It just wasn't commercially profitable with vertical well development.

In 1993, our exploration team had been working a 2D seismic grid in Bowman County, North Dakota, and Fallon County, Montana, looking for structural traps in the Red River "C" and "D" Formations. We had taken quite a few leases and were preparing to test a couple of the identified leads. During the prospect review, I noticed the overlooked Red River "B" horizon on the log cross-sections in that area. It fit all my parameters for horizontal well development. It was a saturated, micro-sucrosic dolomite at eight thousand to nine thousand feet vertical depth with good porosity, but it was limited by low permeability as the porous holes were not connected very well. The Red River "B" was also very thin, averaging only ten feet thick. I believed a horizontal wellbore could be the answer since vertical wells, although productive in this formation, just weren't commercial due to their low production rates.

We initially acquired about twenty thousand acres of leases based on the conventional prospects generated by one of our geologists and geophysicists. We owned over two thousand miles of 2D seismic data and were searching for structural traps where oil and gas could accumulate in the Red River "D" zone.

At the time, conventional wisdom said it would be uneconomical to try to produce oil from the low-permeability dolomite "B." Thanks to the team's efforts, we knew the area was "charged" with hydrocarbons in the low-permeability zones of the Red River Formation, especially the Red River "B" geologic member. Our big bet was based on connecting all the porous rock with a long horizontal lateral to produce commercial quantities of oil. The only way to definitively know was through the drill bit. We began with two drilling rigs. Existing vertical wells drilled in this zone produced only sixty barrels of oil per day. Our hope was to make wells of six or seven hundred barrels or more per day through a one-mile unstimulated horizontal lateral.

Our first well, the Jean Peterson, came in with an initial oil production from a five-thousand-foot uncased lateral producing seven hundred barrels of oil per day—a far cry from the normal initial rate for a vertical well. At that time, horizontal wellbore stimulation was barely contemplated, much less perfected. We believed well-bore exposure (the total surface area of a well) was all you needed to be commercial. Luckily, in this instance, it was.

On one of our first nights of exploration there in 1995, I climbed the metal steps to the floor of Nabors Drilling Rig 557 in North Dakota. The sky was clear and cold as I peered out from the rig. For a moment, I felt how I imagine the early explorers must have felt—knowing something remarkable was out there, feeling it in my bones. And at the same time, wondering if the whole journey would end in utter failure. The weird thing about the view that night from the floor of Nabors 557 was that we had two rigs drilling two test wells on the Cedar Creek Anticline, and you couldn't see one rig from the elevated floor of the other one. On our lease and prospect area map they had seemed so close together. At that point, on that dark night, I was somewhat taken aback by the immensity of this prospect. As Tom Selleck said, "Risk is the price you pay for opportunity." We were about to find out the real price.

Both early tests worked. We immediately leased one hundred thousand additional acres. I spent every penny we had to own what I knew was there. Tom Luttrell, our head Land guy, ran the leasing show with me. The tension and the excitement were unending. From Baker, Montana, to Buffalo, South Dakota, we were in a leasing competition with Meridian Oil Company that required a virtual war room. We eventually amassed over two hundred and fifty thousand acres of leases. In addition, we bought out Koch Oil Company's holdings in the area, including their Red River Units and Medicine Pole Hills Units that I believed were parts of the contiguous field. Cedar Hills proved to be a milestone field for Continental.

But that wasn't our biggest bet. Our team's faith in our technological prowess was the difference maker.

The Jean Peterson well was one of hundreds of wells that were ultimately drilled in the Cedar Hills field—Continental's first giant oilfield. It made history as the very first oilfield in the world drilled exclusively with horizontal wells. Other operators in the Williston Basin were skeptical of Horizontal Drilling at that time and elected not to take part in the drilling or development of the field.

At that time, Horizontal Drilling was just too novel an idea for most in this industry. Only those daring, unconventional, or crazy would try it. We were all three. Meridian and Continental were the only companies to drill wells in the entire field. After the field was developed, I had the opportunity to ask a prominent operator in the Dakotas why his company didn't participate in the development of Cedar Hills.

He replied simply, "I guess I was just burdened by too much knowledge." His statement said so much. Here again, I was glad I did not have that much knowledge. So many people are set against change and always settle for the status quo rather than believing in what could be.

Now on to the next challenge. *If only we could see down there when we're drilling in order to stay in zone.*

Implementing Near-Bit Technology

We used gamma rays to locate the drill string in a particular formation in the horizontal lateral, but the gamma ray tool had to be placed almost one hundred feet behind the drill bit due to the existing technology at the time. Obviously, we needed the tool to be as close to the bit as possible to keep from drilling out of the preferred formation. I called our drill-guidance vendors and invited them to our office in Enid.

Halliburton, Schlumberger, Baker INTEQ, and Sperry-Sun all descended on Enid to meet with us in 1995. We told them about our Horizontal Drilling issue and that we needed a better way to precisely guide the drill bit. I'll never forget the CEO of Halliburton's response.

"Harold, this Horizontal Drilling is such a novel idea, we just can't afford to spend any research and development money on

U.S. Rig Count Orientation by Market Share

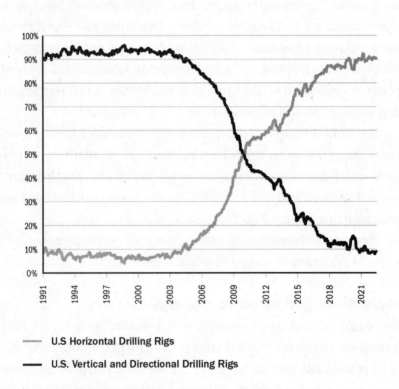

------- U.S Horizontal Drilling Rigs

——— U.S. Vertical and Directional Drilling Rigs

Source: "North American Rig Count," Baker Hughes, accessed December 21, 2022, https://rigcount.bakerhughes.com/na-rig-count

The first one hundred years or so of fossil fuel recovery was tapping pools of oil that leaked from the source beds. Horizontal Drilling revolutionized the way we produce oil and natural gas, so it's no surprise it's pretty much replaced vertical wells.

it." I replied, "That's OK, but whichever company is willing to work on developing this technology and spend research money to do so will receive 100 percent of our business from now on."

Sperry-Sun, a much smaller company, elected to invest in the research and development of near-bit technology, and we gave them 100 percent of our work, as promised. The other vendors had been watching closely for any breakthroughs in research that would provide improvements to the technology. As soon as these improvements were made, Horizontal Drilling took off. The change had started and was beginning to escalate. That year, Halliburton formulated an offer and bought Sperry-Sun as part of its Dresser Industries merger to get the technology they developed for horizontal work. (Yes, they somehow found an even bigger budget for that enterprise. Better late than never, I suppose.) Today, over 90 percent of all wells in the U.S. are drilled horizontally.

Cedar Hills has now been producing for almost thirty years and has been successfully unitized by the North Dakota Industrial Commission. This means all interests in the field are merged into common units for secondary repressurization. We will explore this later, but these units will soon be repressurized with CO_2 for tertiary recovery to yield even more oil and used for carbon capture and storage.

Total field recovery is expected to exceed 250 million barrels of oil; that's considered a major field and a company maker. Continental's portion of the field still produces 7,500 hundred barrels per day after all those years. Not a bad start for wanting to find oil in large quantities—and all thanks to Horizontal Drilling!

Exploration Changed Forever

The Horizontal Drilling phenomenon has been referred to as a miracle, and it will go down in history as one of the top ten technological achievements of the twentieth century. Horizontal Drilling transformed everything connected to energy. It was a revolution compared to vertical drilling techniques, and so much of a complete change that our young superclass of geologists today has asked me to tell them about the vertical days. The Horizontal Drilling transformation is so complete that younger generations can't even envision what was being done before. Miracles like these advancements may take a long time to conceive, but they have an incredibly swift impact on society.

With this new opportunity unlocked, I could begin to hypothesize what else was possible with this technology. Horizontal Drilling had proven to be the key to uncovering the oil bounty of thin-bedded reservoirs. I immediately asked myself and my team, "Where is the next one?"

The answer wasn't hard to find.

CHAPTER 7

Shale Yes! Cracking the Code of the Bakken

" *Harold Hamm, the Oklahoma-based founder and*
CEO of Continental Resources, the 14th-largest
oil company in America, is a man who thinks big.
He came to Washington last month to spread a
needed message of economic optimism: With the
right set of national energy policies, the United
States could be 'completely energy independent
by the end of the decade. We can be the Saudi
Arabia of oil and natural gas in the 21st century.'"

—Stephen Moore, "How North Dakota
Became Saudi Arabia," the *Wall*
Street Journal, October 1, 2011

IN 2011, STEVE MOORE'S HEADLINE IN THE *WALL STREET Journal* aptly dubbed North Dakota the next Saudi Arabia, showcasing for the world my belief that domestic oil production would quickly lessen our dependence on foreign oil—if the industry had the will, investment capital, regulatory framework, and technology to make it work. After the Horizontal Drilling success of Cedar Hills in 1995, we immediately began searching for the next application for this breakthrough technique and found it in the Bakken Formation, beginning in Montana.

Armed with the challenge, Jim Kochick, a geologist from our exploration team, mapped out a large area of porosity within the middle Bakken geological member in 1996. The Bakken Formation contains a mixture of oil-rich organic shales with interbedded, silty dolomites and sand, and it covers about two hundred thousand square miles, including parts of Montana, North Dakota, Saskatchewan, and Manitoba. It was named after Henry Bakken, a farmer in Tioga, North Dakota, who owned the land where some of the first wells in North Dakota were drilled. Oil was first discovered in the early 1950s, but it would take another five decades before Henry's name would become known around the energy world due to our work with Horizontal Drilling and breaking the code of how to produce oil and gas from shale.

We knew the Bakken contained huge amounts of oil and natural gas. Earlier estimates had indicated as much as 450–500 billion barrels of oil had been generated from the Bakken shales over geologic time. Despite this grand estimate, very little had been produced due to the difficulty of producing oil from a shale formation. It was nearly impossible from vertical wells. This was one of the many times where more than a few people around me were saying, "Harold, you know trying to get oil from shale is crazy." They failed to dissuade me. I would try to prove them wrong through the use of our new tool, Horizontal Drilling.

My team and I were determined to find a way to turn the Bakken shale into one of the great producing fields in the lower forty-eight states. Next to my family and friends, I'm always happiest when I'm spending time with the geologists and engineers, poring over logs and working with interpretations and 3D seismic. My office is littered with maps and charts. I probably know more about what's underground than what's above.

In 1996, we had the Bakken all mapped out, and we first began leasing in Montana in 2000. We knew that commercially producing the Bakken required both Horizontal Drilling and reservoir fracture stimulation. But before we could drill the Bakken, we had to drill through regulatory rock.

Montana had a pile of burdensome regulations that had virtually killed the state's energy industry. We set out to change this. First, we received the Governor's blessing. Next, we held many industry town halls and one-on-one meetings to share information with other stakeholders. Then, we sponsored and passed legislation in 1993 to provide an eighteen-month tax holiday for certain types of innovative drilling techniques, including horizontal. We later did the same in North Dakota, working with their governor, industry officials, and other decision-makers. Spoiler alert: lowering taxes and reducing regulations actually increased revenues and boosted the economies for those states in a big way, as it typically does. These changes were instrumental in bringing about exploration in the Cedar Hills field and helpful in kicking off the Bakken play in Montana, where it all began. Removing these regulatory and tax hurdles cleared the way in both Montana and North Dakota to revitalize the oil and gas industry there.

As I look back on the entire sequence of events that brought about this incredible transformation, it strikes me that what we were able to do was nothing short of a miracle. Prior to our work there, the Bakken was considered *noncommercial* by everyone in our business. The interest wasn't there because the technology didn't exist to get oil from shale. For goodness' sake, "everyone knew it was the source bed, not a producing interval, after all." We knew it was going to take a technological leap or two to make it work. It took more than that!

In a portion of the area, Kochick, we mapped a couple of wells and leases that we were interested in and were owned by a Dallas oil and gas operator. We approached them with a joint venture arrangement using Horizontal Drilling and wellbore stimulation.

They declined but took the idea and started Horizontal Drilling operations suspiciously similar to what we had proposed. Not having their own set of rock stars, they flailed for a couple of years, drilling eighteen wells without commercial success.

We watched patiently as they tried various methods and ideas until they reached the point of maximum frustration and one of them tried something we call "pump and pray"—indiscriminately pumping large concentrations of water and sand down the intermediate casing into the uncased but isolated horizontal lateral within the Middle Bakken. Lo and behold, the well delivered eight hundred barrels of oil a day.

You might wonder how we knew so much about what our competitors were doing. It's hard to keep anything secret very long in the oil business. There are public records on rig and well activity, but the number one communication pipeline in the oilfield is the grapevine. It's always the most dependable.

So we again dropped the flag to begin leasing every open acre within the Kochick outline. Our ownership within the producing area of the Bakken in Montana ballooned to about one-third of the overall field size.

In 2002, once we were more certain in our capabilities on the Montana side, we sent Tom Luttrell and his land-acquisition army out to acquire as many leases as we could grab along the Nesson Anticline in North Dakota—a long geologic feature that ran from north to south, from the Canadian border near Tioga, North Dakota, through the state, finally petering out just south of Dickinson, North Dakota. By 2003, we had leased three hundred thousand acres in North Dakota to begin with.

Geologically, we had projected this area as the thermal, overpressured "kitchen," which, during the maturation process, turned the organics trapped in the Bakken shale into oil and natural gas. Here's how it looked to us.

Jeff Hume, who was the head of our operation efforts at the time, will tell you he was scared to death. Truth is, we were all a little twitchy. Every dollar we had was earmarked for additional leases. We were hoping to bring in more partners to help

Bakken Petroleum System

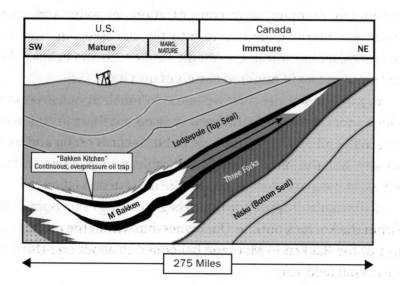

We operate thousands of feet below the surface and across hundreds of miles of geological formations.

us acquire more acreage, but no one was biting. Back in Dallas and Houston, there were chuckles about "Hamm's Folly" in the conference rooms. What did we do? The only thing we could do: we started drilling and wound up with eight rigs in Montana. Completed wells justified the growth. Wells came in producing eight hundred to a thousand barrels of oil per day, and our all-in cost for these producing wells at the time were $2 million per well. They were paying out in six months' time, giving us a great return on investment. But the Montana Bakken was completely different than the North Dakota Bakken shale. On the Montana side, we had a thin, low-porosity zone to help us. On the North Dakota side, the porous zone wasn't there. We were left working with mostly impermeable shale rock.

We tested our concept with one rig on the North Dakota side in 2003. It was the Robert Heuer 1-17R well in Divide County, which became the first fracture-stimulated, commercially successful horizontal Bakken well in North Dakota—but just barely. Those early days of figuring out the magic formula were tough sledding.

Game Changer: Cracking the Code in North Dakota

Most petroleum geology classes assumed that oil, being a liquid, could not be produced from low-porosity rock due to its impermeable nature and the size of the oil molecules. The textbook answer was that only natural gas molecules could pass through the tight rock of the source beds. Once again, I'm glad I didn't read that book. Looking back, cracking the code took determination, lots of trial and error, and intense applied rock-science technology. But more than skepticism around tight rock, we had to overcome the impermeability problem.

In short, we reverted to consideration of the geologic conditions that are unique unto themselves. Our new prospective area was closer to the overpressured basin center, the pressures that it took to stimulate the rock were considerably greater, and there was an order-of-magnitude difference in terms of permeability and porosity. The open hole "pump and pray" was not going to cut it in the North Dakota Bakken. Recoveries were limited and oil and gas production declines were significant and immediate, providing sub-economic returns.

To solve the permeability issues with the shale, our team devised a strategy for the increase of stimulated rock volume (SRV). We did this through the development of multistage fracture stimulation within many isolated, individual segments of the lateral portion of the well through limited perforation clusters using the placement of large quantities of fine-grained sand carried by slick water. The sand enhanced the natural fracturing within the rock.

I also made the call to extend the lateral lengths to two miles, doubling the industry standard for about one-third more cost. Although it took some regulatory work, it proved economical, and this became the new spacing standard for North Dakota drilling.

We had to consistently improve the process over time to increase the return on our investment. At Continental, we do the difficult immediately; the impossible takes a little longer. It sure did prove to be true with breaking the code of producing oil from the Bakken shale in North Dakota. We slowly climbed the learning curve, well after well, as we attempted technological idea after idea to get the job done. All in all, it took us about five years. Like I said, the impossible takes a little longer. But by 2008, we were making some phenomenal wells and finally seeing a giant leap in the rate of return and an equally significant emerging resource. It had worked. We had cracked the code. Another game changer! Just as Horizontal

Drilling was the driver of increased production from tight reservoirs, now shale oil production was a significant lasting game changer as well.

Down-hole steering practices became easier with Measurement While Drilling (MWD) and other advanced technologies. Through better steering techniques, we cut our drilling costs, which improved the rate of returns. With modern directional steering practices, we can now drill over three miles laterally (without any sidetracks) and literally hit a target as small as a penny—or a quarter, adjusting for today's inflation. Drilling time in the Bakken decreased from forty-five days per well to between eight and eleven days. Multistage completion technology now allows up to sixty separate completion stages (sections in the wellbore that extract hydrocarbons, or the "holes in a straw" analogy) compared to one single stage in the beginning.

Three Forks

In 2000, I and other team members visited the state core lab at Grand Forks, North Dakota, to examine all the available Bakken cores. Julia LeFever, core lab director at the University of North Dakota, laid them out for us in a nice, orderly fashion. We were trying to understand all about the rock. Interestingly, we noticed staining in a section of the zone below the Bakken in the Three Forks Formation. I wondered how the oil stain got into that lower section. It didn't seem to be a source rock or have enough organic matter in it. I finally thought, *Someday, we'll just have to test it.*

As the Bakken developed, I had that nagging feeling I needed to test Three Forks. Everybody pushed back. We were doing so well now drilling the Middle Bakken. I insisted, and we drilled the Bice Three Forks well in 2008. It was hugely successful. My crazy idea paid off. A year later, everybody was permitting and drilling the Three Forks interval. The size of the prize grew exponentially as the Three Forks produced commercially from up to three interval geologic members and covered a very large geographical area.

As our May 2008 press release noted, "The Bice 1-29H flowed at an average rate of 693 barrels of crude oil equivalent per day during its initial seven days of production.... We are very pleased with these results. This is our first well designed to test the theory that the Three Forks/Sanish formation may be a separate oil-producing reservoir not drained by a horizontal completion in the Middle Bakken zone above it."

While everyone else was distracted with challenges in the economy, we were amassing a huge acreage position because we could envision the size of the Bakken prize. We leased nine hundred thousand acres between 2008 and 2009, and within a decade, Continental had a majority-lease position in the Bakken oilfield. Our peak leasehold position in Montana and North Dakota for the Bakken was 1.2 million acres. At the time, our combined leases in the Bakken only occupied an area the size of Rhode Island, without the fancy seaports.

Back in 2005, the U.S. Geological Survey said there were 151 million barrels of recoverable oil in the Bakken, but they hadn't updated their data since 1995. That's a nice number, but it didn't get anyone's blood pumping. In the spring of 2008, after a request by the North Dakota Industrial Commission to recheck their numbers, they upped their reserves to 3 to 4 *billion* barrels recoverable utilizing the conventional technology at the time. That puts it among the top fields in the world. The U.S.G.S. clearly wasn't on the same page as everyone else and never seemed to come around to the idea of a huge pool of recoverable oil in the Bakken shale. Consequently, there still weren't many "experts" thinking we had a reason to be so obsessed with the Bakken. But I knew the estimates were way off. The field has already produced over 4 billion barrels of oil and is closing in on 5 billion.

At Continental, our estimates at the time were between twenty and thirty billion barrels in the Bakken, five to seven times more than the government calculated. Time and technology proved us right. Our estimates today are at the higher range near thirty-five billion barrels and could go higher with secondary and, possibly, tertiary recovery, CO_2 injection, and continued advances in technology.

Let me give you an idea of how far we had come as a company. Back in 1992, our CFO, Roger Clement, pushed a piece of paper across the table to our new exploration manager, Jack Stark, and said, "Here's your drilling budget for the year." It was $4 million. He added, "Don't waste it."

When you start out the way I did, $4 million was an eye-popping number.

Today, one well in the Bakken is a $7 million spend alone. As our budget grew to $5 billion over the next thirty years, this story remains one of Jack's favorites to tell.

But perhaps most impressive, and thanks to our band of rock stars, the Bakken changed the trajectory of energy in America. It propelled us to energy independence in the U.S.

In general, we are producing more oil domestically than we're consuming, lessening our long, expensive reliance on foreign sources of oil. The light, sweet crude found in a barrel of Bakken oil has no sulfur content, very little asphaltic bottom sediment, and a large amount of middle distillates, making it perfect for diesel, jet fuel, and gasoline. As a result, diesel prices dropped from $4.50 a gallon to under $2.50 by the end of 2020. Before the Biden administration, U.S. gas prices were the lowest unsubsidized prices in the industrialized world.

But, most importantly, it provided proof that crude oil could be produced from shale source beds in huge quantities. As a result, that one breakthrough in technology has been applied to numerous shale reservoirs across America. Oklahoma's own Woodford Formation is a prime example.

Horizontal Drilling unlocked those "immobile" barrels Michael Ray talked about in his thesis long ago. This process is directly responsible for the creation of the American Energy Renaissance. In the century before this technology was developed, we were literally scratching the surface. I am thankful to have enjoyed a role in the process of expanding the natural gas and oil production in our world, and I'm thankful for the dedication and ingenuity of my colleagues.

The *culture of the possible* has been core to my convictions and our company's core values for the past fifty-five years. We embody the old saying, "The difficult is done at once; the impossible takes a little longer." I believe this will stand the test of time.

Thanks to Horizontal Drilling, millions of jobs were created. We have a bountiful and reliable supply of energy. Production tax dollars flowed to federal, state, and local coffers, and our nation has enjoyed a $1 trillion swing to the positive, meaning a $1 trillion surplus back into the pockets of consumers of the world, all because we are exporting energy and keeping our energy dollars at home.

Our company helped produce a large cadre of new millionaires in Montana and North Dakota from the new jobs and mineral royalties. Not bad for a bunch of rock star explorers from Enid, Oklahoma.

At the beginning of the book, I told you we bet the farm on going public in 2007 at $15. Did it pay off? It paid off indeed. Those investors that took the risk with us as we validated the Bakken were rewarded within sixteen months, with a stock price of $81.68. Going public had proven to be the right thing to do at the right time, even though it hurt and was a very difficult decision to make.

Exploration in America

Because we zigged when the "experts" zagged, we found the reservoirs and developed the technology to extract the goods. You may have noticed in all these details that no large oil company names are mentioned when it came to the development of the shales in the past twenty years. For them, they just couldn't believe it would ever be big enough to affect their bottom-line financial results.

Recently, that narrow view changed drastically as they witnessed the magnitude of shale development across the major producing basins of the continental U.S.

As I like to say jokingly, *When Big Oil's ship came in, they were at the airport!*

They've since come back home and spent billions buying back into ownership positions within the major shale-producing basins of the U.S. Most of the large oil companies have made multibillion-dollar acquisitions for oil and gas production, future development opportunities, and infrastructure in shale basins.

In addition to the gifted colleagues whom I mention in this book, there are scores of others whose talent and dedication changed the game—not only for Continental Resources but for every citizen of this country. Thank you. My hard hat is off to you.

Groundbreaking

If not for Horizontal Drilling, this nation and our daily lives would look much different. Would gasoline prices be over $10

Evolution of Drilling & Completion Technology

1800s
1st well drilled in 1859

Conventional Vertical Wall

~60 sq. ft of reservoir exposed to the wellbore.

In 2000
8% of wells are horizontal

8%

1940s

Vertical Well + Stimulation

~12,000 sq. ft of reservoir exposed to the wellbore.

↓

200x more efficient.

Today
94% of wells are horizontal

94%

1990s

Horizontal Wellbore

2 miles

80,000 sq. ft of reservoir exposed to the wellbore.   ⟶   **1,000x** more efficient.

2000s

Horizontal Wellbore + Fracture Stimulation

2 miles

12,000,000 sq. ft of reservoir exposed to the wellbore.   ⟶   **200,000x** more efficient.

Source: Enverus, subscription, accessed December 21, 2022, https://app.drillinginfo.com/production/#/default

The point I relentlessly make is, technology evolves and continually improves, unlocking more energy, more economically.

a gallon? Probably. Would we be looking for oil in all the wrong places? Definitely—all while boosting the bank accounts of some pretty dangerous regimes.

Starting in the early 1900s in Titusville, Pennsylvania, pundits have told Americans that we have a limited supply of oil and gas in America that is on the verge of running out. Yet independent oil and gas producers in America have proved them wrong time and again as additional reservoirs are found and new technology enables more discoveries.

Horizontal Drilling means members of the herd have to change their thinking and admit they are wrong about U.S. oil and natural gas potential. After centuries of using rudimentary drill bit measures, we can now realize the huge oil and gas resources that we have for our consumption in the U.S. and around the world.

As we continue to disprove the pundits of the past and provide reason to give them pause when viewing predictions of the future, I can proudly say that today, America is the leading producer both of oil and natural gas in the world. Will we ever face an oil and gas shortage again? Probably due to politics but not due to America's geologic resource.

CHAPTER 8

The Renaissance: America Achieves Energy Independence

L ET'S TAKE A MENTAL FIELD TRIP AND DRILL A LITTLE deeper into what drives our way of life.

Your alarm just went off. Alexa's voice is softly suggesting it's time to get your butt out of bed. The Amazon Echo device she's housed in is made of plastics and artificial fibers. She's powered by a server farm and your connection to the electrical grid.

Twenty percent of the electricity you're using this morning might come from renewables. Maybe there's some wind and a bit of solar. You flip back the sheets and blanket, made by people in Vietnam, shipped in huge cargo ships, and then trucked to retail stores across America. Most likely your mattress, bedding, and towels are a blend of natural and synthetic fibers.

You lace up your running shoes, which are made entirely of petroleum-based synthetic materials. The smartwatch you're wearing, the moisture-wicking fabrics in your running clothes, and the pavement you're pounding are all composed of hydrocarbons.

You return home. The coffee machine is set to brew at exactly 7:15 a.m. The aroma of freshly ground coffee wafts through your home. The beans originated in Costa Rica and were delivered by container ship, and those big boats are definitely not wind-powered. The brewer has a smart chip produced in Taiwan. The machine itself was manufactured in Germany and is made of petroleum products imported from the Middle East.

You stumble down the hallway made of a petroleum-based laminate and flick on the nifty lights your spouse installed last year. They're LED energy savers. Good for you, but the bulbs are mostly made from fossil fuels.

You open your refrigerator. Now, I would guess nothing in it is grown, harvested, killed, or field-dressed by you or your family. Thanks to the best hydrocarbon-powered logistics and transportation network in the world and the fertilizers used in farming, you have fresh strawberries from California, grapefruit from Texas, cherry tomatoes from Mexico, and organic herbs from a farm downstate. The security of our food supply relies on natural gas.

Go ahead, crack a couple of eggs, and turn on the burner. What's that? Oh, it's the glowing blue flame of clean-burning natural gas piped a thousand miles or so from the Marcellus Shale in western Pennsylvania.

Back up the stairs for a quick shower. The new PVC piping behind the walls is, well, you guessed it, sourced from hydrocarbons. The sun is just coming up over the horizon, so no real contribution from solar yet, and millions of your fellow Americans are making similar demands on the grid. The country is waking up, and energy demand is beginning to spike, but that's not your problem. You just want a hot shower.

Maybe you turn on the sixty-inch smart TV—a miracle of petroleum-based engineering that would have astounded our great-grandparents.

You reach for your phone and laptop that have been charging all night, courtesy of the hydrocarbon-backed grid that stays on despite the sun's overnight departure. Your devices are mostly hydrocarbon-based technology that didn't exist two decades ago and are adding about 1 to 2 percent demand to the grid annually.

The devices are connected to the Internet, which is powered by huge server farms gobbling incredible amounts of energy to run and keep cool, yet again the result of the hydrocarbon-generated electricity.

You climb in your car. It's gas powered. You considered a hybrid or EV but decided not to pay the extra twenty grand to join the mystical Elon Musk club. It's comfortable, it's powerful, and most of all, its ridiculously convenient to drive, fuel, and maintain. And you may not spend much time thinking about it, but compared to the car your parents drove, it's leagues ahead from an emissions point of view, and you are glad you made the right choice as the Musk–Tesla fantasy meltdown takes place.

As the day advances, so does our world's dependence on hydrocarbons. Office buildings wake up, as do restaurants and stores. The demand for electricity begins to surge. The first flights of the day begin to cycle out of airports, moving hundreds of thousands of people around the world. You can't fly from here to there without oil-derived jet fuel.

Think of all the infrastructure and jobs it takes to make all that travel possible and affordable to virtually every American. There are no solar-powered or battery-operated planes capable of flying two hundred people fifteen hundred miles at speeds of six hundred miles per hour, and there won't be for decades to come, if ever.

But today you're driving, not flying. Your commute has cost about five bucks in fuel. It takes fewer than five minutes to give your vehicle over three hundred miles of range, thanks to all the energy locked up in gasoline.

Next, you swing into the parking lot of your workplace. For the next eight to nine hours, you are dependent on hydrocarbon-generated electricity. Just about everything in the office was made or transported by hydrocarbons. Your desk, your fancy chair, the noise-canceling panels, the carpet and tile, the copy machines—it's all fossil-fuel based.

Maybe you're scheduled for a couple of Zoom calls. Your client and your company's folks are in eight different locations across the country, all of them linked by a sophisticated electronic network that didn't exist even a few years back.

It's now about 5:00 p.m., and you have just enough time to make it to the grocery store before heading to your kid's soccer game. Every grocery cart tells a story. Yours is a testimony to the greatest just-in-time logistic network devised in human history, all powered by hydrocarbons. Fact is, it's not just *powered* by them; the essential ingredients are petroleum-based, beginning with the fertilizer that drives the miraculous yields of modern agriculture.

You grab fresh fruit and vegetables, newly baked bread, milk, and chilled meats. All were delivered during the day and set in the refrigerated section or on the shelves, thanks to hydrocarbons.

As you head home to pick up your daughter for her soccer game, demand for electricity is increasing. Millions of homes are using their air conditioners, and dishwashers and washing machines crank up. As the sun nears the horizon, solar power ebbs and winds diminish. Yet the demand for electricity is surging.

High above you, the International Space Station moves into the night side of earth. The astronauts look down and see a wondrous sight—a brilliant display of lights outlining the cities of North America, most of it courtesy of hydrocarbons.

We are a very long way from being able to dramatically "decarbonize" ourselves and still enjoy a modern life—although we've definitely started making big strides toward that end, starting with carbon capture and underground sequestration (CCUS) and other measures. Given time and intellectual order, it can be achieved—but the folks who believe we can stop using fossil fuels in five, ten, or twenty years are delusional, ignorant, or have another agenda.

Consider one other factor when it comes to the lifestyle we take for granted: for far too long, it ran on oil and natural gas imported from other countries.

The American Energy Renaissance

What comes to mind when you hear the word *renaissance?* Maybe you think of some strikingly dressed medieval thinkers and artists who propelled humankind out of the Dark Ages— mostly by upsetting conventional wisdom and pointing out to those in charge that much of what they believed was hogwash. Challenging conventional wisdom, in any period of human history, is often a risky undertaking. Ask Galileo.

We are living in the midst of another renaissance. Some might argue that it's mostly a tech revolution centered on the rise of handheld computing, social media, and global networking.

But there's another renaissance that's powering it: the American Energy Renaissance. In a little less than two decades, and under the radar of the town criers and court jesters, the U.S. became an energy superpower. The focus has been on the Silicon Valley tech giants who created products and services that met the never-ending human need to connect. Meanwhile, a handful of energy entrepreneurs and innovators, with the help of thousands of men and women in hard hats, helped fuel it all.

The American Energy Renaissance is real. We are only in the first one hundred and fifty years of humankind's hydrocarbon era. And, as I've said, we've only scratched the surface—literally—using about 15 percent of the available energy in those first fifteen decades. But what happened, right under everyone's noses, is the largest economic and geopolitical shift in recent history. This is something Dr. Yergin got right in his most recent book, *The New Map.*

And just like our heroes of the Middle Ages who changed the world for the better and propelled civilization forward, our early twenty-first-century entrepreneurs looked at the prevailing landscape, saw unearthed possibilities, and acted accordingly. There's still a lot of hydrocarbon energy to be found and produced. I like to refer to it as ancient wealth or hidden treasure, locked up until someone finds and shares it. As I often say, if you don't have a giant oilfield, find one.

During the early years of my life, being born in Oklahoma didn't always seem like a blessing. But maybe it was destiny. The Oklahoma Territory became the largest oil-producing region in the world even before it became a state—America's first energy renaissance. And it's probably no accident that Oklahoma was home to many of the pioneers of the most recent energy renaissance in America.

The world's most vibrant economy needed energy, and lots of it. As politicians, policymakers, and experts grappled with the realities of the modern world—mostly coming to the wrong conclusions—a handful of unconventional thinkers were experimenting and innovating to meet our nation's hunger for energy. They were mostly independent in mindset *and* operation. They didn't see any reason to go into parts of the world where business wasn't welcomed, sink billions offshore, or go into the Arctic where nothing worked at fifty degrees below zero.

Just like the unconventional thinkers of centuries ago, our new ideas were met with derision and scorn. Too much was—and frankly, still is—at stake.

Thinking Bigger

Thanks to Horizontal Drilling, beginning in 2010, America was producing more oil than at any time in its history, bringing tens of millions of barrels of the highest-quality light, sweet Bakken crude oil to market. And thanks to the huge new volume of oil enabled by Horizontal Drilling, my team and I championed ending the oil-export ban. The ban on oil exports was a legacy of the wrong-headed thinking of the seventies when all the "experts" were sure our geological gas tank was on empty and would remain that way.

Their reasoning was simple: we don't have much left so we better not sell it to anyone. How archaic and small is that? More importantly, they were dead wrong. We had the oil, but we were not allowed to export it. And the major oil company refiners had long since given up on finding oil in the lower forty-eight states. They had converted their refineries to process mostly heavy bitumen oil from the Canadian tar sands and Mexico. Because of the lack of U.S. refining capacity for light, sweet crude, the downstream refiners were forcing us to discount the value of our oil up to $27 a barrel. Of course, that made it hard for us to stay in business. Even more, light, sweet crude is *more* valuable than heavy oil. It was widely understood we needed to lift the ban on exports, but the "why" was less apparent. It was the abundance of oil, lack of domestic refining capacity, and global demand for our type of crude oil in refineries around the world, but primarily in the U.K.

By 2014, I had put together our case for Congress. Working with the Domestic Energy Producers Alliance (DEPA) and several other organizations, we set out to pass new legislation to correct this injustice. Most thought we had no chance. The optimists predicted it would take three to five years and a friendlier administration. The pessimists didn't think we had a shot. While the optimists and pessimists wrung their hands, I made thirty-five trips to Washington, D.C., in fifteen months, talking with U.S. House and Senate members, their staffs, and many other agency and regulatory bodies. I was relentless because our industry needed to thrive for the U.S. to become energy independent.

Miracles do happen, especially when they have a little push in the right direction. We made our case, and, with a little horse trading, our bill was included in the Omnibus Spending Bill that the Obama administration had to get passed. The export ban was lifted on December 18, 2015, and the results have been spectacular. We achieved our goal in fifteen hard-fought months. For me, Christmas had come early. I was overjoyed. Our Senior Vice President of Government and Regulatory Affairs, Blu Hulsey, and I fielded congratulatory compliments from around the world and toasted with the very best Scotch whisky as financially challenging 2015 finally came to an end.

There was a huge global market for American crude. Billions in investment flowed to the Gulf Coast, and jobs were created across the country as infrastructure was put in place to compete in the global crude oil market. In just a matter of months, the U.S. had created a $1 trillion swing in its favor.

We predicted, with gratifying accuracy, not only that the United States was *not* going to run out of oil but that we could achieve energy independence and erase the market differential. We told anyone who would listen that all we had to do was ship our oil directly to markets around the world. In 2015, my prediction came true thanks to our Horizontal Drilling innovations. In eleven hours of trading, that differential went to zero. The technology returned

tay here, in our pockets, no longer funding the agendas of rogue
egimes and dictators.

Energy-producing states started running big budget
surpluses because of tax dollars collected from oil and natural
gas production. Those tax dollars flowed to education and
created jobs, not just in energy industry but in construction,
transportation, and the trades.

Global Oil Supply, Demand, and Imbalance (mb/d)

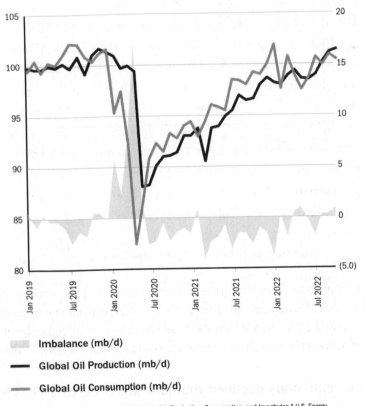

Imbalance (mb/d)

▬ Global Oil Production (mb/d)

▬ Global Oil Consumption (mb/d)

Source: "3a. International Petroleum and Other Liquids Production, Consumption, and Inventories," U.S. Energy Information Administration, accessed December 21, 2022, https://www.eia.gov/outlooks/steo/data/browser/#/?v=6

The world's thirst for oil was only temporarily interrupted by COVID-19. It took no time to get back to a world where energy demand is increasing.

America to the status of an energy superpower. Severa
in 2019, we achieved energy independence.

Made in the U.S.A.

A few years back, at Continental, we framed this ph
lobby of our headquarters: "Good things flow from Am

Perhaps it should have read: *Extraordinary, incred
changing, life-improving things—for all citizens—f
American Oil.*

Here are just a few of the benefits from the dramatic
in domestic oil and natural gas production:

The U.S. became the largest energy producer on th
leading Saudi Arabia and Russia on oil and natural gas pro
to the tune of thirteen million barrels of oil per day in 201
billion cubic feet per day of natural gas. After surviving the
of COVID-19 and more than two full years of the Biden adm
tion, we are currently producing 101 billion cubic feet of natu
each day and more than fourteen million barrels of crude oil
as of this writing. If President Biden would repeal his federal
leasing ban, we could once again become energy independe
surpassing the thirteen million barrels threshold set in 2019.
explain this in greater detail in the following pages.

In 2019, we became a net energy *exporter.* In other word
were energy independent and able to sell the overflow of bot
and natural gas overseas to our global allies. The U.S. is curre
exporting more than eleven billion cubic feet of natural gas per
to our allies around the world as Putin chooses to use his count
natural gas as a military weapon. Expanding the sale of Americ
energy to our allies in Europe and Asia is probably the most eff
tive tactic against Russia's plans to dominate the European ener
market, and the most effective way to boost our economy. Dolla

U.S. Net Energy Imports
(Quadrillion BTU/month)

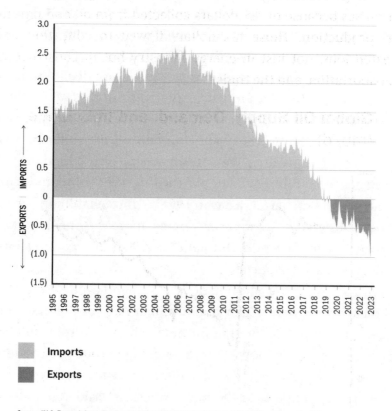

Imports

Exports

Source: "U.S. Energy Information Administration Short Term Energy Outlook Data," Bloomberg, subscription, accessed May 3, 2023

On a total Btu basis, considering the amount of LNG exports we're now sending abroad, the U.S. is actually net positive energy. It has been difficult to maintain at times since 2021 when federal leases and permits were limited by the Biden administration. This could never have happened without Horizontal Drilling.

CO_2 emissions declined dramatically, back to 1990 levels, thanks to clean-burning natural gas replacing coal as the electricity-generating fuel of choice. Today, the U.S. enjoys some of the cleanest air in the industrialized world.

We also strengthened our position in the world. The Middle East countries will always have their oil, as will Venezuela and Russia. But we no longer need it. Every barrel of oil we produce here is one less barrel we need to buy from overseas. We no longer need to bow to dictators, and we reduce the flow of oil revenues that are financing Russia's war chest.

The booming U.S. economy provided Americans with an extra $6,000 in income annually. American families were able to save more as they spent less on gasoline, heating oil, and electricity. Here at home, the era of abundance was producing very strong economic results. We were increasing oil production at an unprecedented rate. For example, the U.S. went from producing about six million barrels a day in 1995 to thirteen million barrels per day in 2019. We were producing more oil and gas than anyone else in the world. Our nation went from becoming a net importer to a net exporter.

In 2023, with the addition of WTI Midland Crude, American oil has become part of the global benchmark for the first time ever as the Brent oil pricing formula, which is responsible for setting the price on more than 75 percent of crude transactions globally, will now include an American crude input. Lifting the ban on exports literally made American crude oil a global commodity.

American Employment

The domestic oil and gas industry is directly responsible for over ten million jobs. The Democratic Party seems bound and determined to decrease the number sharply. My industry contributes 7 percent of our gross domestic product, but in my home state of Oklahoma, it's upward of 30 percent.

Imagine, then, a world in which our American Energy Renaissance never happened. America would have mortgaged its future to hydrocarbon-producing countries. We wouldn't have the cheap and abundant fuel to power growth. Manufacturing would flee the U.S. once and for all, and with it, all those jobs. Our very freedom to move about the country would be at risk as transportation costs would skyrocket. The cost of running a small business would rise dramatically, crushing job creation and healthy competition. Taxes would increase to make up for the shortfalls from levies on energy production and use.

But the miracle did happen! We truly did open up an era of abundance and it remains today with great resilience.

I find it ironic that America is now energy independent thanks to oil and natural gas, while at the same time, it's being thrust politically into an EV world, forced into dependence on China for over 80 percent of the precious metals required for them. One might ask, is it ironic or intentional?

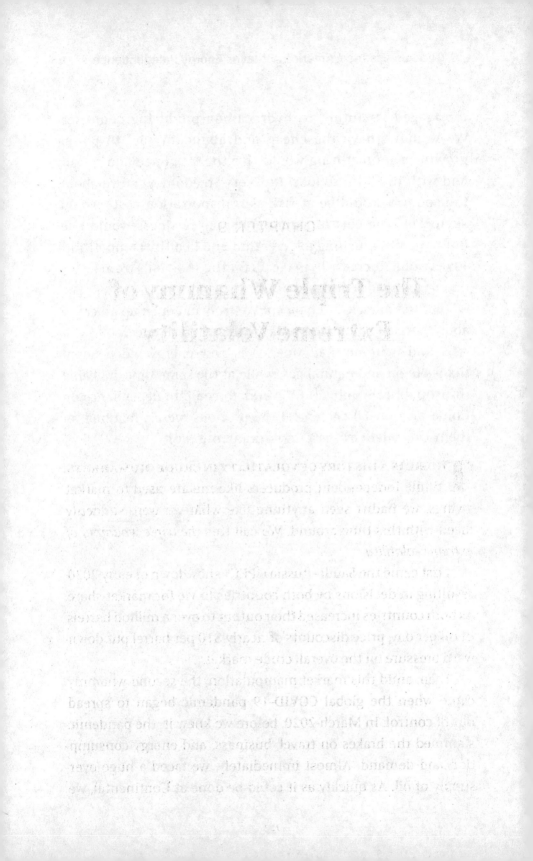

CHAPTER 9

The Triple Whammy of Extreme Volatility

THERE IS A HISTORY OF VOLATILITY IN CRUDE OIL MARKETS. While independent producers like me are used to market swings, we hadn't seen anything like what we were suddenly faced with this time around. We call this *the triple whammy of extreme volatility.*

First came the Saudi–Russia OPEC+ showdown of early 2020, resulting in decisions by both countries to vie for market share. As both countries increased their output to over a million barrels of oil per day, price discounts of nearly $10 per barrel put downward pressure on the overall crude market.

Then, amid this market manipulation, the second whammy came when the global COVID-19 pandemic began to spread out of control. In March 2020, before we knew it, the pandemic slammed the brakes on travel, business, and energy consumption and demand. Almost immediately, we faced a huge oversupply of oil. As quickly as it could be done at Continental, we cut production and drilling accordingly as oil prices fell with demand. Times were very uncertain. Many businesses of all types were forced to close. Others trimmed their workforce. In our industry, exploration slowed to a crawl. On April 20, 2020, oil went negative for the first time ever and sold for -$37.63 at the close of business.

At the start of 2021, activity returned as COVID-19 waned and OPEC+ finally got its act together as a price-setting monopoly once again. Demand began rising as the world economy reopened and world trade was reestablished. However, the third triple whammy came when Joe Biden assumed the presidency. While the first two whammies impacted prices negatively, this third whammy caused commodity prices to begin to escalate at the expense of the American economy as supply growth was immediately limited with his punitive executive orders, starting on day one, in his attempt to eliminate U.S. oil and gas producers as he'd promised he would.

Through the Biden administration's rhetoric, regulations, and policy restrictions against the oil and gas industry, the price of gasoline and diesel immediately began to rise as the market sensed a new era of underinvestment beginning to bring about scarcity of supply. His first executive order was a ban against leasing and drilling on federal lands. By the summer of 2022, the price of gasoline and diesel had doubled, and the cost of electricity had risen.

The week Biden took office in January 2021, the national average gasoline price was $2.30 per gallon. By February 2022, prior to the Russian invasion of Ukraine and contrary to the Biden administration's narrative, gasoline prices were already averaging $3.61 per gallon. By June 2022, the national average crossed over the $5.00 per gallon level for the first time in history.

With the third whammy of Biden's failed energy policies, creating the *Biden premium* on transportation costs, we were also headed for record inflation not seen since the Carter era in the 1970s. More parallel universes.

In addition, what the world did not see coming was the impact of the Russian invasion of Ukraine, which quickly accelerated the whole world into an era of oil scarcity. In less than eighteen months, America went from an era of oversupply to scarcity. The world had already left itself vulnerable by too quickly attempting an energy transition, so when one country used energy as a weapon, it put the world into peril, something we had predicted all along.

Parallel Universes

There's always a mindset behind policy decisions like the Fuel Use Act, and it's rarely based on logic and most generally is punitive. Officials in Washington, D.C., are always looking for ways to generate political power. And there's a bias against the oil and gas industry because those who are employed in this sector are perceived as being "conservative." Many in the establishment don't like our industry and certainly don't talk with us before making bad decisions. If Jimmy Carter had talked with me in 1977, he would have learned that there was plenty of oil and natural gas available to power our nation's growth into the twenty-second century. In fact, I, and other energy professionals, made presentations to the Energy Congress in the winter of 1977 in Washington, underscoring that very point.

The Fuel Use Act was the most egregious early example of the war on energy and the start of our government picking winners and losers, thereby forcing unfavorable decisions on American consumers. It's the same today, as President Biden revealed in May 2022. Jimmy Carter could've probably sued him for plagiarism. Biden announced, "Here's the situation. When it comes to the gas prices, we're going through an incredible transition that is taking place that, God willing, when it's over, we'll be stronger, and the world will be stronger and less reliant on fossil fuels when this is over."

In 2023, with this singular-focused, failed green energy policy, humankind is back on a path to record-high levels of coal use. And as Ronald Reagan said, "Here we go again."

One side sees the oil and natural gas industry as obsolete at best—and a threat to human existence at worst. But hydrocarbons are the reason we have a modern world, lifting billions out of poverty, helping us advance faster in the past hundred years than we have in the previous ten thousand. Oil and natural gas have transformed civilization and made energy affordable and stable.

Our esteemed climate envoy, John Kerry, spends his time jet-setting around the globe, pressuring financial institutions to reduce their commitments to U.S. oil and natural gas companies. He wants them to join something called the Net Zero Banking Alliance, an agreement to shrink or terminate their financing of American oil and gas companies. When mandates, regulatory bodies, laws, and regulations aren't enough, some old-fashioned arm twisting cloaked in virtue-signaling is the perfect ploy.

Choking off capital is one way to hobble the domestic energy industry. Taken to its extreme, it might be the most effective way. What's left unsaid is that banks and financial institutions are chartered or regulated by the federal government and are making billions off the paper peddled by the feds. The pressure to fall in line is enormous.

In my universe, domestic energy exploration isn't the problem; it's the solution. We directly create millions of jobs; pay hundreds of billions in taxes; generously donate to the greater good to fund medicine, research, schools, and the arts—and we make the economy go. Plus, we're constantly innovating to reduce our environmental footprint.

War against Consumers

As I write this book, the U.S. transportation secretary recently declared that Americans will endure high gasoline prices until we "achieve a form of energy independence that is based on clean energy created here at home." In 2021, Secretary of Energy Jennifer Granholm said high gas prices would not be "affecting" Americans if they drove an electric car.

The equivalent of war is still being waged by some in government. And they are so against oil and natural gas that they are blocking the construction of a natural gas pipeline that would help power plants on the East Coast switch from burning coal or fuel oil to natural gas. The Mountain Valley Pipeline is 90 percent built. But this crucial natural gas transportation infrastructure has been stalled by special interest groups for many years.

The Biden administration, like so many before, is trying to change our energy system to fit its political agenda. First, Carter's administration promoted burning coal on a sky-blackening scale while prohibiting the use of clean-burning natural gas, despite being forewarned by an Environmental Impact Statement (EIS) of the consequences to come. Now, President Biden has nearly done the same, succeeding in doubling the price of gasoline and diesel, which pumped up inflation to the forty-year highs of the Carter administration—and he keeps doubling down! President Clinton is known to have said, "When you get into a hole, stop digging." Seems President Biden hasn't learned that one yet.

But trust me. The oil and gas industry will have the last word. We've been changing society for the better for decades, and we won't stop now.

Domestic Production since Joe Biden Assumed Office

It was one thing to fight a global pandemic, but our industry was further complicated by our own government as newly elected President Biden declared his efforts to end fossil fuels. While our industry was working to climb out of an unprecedented global pandemic, President Biden enacted the most punitive executive order in my lifetime, which strangled our ability to produce on federal lands. Federal lands are owned by the American people and make up 28 percent of the land mass and one-third of U.S. productive capacity.

By late 2020, global demand began to recover. Yet, while American oil and gas production has increased, the *rate* of recovery under Biden's administration has been blunted because of the punitive regulatory and permitting framework that is now in place. It is necessary to grow production to meet growing demand, or prices will be impacted as they were in the summer of 2022, when crude oil went up to almost $120 a barrel and natural gas reached $10 per mcf. The Biden administration's ill-advised strategy to choke American production backfired, and American production plummeted right along with Biden's polling.

Then, in a totally political move, Biden began releasing oil from the Strategic Petroleum Reserve. Without regulatory relief, we should get accustomed to the price fluctuations we see today.

Here are a few more highlights from candidate and then President Biden and his administration as of this writing:

- July 31, 2019 – When asked if there would be any place for fossil fuels in a Biden administration, Biden responded, "No … we would make sure it's eliminated and no more subsidies … (for) any fossil fuel."
- December 29, 2019 – Biden stated, "Doing away with any subsidies for fossil fuel … holding them liable for what they've done."

- January 25, 2020 – When asked about stopping new pipeline infrastructure, Biden responded, "Yes, yes."
- February 5, 2020 – Biden stated, "We are going to get rid of fossil fuels."
- March 15, 2020 – Biden said, "No more drilling on federal lands. No more drilling, including offshore. No ability for the oil industry to continue to drill, period."
- October 22, 2020 – Biden stated, "It has to be replaced by renewable energy over time, over time. And I'd stop giving to the oil industry. I'd stop giving them federal subsidies."
- October 22, 2020 – Biden said, "No fracking or oil on federal land."
- January 20, 2021 – On the day of his inauguration, President Biden revoked approval for the Keystone XL pipeline.
- January 27, 2021 – President Biden imposed a moratorium on oil and gas leasing on federal lands and waters.
- February 26, 2021 – President Biden inflated the social cost of carbon to justify the onerous regulation of fossil fuels.
- March 2, 2021 – Democrats introduced a bill to increase the cost of oil and gas production on federal land.
- March 19, 2021 – Democrats introduced a bill to make it prohibitively expensive for American energy companies to produce oil and gas.
- April 1, 2021 – Democrats proposed a national energy tax on oil, gas, and their by-products.
- May 28, 2021 – President Biden proposed a budget that would increase taxes on energy producers by $35 billion.
- August 11, 2021 – President Biden asked foreign operators at OPEC+, not domestic producers, to increase supply to address rising gas prices.

- October 28, 2021 – President Biden and Congressional Democrats proposed a methane fee, essentially a tax on production.
- November 17, 2021 – President Biden sent a letter to Federal Trade Commission chair Lina Khan requesting an investigation into oil and gas companies.
- February 17, 2022 – President Biden's FERC Chairman pushed through changes, making it next to impossible to build or upgrade pipeline infrastructure.
- March 11, 2022 – Democrats, who seemingly missed the president's memo requesting energy companies increase production, introduced a bill that would implement a massive new tax, destroying any incentive to produce more oil.
- March 21, 2022 – The Biden administration's Securities and Exchange Commission proposed a rule change to divert investment away from carbon energy.
- March 28, 2022 – President Biden, in the middle of an energy crisis, once again proposed a tax increase on domestic oil and gas producers, totaling nearly $45 billion.
- March 30, 2022 – The FDIC Chairman proclaimed that carbon-emitting sources of energy present risks to the safety of the financial sector.
- October 2022 – The Saudi government released the following statement following its announcement to cut production: "The Government of the Kingdom clarified through its continuous consultation with the U.S. Administration that all economic analyses indicate that postponing the OPEC+ decision for a month, according to what has been suggested, would have had negative economic consequences."

Biden's War on Oil Hits Consumers

By May 2022, consumer prices had increased 8.6 percent to their highest level in forty years. Food prices had risen by 10.1 percent, and energy was up 34.6 percent. Self-imposed inflation was rampant. The American energy industry stood ready, if only Washington would allow us to help and stop trying to put us out of business.

Gasoline prices soared to the highest prices we have seen, surpassing my $6 prediction. Biden's SPR releases lowered gasoline prices temporarily, but they failed to meaningfully decrease diesel prices. Diesel prices are the clearest indicator of the Biden administration's punitive policies. SPR releases are heavy sour crude with very limited amounts of middle distillates suited for the production of diesel. Diesel prices are the primary drivers of inflation for truck and train transportation. Americans need relief in the form of more U.S. light crude oil, and one thing stands in the way: President Biden's unwillingness to reverse course on his administration's commitment to put the American oil and gas industry out of business at the consumer's expense by shorting the market.

Freezing new drilling leases on federal land and banning federal permits puts our national security at risk. There is no good reason for America to become more reliant on foreign imports of oil and gas. Such reliance constrains our policy choices, forces us to cede our national security to foreign players, and enriches those who would do us harm. The Biden administration is working with the Saudis, Venezuelans, and even Iranians to come to the rescue. Why this foolishness? It is maddening to me that America has an abundance of oil and natural gas that Americans need—along with our allies, who are in desperate need—and we are being prohibited from producing it while we cede power to rogue regimes.

Their plan will mortgage our energy security—and economic security—while coming no closer to ending our dependence on hydrocarbons. The recent past tells the story.

Modern life in the world is predicated on cheap, abundant, and reliable energy. Why have politicians and pundits manufactured scarcity and mandated insecurity around the globe? Energy prices are rising everywhere, and Biden's release of 180 million barrels of oil from our strategic reserves was a temporary patch to repair his poll numbers, which had plummeted because of his ill-advised energy policies, and to try to maintain a majority in Congress. The SPR release will not impact the fundamentals of supply and demand in the long term—and its only achievement was to reduce the reserve to about half its capacity, making our national security even more vulnerable should a true emergency arise. By the way, the largest strategic reserve in the world is located in our American oil basins. We're sitting on a $50 trillion treasure chest of available energy. There is no energy shortage; America is an energy superpower.

We all need real-world solutions to America's energy policy.

I wrote an op-ed for the *Wall Street Journal* in March 2022. The premise of the article lies in these three simple actions that can restore American energy independence:

- First, make it official U.S. policy to use all sources of available energy in America. Announce the intent to bring on more supply of oil and gas in the U.S. This provides certainty for producers to bring new capital and supplies to the market, meeting world demand.
- Second, reopen federal lands for energy development. Public lands have been available for development and have contributed to our national energy security for more than one hundred and fifty years.

- Third, support critical energy infrastructure, including pipelines to transport natural gas, oil, and CO_2 safely. Projects such as the Mountain Valley Pipeline would increase energy availability and enhance our ability to export to our allies—providing a cost-effective incentive for allies to switch from coal to clean-burning natural gas.

Since President Biden took office in 2021, we have made every effort to meet with the administration to offer insight and expertise on how we can help. Our efforts have been rebuffed, and sadly, the damaging policies continue.

Well before Putin's invasion of Ukraine in February 2022, oil supply had started to shrink and prices to rise. By the end of 2021, the price of oil had already gone over $80 per barrel.

Just prior to the invasion, oil had increased to $96 per barrel. Russia invaded Ukraine and ratcheted up oil and gas as a political weapon. With President Biden's lifting of sanctions on the Nord Stream pipeline, Putin now held all the cards. With this invasion, prices skyrocketed to almost $120 per barrel.

Self-Inflicted Economic Pain

In April 2022, leaders of many American oil companies were hauled before a congressional committee to defend their industry—scapegoats sacrificed in a midterm election year. I escaped the interrogation, but here's what I would have said given the chance:

The current energy crisis is one of your own making.

America is blessed with an extraordinary amount of natural resources, including some of the largest oil and natural gas reserves on the planet. Thanks to a huge leap in technology and innovation centered on Horizontal Drilling—and despite decades of hostile policies—America became an energy powerhouse. We broke the code and brought tens of billions of barrels of oil and natural gas equivalents to the marketplace.

Most important, it was *American* oil and natural gas.

On June 30, 2022, White House economic adviser Brian Deese was asked about high gas prices with the assumption that the war in Ukraine was the cause. Referring to the president's position that consumers would pay a premium at the pump "as long as it takes," Deese said, "What you heard from the president today was a clear articulation of the stakes. This is about the future of the liberal world order, and we have to stand firm." My translation: *American consumers be damned—we're on a globe-changing mission.*

And it's not just the pundits weighing in on questionable policies. On July 2, 2022, President Biden tweeted: "My message to the companies running gas stations and setting prices at the pump is simple: this is a time of war and global peril. Bring down the price you are charging at the pump to reflect the cost you're paying for the product. And do it now."

This was too much, even for Jeff Bezos, who replied, "Ouch. Inflation is far too important a problem for the White House to keep making statements like this. It's either straight ahead misdirection or a deep misunderstanding of basic market dynamics."

Think I'm being dramatic about our situation? Here's Secretary of Energy Jennifer Granholm's insights from June 15, 2022:

What we're saying is today we need that supply [of oil] increased.... Of course, in five or ten years—actually, in the immediate, we are also pressing on the accelerator, if you will, to move toward clean energy so that we don't have to be under the thumb of petro-dictators like Putin or at the whim of the volatility of fossil fuels.... We really want to see us move to clean energy, but we also need to see this increase right now.

Follow that logic? Me neither. Here's my translation:

We want the energy industry to hurry up and invest billions on projects that require several years to develop—but we won't tell them what lands might be suddenly closed for exploration. We're accusing them of profiteering and threatening executive action to make them produce more oil and natural gas because it's an election year, after all. And while we're plotting the demise of oil, we're increasing imports, and we're chumming it up with Venezuelans and Saudis.

Still doesn't make sense, does it?

Yelling at Yellen?

Consider these comments from U.S. Treasury Secretary Janet Yellen on June 19, 2022:

Well, I don't think that [Biden's] policies are responsible for what's happening in the oil market.... Actually, consumption of gas and fuels are currently at lower levels than pre-pandemic, and what's happened is the production has gone down. Refinery capacity is declined in the U.S., and oil production has declined. I think that producers were partly caught unaware by the strength of the recovery in the economy and weren't ready to meet the needs of the economy. High prices should induce them to increase supplies over time....

And look, as a medium-term matter, the way in which we can assure reasonable energy expenses for households is to move to renewables to address climate change, as a medium-term matter. That's the way to free us from geopolitical movements in oil prices.

It's not my nature to yell, but please allow me to offer some play-by-play commentary on these statements, one sound bite at a time.

Yellen: "I don't think that [Biden's] policies are responsible for what's happening in the oil market."

My response: Secretary Yellen, you're an economist for goodness' sake. Don't you realize the vast amount of damage done to the oil and natural gas industry during the COVID-19 shutdowns? This president cut off millions of acres of land from oil and natural gas production and is making it more difficult to produce energy! His energy secretary wants us to be gone in ten years!

Yellen: "Actually, consumption of gas and fuels are currently at lower levels than pre-pandemic."

My response: Don't you think record-high prices for gasoline might persuade people to reduce consumption? It also persuades people to cut back on other purchases, including necessities.

Yellen: "Production has declined. I think that producers were partly caught unaware by the strength of the recovery in the economy and weren't ready to meet the needs of the economy. High prices should induce them to increase supplies over time."

My response: We were unaware of the extent to which the administration would wage war on the energy industry, especially as inflation soared and the economy slowed! Do you want high prices to result in increased oil production or to move us away from oil?

Yellen: "The way in which we can assure reasonable energy expenses for households is to move to renewables to address climate change."

My response: The price of electricity is skyrocketing, and most electricity is produced by hydrocarbons. And your agenda is showing, Ms. Yellen—you're willing to crush the economy and burden tens of millions of citizens with higher energy prices as long as you can feel good about renewables! Ms. Yellen, you and the Biden administration are willing to have Americans endure a recession in your emotional quest for renewables. I'm not against diverse ways to generate electricity. I'm against delusion that impacts our citizens. The delusion is this: over 80 percent of our electricity is generated with hydrocarbons, yet you believe $10 gasoline will somehow help us "transition" to solar and wind.

Yellen: "That's the way to free us from geopolitical movements in oil prices."

My response: In case you haven't noticed, under this administration, our country has become *more* dependent on oil from hostile nations like Venezuela. Beg your pardon, Madam Secretary, but in Oklahoma we call this kind of talk *bull puckey.*

One of the saddest facts about her remarks is that Secretary Yellen is tasked with "formulating and recommending domestic and international financial, economic, and tax policy, participating in the formulation of broad fiscal policies that have general significance for the economy, and managing the public debt."

And here are some more facts. In the past twenty years, our nation's Gross National Product has increased steadily (with the exception of the 2009 government-inflicted financial collapse) along with a per-capita increase. Most people wouldn't be surprised by this. But did you know that per-person consumption of energy has continued to go down? It is possible for our economy and population to grow, along with more efficient energy consumption.

World War

Contrast the gains we've made in this country with what's happening in many parts of Europe. In the Netherlands, tens of thousands of farmers and their supporters have staged huge protests against government regulations on fertilizer. (Most chemical fertilizers are produced from natural gas, by the way.) Dutch politicians are trying to please European Union elites and slash emissions from ammonia and nitrogen by 50 percent by 2030. So they're mandating reduced use of man-made fertilizer and even requiring fewer head of livestock.

In a smug statement, the Dutch government said, "The honest message … is that not all farmers can continue their business." How out of touch with reality do you have to be to shrug your shoulders about policies that put farmers out of business? Is food now a luxury?

What happens if the government makes fertilizer illegal? We don't have to wonder. We can look at the nation of Sri Lanka. In 2021, the president of Sri Lanka enacted a ban on agrochemicals, which included weed killers, pesticides, and fertilizers. In short order, the farming sector collapsed. Rice crops dropped by 20 percent, and prices went way up. This policy not only ruined many farmers but also added crippling debt to a nation already in huge financial trouble. Fuel shortages made life hell for farmers in a country that had been self-sufficient in food production. Some predict agricultural production will decrease by 50 percent, and it is all due to the stunning ignorance of these aggressive policies.

As of July 2022, that president is now the *former* president who fled the country after protests reached his luxurious palace. As usual with elites, he is probably living it up in Western Europe, while his former countrymen struggle to feed themselves.

War or Peace?

Growing up in the heartland of America, being a patriot is ingrained in who I am. So it was especially meaningful, and I was greatly humbled, when I received a signed photograph from Vice President Mike Pence of a quote by former Senator Daniel Webster, one of the greatest orators and statesmen of the early nineteenth century. It was a token of thanks for the contribution that I have been blessed to make to the American Energy Renaissance. The quote is inscribed over the entrance of the U.S. House chamber in our nation's capital, and reads, "Let us develop the resources of our land, call forth its powers, build up its institutions, promote all its great interests, and see whether we also in our day and generation may not perform something worthy to be remembered." This has been my life's mission.

Yet there are those who choose to ignore the principles on which our nation was founded and meant so much to those who established our great country. As a geologist, I am a natural historian. When I think about the American government and why it was formed, I go back to the preamble of the U.S. Constitution,

"*Insure domestic Tranquility, provide for the common defence, promote the general Welfare, and secure the Blessings of Liberty to ourselves and our Posterity.*" Our Founding Fathers fought a brutal war to flee from tyranny and protect the rights of our people. But like the proverbial frog being boiled to death, do we realize that today, our government is making decisions to take away our freedoms, our security, and our prosperity? All the way down to how you are allowed to prepare food in your own home, with a recently proposed gas stove ban.

Who wants to invest in a business that's in the political crosshairs of powerful government entities? Who wants to work in an industry that might not have a future? Who wants to defend companies that are depicted as humankind's biggest enemy?

From what we hear on the news and from our politicians, you'd think we Americans should be ashamed of our way of life—right along with those "planet choking" energy producers. But freedom and innovation always surprise those who fear the worst. As Victor Davis Hanson recently wrote, "Under the Biden energy logic, we must destroy the American economy in order to save it."

Let's stop waging war—moral and economic—against ourselves.

The clothes we wear, the medicines we take, the food we eat and how we cook it, and the way we move about our world are all interconnected with the product of my industry. Higher energy costs make everything more expensive and harm those most who can afford it least. There are no current substitutes for American oil and natural gas. To claim otherwise is disingenuous. History has proven that punitive government intervention hinders progress and free enterprise.

We can replace scarcity with abundance. We can secure our energy and economic future. We can lead the world with production efficiencies that will protect the environment. We can make energy more affordable to hardworking Americans.

There is no reason to beg despotic regimes for more oil so they can line their pockets. It's silly—and dangerous—to empty 40 percent of the SPR to save a few congressional seats.

The people of American oil and gas are not the problem. We are the solution. Put us back to work, and the American Energy Renaissance will do the rest. The winners are the consumers, not politicians.

U.S. Sector Total Return Analysis

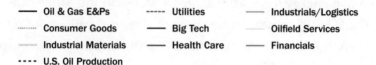

- —— Oil & Gas E&Ps
- ---- Utilities
- —— Industrials/Logistics
- ······· Consumer Goods
- —— Big Tech
- —— Oilfield Services
- —— Industrial Materials
- —— Health Care
- —— Financials
- ---- U.S. Oil Production

Prompt WTI Oil Price ($/bbl)

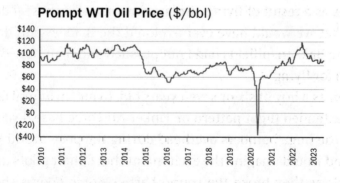

Source: "U.S. Energy Information Administration Petroleum Supply Monthly Data," Bloomberg, subscription, accessed May 25, 2023; "Prompt WTI Oil Price Data," Bloomberg, subscription, accessed May 30, 2023

I've been asked countless times over my career about the price of oil. I believe that cheap and abundant energy has underpinned American economic growth since the turn of the twentieth century. Affordable energy is crucial to the continued flourishing of America. Our research indicates that a sustainable price is around the mid-$80 per barrel mark.

CHAPTER 10

Free to Fly: Giving Our Company Wings

AS I REFLECT ON MY LIFE, SOME OF THE MOST IMPACTFUL developments came about almost as happenstance. My findings as a result of flying airplanes are some of those. I don't know that we would have ever explored the Rockies and developed the Bakken oilfields had I not pursued and maintained my passion for flying.

Even as a boy of six or seven years old, living on a rural farm in the extended flight pattern of Tinker Air Force Base, I was in awe of the huge bombers overhead during the post–World War II era and would imagine the excitement that fighter pilots must have felt as they broke the sound barrier. Sonic booms shook the windows of our old farmhouse and rattled dishes in the cupboard. I was envious of the freedom a pilot experienced.

It wasn't long before I was able to bum a ride in a small plane from a guy who had a hangar near the grass strip of the small airport at Lexington. As soon as the wheels left the ground, I knew I had to be a pilot. I never forgot the thrill of that first flight.

In 1970, I began flying with a friend named Bill Wriston, who owned a Piper Comanche single engine. In addition to operating his drilling mud company, Bill loved to fish. It was during those fishing trips to Toledo Bend Lake in Louisiana and Lake Amistad on the border of Mexico that he let me fly as he navigated the route. Those flights ignited the fuse, and it wasn't long before I was in flight school. In 1973, I received my pilot's license. After I made enough money, I bought a small 1968 Mooney Executive plane to start logging flight hours. At the time, I was living in northwestern Oklahoma, over one hundred miles from a commercial airport, so flying was considered a necessity instead of a luxury. As our service company operations became increasingly spread out across the state and our drilling company grew, having access to an airplane became even more important. I split my time between sales calls and operational tasks. It wasn't long before the cockpit became my office.

Hamm Time on Jet Fuel

My first experience with utilizing a jet aircraft was quite unusual. Ironically, it involved Continental Airlines—not my Continental Resources. Continental Airlines owned a Sabreliner 65 corporate executive jet that Bob Six, its founder, and Audrey Meadows, the famous actress, flew around the world. Continental Airlines was in financial trouble and, as a result, was forced to restructure to avoid bankruptcy. A crucial part of its restructuring plan involved over one hundred million dollars in concessions, which could be gained from the employees' union in wage reductions for pilots, attendants, and maintenance personnel. To offset this, management eliminated corporate perks, such as the founders' executive jets and salaries.

To effect a quick sale and the removal of the aircraft from Continental Airlines' Los Angeles facility, I participated in a deal between a national petroleum products transportation firm to trade jet fuel across Continental Airlines' flight route in an equal value amount in exchange for the Sabreliner.

As Continental Airlines' final negotiations were taking place with the unions, the executive aircraft was a sticking point. As a result, Continental Airlines' management was pestering us to get it out of their hangar. I was busy and unable to pick up the plane and suggested they just paint our name on the plane. We named it Conacasta USA. They did, and the union's negotiation was finalized.

The aircraft was pledged to my bank in security of a note as funds for fuel purchases were drawn against it. A transaction was made, the plane was delivered to Oklahoma City in preparation for resale, and fuel transfers began.

Enter Frank Lorenzo with Texas Air. Attempting a hostile public takeover of Continental Airlines, the much smaller Texas Air was trying to swallow the bigger airline, reluctant management included. Frank was displeased to find the small but luxurious corporate airplane, with only three hundred and five hours of air flight time, was gone. He immediately filed a lis pendens lawsuit with the court to halt the transaction of the Sabreliner, which prevented us from reselling the airplane. I had gone from being a financial backer of the deal, alongside the bank, to the owner of an aircraft that could not be resold. I figured if it was just going to sit there, I'd put it to good use for myself and our company as we fought to untangle the mess Lorenzo had created.

It didn't take long for me to start seeing this unwanted challenge as an awesome opportunity! We hired two great pilots and put it to work. The jet gave us the ability to make quick deals across the oilfield and capitalize on oil properties that were being sold for less than their value in the early 1980s. Company after company fell victim to high debt, interest payments, and falling commodity prices. Using the cash from my earlier drilling company sale in the 1980s, we made oil and gas acquisitions popular before it was in vogue.

As an example of the time-is-money advantage the aircraft provided, one day I left Enid at 8:00 a.m., flew to Denver and bought a nice package of properties from a distressed owner, flew on to the West Coast for another meeting with principals of another company, returned to Denver to pick up all the well and land files on the properties I had purchased earlier that day, continued on to Enid, and had the plane back in the hangar by 8:00 p.m. the same day!

I was awestruck with what I could accomplish in one day. Even my kids were impressed. My daughter Deana still tells the story that we left Enid on a very cold January day and four hours later, landed in the warm Virgin Islands. The freedom and ability it gave me not only to conduct business but also to spend time with my family were monumental.

Lorenzo's attempt to take over Continental Airlines ultimately failed, and his ruthless conduct was brought to the attention of the Civil Aeronautics Board. They revoked his operating authority and forbade him from ever having anything to do with another airline in the future. When the lawsuit ended, I was able to sell the beautiful new Sabreliner as planned.

The experience I gained from flying the Sabreliner taught me the efficiency with which I could work and have access to all the oil basins in the U.S. and Canada.

Our company had wings.

Taking Control

As I gained my own hours as pilot-in-command, I achieved additional pilot ratings. First, I got my instrument rating for weather, which was important because the majority of our work was north of the 39th parallel, where most of the challenging weather is located. Next, I received the twin engine rating, which was motivated by many nighttime return flights from North Dakota in my single engine plane. In my imagination, I often heard that lone single engine knock as I flew over the very isolated Nebraska sand dunes. Finally, I achieved my pressurized cabin class and jet aircraft rating, which enabled us to safely fly above inclement weather with the reliability of turbine engines.

Over time, I logged six thousand total hours as pilot. Much of it was done in a single engine airplane, which required five hours one way to Montana or North Dakota. During that time, we grew from a small independent oil company headquartered in Enid to a top ten oil and gas producer in the U.S. with operations in many of the major producing basins of the country.

Quick and direct access served us well in the oilfield. The Bakken grapevine leaked news that a new well had responded favorably to a "pump and pray" stimulation technique (as we called it then) and was producing eight hundred barrels per day. This volume would be enough to make the well commercially attractive. We were attending a North Dakota Industrial Commission hearing in Bismarck that day. As soon as it ended, we flew to Sydney, Montana, borrowed a car from the airport, and drove to the location of the well. We confirmed the flow rate and the flowing pressure. Sure enough, the grapevine was right, and we dropped the flag to begin leasing every open acre we could find.

On March 1, 1985, we purchased six hundred well interests from Petro-Lewis Company. Unbeknownst to us at the time, about seventy of the wells in Major and Blaine Counties in Oklahoma that were part of the purchase had a thin dolomite zone "behind the pipe," meaning they were cased through with pipe and cemented in place, making them easier to access. This was known as the Inola Formation. Upon discovering the existence of this prospective formation, we began qualifying the gas under Natural Gas Policy Act rules as "stripper gas," perforating the casing opposite the zone and using breakdown fluids to open it up for production. Being of low porosity, some produced gas initially and some didn't. It was baffling to me as to why they both had the same electric log characteristics. The answer to this question became clear to me on a flight over Inola, Oklahoma, on my way to Branson, Missouri.

I was interested to see what the Inola would look like from the air. The Inola Formation crops out at that geographic location on the surface. Looking down from about 3,500 feet, lo and behold, I could see a block design pattern on the weathered rock. The block sizes appeared to be ten to fifteen feet across from one exposed joint to the next joint, giving it a wafflelike appearance from the air. This made it clear how a randomly placed wellbore, which intersected this jointed fracture system, could be connected to a widespread producible network. And a wellbore that was in the center of one of the blocks of tight dolomite would not be connected to the network and therefore would produce poorly. The task then became how we could overcome that isolation. We designed a phased-in stage treatment of wellbore cleanup fluid followed by larger volumes of retarded acid to reach the block fractures. It worked and we were able to better develop the field. The visual perspective from the air made all the difference.

I've owned and flown several single-engine airplanes, in addition to those owned by the company. I also loved flying the bi-wing acrobatic planes built in Enid by Doug Champlin's company and powered by 185 HP Lycoming engines. They would literally climb straight up for four thousand feet or more! Jerry

Suits, my drilling superintendent, and I would try to wring each other out with rolls, spins, and other acrobatics. I don't know about him, but I sometimes wanted to kiss the ground after an hour or two of those maneuvers.

When I turned sixty-five, Continental Resources' public board of directors urged me to stop flying. Of course, I valued my board's opinion and accepted its recommendation, but it took me nearly a year before I could bear to sell the Cirrus SR-21 I had just purchased and accept the fact that I wouldn't be pilot-in-command again. I hated giving up what I had always loved, but I knew they were looking out for my safety and the well-being of the company. These days, I am relegated to the back seat, free to enjoy a glass of Scotch as we come back from a trip to Bismarck or Houston, but I will always miss the personal freedom piloting brought me.

CHAPTER 11

Pipelines of Power

I'D RATHER GO TO AN OKLAHOMA STEAKHOUSE THAN THE White House, unless a meeting with the president and staff accomplishes something worthwhile. Then I can go have a steak and celebrate a good day's work.

I've had the honor of visiting with several sitting U.S. presidents—George H. W. Bush, Bill Clinton, George W. Bush, Barack Obama, and Donald Trump. I've also advised several candidates about energy policy. There is a part of me that gets excited about these opportunities to share why energy is the key driver of America's economy and what is needed politically to keep the engine running. I suppose that's because I'm a farm boy at heart, always an optimist believing that good things will come from those interactions, and because maybe I will inspire the next generation, that their voices can also make a difference.

In one meeting with President Obama, I was energized to discuss the momentum that Horizontal Drilling was bringing to domestic energy production. We had the potential to increase national security and boost the economy out of a recession through energy independence. I was very excited to share this good news with him. I asked him if he was aware of how Horizontal Drilling could eliminate our dependence on foreign oil—which had sent trillions of dollars overseas. He seemed to have some understanding of the technology and acknowledged we were going to be dependent on hydrocarbons for the near term, but said, "I have been assured by my Department of Energy Secretary Steven Chu, that we will have a battery perfected within five years that will allow people to go to electric vehicles, so we no longer need fossil fuels." That meeting was in 2012. I'm still waiting on that battery.

In 2018, former President Obama remarked, "You wouldn't always know it, but [domestic oil and natural gas production] went up every year I was president. . . . Suddenly, America's like the biggest oil producer and the biggest gas [producer]. *That was me*, people. . . . Just say thank you, please."

I have a long list of people I thank for the U.S. becoming energy independent, and, respectfully, President Obama is not on that list. He did become famous for his burdensome regulations we called "Death by a Thousand Cuts" as he tried to hobble our industry further.

That meeting, like many others with D.C. power brokers, highlights the attitude that has kept the U.S. from realizing its potential—especially in the energy sector. They ignore the oil and natural gas industry because they don't like us politically and refuse to face the reality that we will need hydrocarbons for the next fifty years and beyond. Who suffers? You guessed it—the consumer.

Meanwhile, crucial-but-boring infrastructure is also ignored. Like pipelines and America's need for them.

Pipelines: Our Circulatory System

America has the largest network of oil and natural gas pipelines in the world. There are 190,000 miles of pipes transporting oil and over 320,000 miles of pipes transporting natural gas. All of it is unseen, buried beneath our feet. There are thousands more for refined products as well. In contrast, the Interstate Highway System is about 47,000 miles. Oil and gas infrastructure represents decades of work and hundreds of billions of dollars' worth of *private money* investments. America relies on its pipelines to fuel virtually everything that moves, not to mention everything we make. They are miraculous networks of engineering that provide 24/7, on demand, and continuously flowing arteries of liquid energy to meet the growing demand of the consuming public. But there are large portions of our nation that are being deprived of the tremendous benefits of clean-burning natural gas are forced to use fuel oil, coal, and wood to heat their homes and businesses, causing increased amounts of harmful emissions. A large portion of the coldest part of America's heavily populated Northeast is included. So-called environmental activists have denied access to the Mountain Valley Pipeline, which would service this area, for almost a decade, leaving residents in need of a reliable, clean source of fuel and a large part of our nation emitting a lot more CO_2 than is necessary. One might ask why this situation has been allowed to evolve. It's really quite simple: those powerful folks who wish to stop oil and gas development devised a devious plan. Eliminate the pathway for oil and gas operators to move their product to the next market and you take them out of business—regardless of who you hurt along the way and the harm done to the environment and the economic world we live in. It's not working but they are sure locked in on continuing the effort.

Pipelines aren't just *good*—they are necessary. Without them, our whole way of life would come to a crashing halt. They are the safest, most cost-efficient, environmentally friendly method to keep energy flowing, and they need to be protected. Think I'm overdramatizing?

Russian hackers attacked the Colonial Pipeline in May 2021. You can come to your own conclusion as to whether it was a state-sponsored attack. Putin stared into the cameras and denied any culpability, but there's no question in my mind that the ransomware intrusion originated from Russia.

The Colonial Pipeline is 5,500 miles long and connects the refineries of the Gulf Coast with the energy-hungry states of the Atlantic Coast. Forty-five percent of the eastern states' fuel, or 2.5 million barrels per day, flowed through Colonial. In a matter of hours, everything got dicey. Politicians squirmed and then threatened the companies—not the perpetrators responsible—for transporting and distributing the fuel. The media went into a frenzy. The talking heads sputtered ignorantly on yet another "apocalyptic" event, and shortly thereafter, the lines for gasoline formed.

No one, to my knowledge, talked about resiliency and reliability being necessary to protect our future, or how the federal government and all its regulatory tentacles have made it nearly impossible to add additional energy infrastructure.

While energy demand continues to climb, the Biden administration is busy canceling U.S. pipelines (such as the Keystone XL and the Atlantic Coast Pipeline) or trying to get a judge to shutter the Dakota Access Pipeline—570,000 daily barrels of energy sorely needed by the Gulf's refineries. All of this while the administration waives sanctions on the Nord Stream 2 pipeline, effectively telling the Russians, "Hey, go ahead, make Germany and much of Europe utterly dependent upon Russian natural gas." It is my strong belief that pipelines are central to American energy security and should be protected to ensure all Americans have access to affordable energy.

Oh, Canada

Back in the early 2000s, the major oil companies were all convinced they were going to be dependent on offshore oil and gas and foreign fields such as the Canadian Tar Sands. For a country as environmentally "woke" as Canada, it's always been amazing to me how they produce the dirtiest of all sources of hydrocarbons on the planet. Their oil (bitumen) is dirty, full of contaminants such as sulfur, and a land-management night-mare. But they have a lot of oil in the tar sands, and I guess it helps pay for national health insurance, so they decided to build another large intercontinental pipeline.

This is one guy's opinion, but the refiners have a penchant for getting it wrong—on a recurring basis, by the way. In this case, they were betting on the lousy-but-cheap Canadian oil and messy Mayan crude to meet demand and increase their margins. So what did they do? They started to retrofit all of their refineries to handle the heavy, contaminated crude coming out of Mexico and bitumen (tar) from Canada at a cost of many billions of dollars. Meanwhile, they were paying little or no attention to the revolutionary possibilities of Horizontal Drilling and what we independents were up to in the Bakken and Permian.

In 2008, our production in the Bakken was increasing dramatically. We were producing light, sweet crude but relying on railroads and undersized, inadequate pipes to move our product. We needed a whole lot more capacity to move our oil to the Gulf Coast or at least to Cushing. We knew Keystone was in the planning and permitting stage and felt like this was a golden opportunity to build a spur connecting it to the Bakken or to reroute it slightly to intersect the field just to the south of their proposed route.

Off Ron Jones, a former Continental employee, and I went to Calgary, in our modest company plane, confident TransCanada would see the financial and industry benefits of transporting our three hundred thousand barrels a day to the Gulf. We had contracts. We could help with permitting and rights of way. All of our ducks were in a row, but theirs, apparently, were not. They claimed, with a straight face, to be fully contracted for the rest of time with their Canadian customers. In short, they blew us off. I felt as if they were simply dismissing us as Americans whom they weren't interested in helping.

I have walked away from any number of deals in my life without regret and animosity. But that one got under my skin. Energy demand was growing. The U.S. and Canada are joined at the hip economically and had the opportunity to work together to make North America its own sphere of energy influence. But that's not how it went down.

On the flight back, I decided we needed to make a little noise. Next step was pointing out to the then governors of Montana and North Dakota how unreasonable TransCanada had been. Governor Brian Schweitzer of Montana, a Democrat, got the point immediately, as did his Republican counterpart in North Dakota, Governor John Hoeven. The right of way cut through both states and touched a whole lot of landowners and voters. Governor Schweitzer attended one of our meetings in a flannel shirt and jeans with his herd dog by his side. Both governors (and the dog, too, I'm sure) came to the same conclusion. To paraphrase them, "They shouldn't be allowed to come through our state with their oil if they're not going to carry ours!"

TransCanada had a sudden change of heart given that opposition was beginning to build, and Montana and North Dakota were too big to bypass. The usual suspects started to nibble at the whole idea: concerned landowners, Native American tribes, and environmentalists—some motivated by money and some by a "higher calling."

But you can't paint the full picture of this negotiation without some basic pipeline logistics. Assuming Keystone would be built, the landlocked Cushing storage space in Oklahoma would have been quickly overwhelmed and overrun with Canadian oil. We and others argued Keystone should build a Cushing-to-Houston extension to handle the flood of oil that would be coming to Cushing in order to not disrupt the market. If they did this and gave us access to their pipeline, all would be forgiven, and we would remove our protest and embrace the idea. They agreed. Finally.

In 2012, President Obama came to Oklahoma to celebrate all the high-paying union jobs the Keystone pipeline would create. One of my buddies spent nearly $1 million to prep the site for this presidential moment in Oklahoma. He prepared it with a dozen guys festooned in hard hats and lots of infrastructure and technology decoration celebrating American labor and energy know-how. The president's speech lasted eleven minutes and forty-eight seconds. To this day, my buddy claims it's the worst return on $1 million he ever witnessed.

In typical fashion, the optics were different than the intention. Three days later, buried inside an article in the *Wall Street Journal*, the president was quoted as saying he didn't have the authority to "approve" Keystone. He hid behind his regulatory appointees, and the project continued to languish for his entire presidency, giving the opposition life support—until a newly elected President Trump rediscovered the authority to move it forward. It didn't stick long enough to get built before Joe Biden found the "authority" in January 2021 to put Keystone out of its misery once and for all.

What was the result of nearly twenty years of silliness? Well, one good thing happened. There is a pipeline from Cushing to Houston, capable of transporting half a million barrels a day to the Gulf and keeping Cushing's oil inventory completely drawn down most of the time.

On the downside, billions of dollars of investment were frittered away. Huge amounts of time and talent were wasted, not to mention that a bunch of contracts—including a few of ours—were voided. Pipe and construction materials that were being staged for completion are now strewn all over the countryside. Thousands of high-paying jobs vaporized. The Biden administration stiffed the Canadian government big time. And we missed yet another opportunity to strengthen our national and economic security. TransCanada's unwillingness to listen and deal with two guys from Enid, Oklahoma, ultimately cost them a long delay and the opportunity to build the Keystone XL Pipeline. Oh, Canada.

Political Pipes

I mentioned earlier the Mountain Valley Pipeline. It goes in and out of the news because it has been stalled for many years, with fewer than forty miles left to complete and connect new and existing pipelines that fuel many parts of the East Coast. If completed, it could help utilities convert from coal-burning electricity generation to 2 million dekatherms of natural gas a day. (Don't know what a dekatherm is? Trust me, it's a lot.) Thankfully, this much-needed infrastructure may be allowed to continue in the near future.

In January 2022, the Biden administration found another pipeline it didn't like. The president inexplicably decided to withdraw support for a pipeline project designed to deliver

Israeli natural gas to Europe. In the early 2000s, an American company drilling in Israel discovered offshore gas fields, the Tamar and Leviathan. There is enough natural gas in these fields to meet Israel's needs domestically for decades to come, and with extra to export. The pipeline would have been a win-win for all involved. Europe would have an alternative to Putin's natural gas, and Israel would strengthen its trade with Europe.

But the Biden administration determined the reversal was in keeping with its policy of encouraging renewable energy, putting its myopic devotion to all things green over the energy security of our allies. They added that the U.S. is all about promoting clean energy technologies and is preparing the region for clean energy transitions. So now we are telling our allies how to manage their own affairs when it comes to their energy policies.

The practical effect of the reversal of U.S. policy was to strengthen the hand of the Russians yet again. The Biden administration gave a big thumbs-up to the Russian-inspired Nord Stream 2 pipeline system by waiving sanctions on the companies behind the project, never once mentioning "renewable energy." So Russian pipelines = good; American and Israeli pipelines = bad?

We need more pipeline infrastructure, not less. We need to fortify our infrastructure against cyberattacks. We can and need to do everything to ensure America's energy security is front and center.

Political Frackers and Flip-Flops

There seem to be a lot of frackers in politics. In case you haven't noticed, many power brokers also perpetuate the myth that hydraulic fracturing (which they dubbed *fracking*) is bad. Or not that bad, depending on the wind generated by public opinion and the price of gasoline.

Here's a partial list of recent examples where the Biden administration seems to have more flip-flops than a beachside shoe store:

September 4, 2019 – CNN Town Hall:
Kamala Harris: "There is no question I am in favor of banning fracking."

September 6, 2019 – Speaking to an activist in New Hampshire:
Biden: "I want you to just take a look ... I want you to look at my eyes. . . . I guarantee you we're going to end fossil fuel."

March 15, 2020 – Democratic presidential debate:
Biden: "No more, no new fracking."

August 31, 2020 – Campaign event in Pittsburgh:
Biden: "I am not banning fracking. Let me say that again. I am not banning fracking. No matter how many times Donald Trump lies about me."

October 7, 2020 – Vice presidential debate:
Harris: "Joe Biden will not end fracking; he has been very clear about that. I will repeat, and the American people know that Joe Biden will not ban fracking. That is a fact. That is a fact."

October 7, 2020 – Kamala Harris tweet:
Harris: "Joe Biden will not ban fracking. That is a fact."

October 8, 2020 – Biden campaign press release:
Biden: "Joe Biden has been clear: he will not ban fracking."

Harold at four, ready to take on the world.

Harold's parents, Leland and Jane Hamm, at their home
in Lexington, Oklahoma, in the early 1960s.

As the last of the brood, Harold was raised by his six loving sisters.
(Left to right: Carolyn, Clara, Ann, Flora, Fannie, Lois, and his mom, Jane.)

Harold, during his senior year of high school, sporting
the "flat top" hairstyle of the times.

Harold and Les Phillips with one of their first oil services trucks. Notice the logo; even then Harold knew the importance of branding and image building.

In the kitchen of Harold's first apartment in Enid, cramming in a midnight study between attending high school and his sixty-hour work week.

The first airplane. Harold loved flying, eventually logging six thousand hours crisscrossing the oilfields of the Mid-Continent.

Before starting this book, the team plotted fifty years of
American oil and gas history. You can see the many attempts
of government intervention throughout the years. Every
policymaker in America should come by to see it.

Continental registered the trademark for the Eco-Pad® in the 1980s,
a technology that shrank its drilling footprint and unlocked massive
amounts of oil and gas, made possible through Horizontal Drilling.

The thirteenth son of an Oklahoma sharecropper humbly found himself considered among the world's most influential people in 2012, the year the world finally took notice of the technology this nationally known wildcatter had produced.

There was a time, in the not-too-distant past of 2014, when finding more American oil and natural gas was celebrated.

Speaking before the Republican National Convention in 2016
on national security and American Energy Independence.

Harold was diagnosed with Type 2 diabetes in the early 2000s. He set on a mission to find a cure and provide affordable medication while searching for that cure. Progress is being made at the world-renowned Harold Hamm Diabetes Center at the University of Oklahoma.

Harold celebrating with students from the University of North Dakota Hamm School of Geology and Geological Engineering, the next generation of "explorationists."

The Hamm Institute for American Energy opened its doors in 2021 with a simple mission: Inspire the next generation of energy leaders to responsibly produce the energy America and the world need.

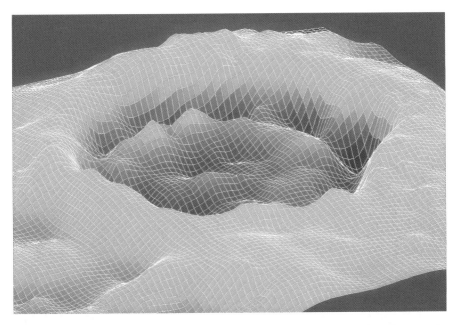

Advances in technology allowed Harold and team to find oil and natural gas in, of all places, a 450-million-year-old meteor strike called Ames Hole.

NBC's Harry Smith joined Harold in front of his childhood home. Harry was in town to learn about Harold's efforts to make affordable insulin available to people living with diabetes.

The older one gets, the more often someone gives you an excuse
to wear a tuxedo. Harold was inducted into the Oklahoma Hall
of Fame in 2011. He is pictured with former Democratic Governor,
Senator, and President of the University of Oklahoma, David Boren,
who presented him with the Oklahoma Hall of Fame Medal.

An illustration that accompanied the article from the WSJ titled, "How North Dakota became Saudi Arabia," from October 1, 2011, predicting America's Energy Renaissance and Independence brought about by Horizontal Drilling.

Horizontal Drilling changed everything. Here's one of Continental's rigs in the Bakken field in North Dakota, where there is still an estimated thirty billion barrels of recoverable oil.

Harold will tell you his greatest accomplishment
will always be his five children.

The Hamm family name is associated with the best educational institutions across America. Here Harold is celebrating his family's contributions to the University of Mary in North Dakota, where the Hamm School of Engineering was recently established.

Still in the dark about these conflicting policy positions? It's because they are not based on science.

Allow me to shed some light on what really happens thousands of feet below the surface—naturally, and with a little help from explorationists.

Over millions of years, organic material in rock goes through a process where it becomes much larger as the molecules mature into hydrocarbons. Whether it's natural gas or oil, as it forms, it expands—sometimes as much as 200 percent. What happens when the oil and gas expand? The host rocks fracture. You can actually see it when studying their composition through a microscope.

Yes, it's a frack of nature.

When we use fracture stimulation with fluids when completing wells, we're simply augmenting the process of fracturing in the rock surrounding the wellbore. This opens up those fractures and keeps them propped open, which enhances the ability for that rock to yield oil or natural gas. It's that simple. We've always called it "wellbore stimulation fracture treatment."

So what's the big deal about this game-changing technology? In my view, the problem is how well it works, from the perspective of a rival energy-producing nation.

The Russians and other nations looked at the technology and realized, *This is going to turn loose a lot of gas and open up competition in Europe and the Americas.* Their response, which has been verified with evidence from the North Atlantic Treaty Organization (NATO) and the U.S. House of Representatives, was to cook up a massive public relations campaign to cancel wellbore stimulation. They tabbed it with the "F" word: fracking. And the PR wasn't cheap. The cost was later estimated by some to be $500 million initially. One can sway more than a few opinions with half a billion dollars.

Anders Fogh Rasmussen, former secretary-general of NATO and former premier of Denmark, confirmed this in a meeting with the Chatham House think tank in London in June 2014: "I have met allies who can report that Russia, as part of their sophisticated information and disinformation operations, engaged actively with so-called non-governmental organisations—environmental organisations working against shale gas—to maintain European dependence on imported Russian gas."

Former Secretary of State Hillary Clinton, in a private 2014 speech, said, "We were even up against phony environmental groups . . . funded by the Russians to stand against any effort, 'Oh that pipeline, that fracking, that whatever will be a problem for you.'"

A 2018 investigation by the U.S. House Committee on Science, Space, and Technology reported on Russian attempts to sway U.S. energy markets through the use of social media. One of Russia's most ingenious moves was to promote the label of "fracking"—and the term stuck for many reasons. Those opposing the increased energy output that Horizontal Drilling enabled wanted to make the technology a "four-letter word" to sour public opinion. And they did.

While Russia was warning Europe and the U.S. about the cataclysmic impacts of fracking, they were trying to advance their capabilities. Unsurprisingly, Russia uses this technology today.

As I've said before, energy policy is always connected to power—*political* power. Keep that in mind when you peruse the news.

Where is the U.S. gonna go with energy policies? How fast is Europe going to be able to pivot away from the impacts of the war with Ukraine? What does going green mean, and in particular now that we've seen some of the shortcomings of policies that were out of sync with reality and the devastating impact on consumers? . . . Energy policy both in the U.S. and Europe has been just a train wreck for the last couple of years.

—CITADEL CEO KEN GRIFFIN IN A MAY 2022 INTERVIEW

CHAPTER 12

It's Easy Being Green

ZERO HAS BECOME THE NEW MANTRA OF THE CLIMATE change alarmists. The Zero Movement—or Net Zero, as advertised—has *zero* chance of working. Meanwhile, a handful of environmental elites will make tens of billions of dollars from it.

But the concept sounds good, right? *Let's get to zero emissions!* Lots of hot air is being released about how we might get to the mythical zero. Who can possibly be against zero emissions? Not any rational citizen of the planet.

I'm for reducing emissions—and as you'll learn, my companies and colleagues are doing, everything we can to decarbonize our operations, and we're writing big checks in the process. But the modern world will never reach true zero emissions. Humanity emits. That said, the U.S. *is* moving in the direction of zero (thanks to domestic natural gas), while China and India are rapidly going the opposite direction.

U.S. Primary Energy Consumption and CO_2 Emissions

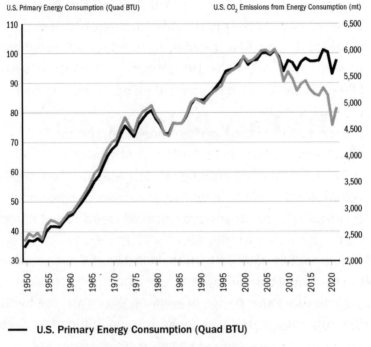

U.S. Primary Energy Consumption (Quad BTU)   U.S. CO_2 Emissions from Energy Consumption (mt)

— **U.S. Primary Energy Consumption (Quad BTU)**

— **U.S. CO_2 Emissions from Energy Consumption (mt)**

Source: U.S. Primary Energy Consumption and CO_2 Emissions, U.S. Energy Information Administration, accessed December 21, 2022, https://www.eia.gov/totalenergy/data/browser/index.php?t-bl=T01.01#/?f=A&start=1949&end=2022&charted=4-6-7-14; https://www.eia.gov/totalenergy/data/annual/show-text.php?t=ptb1101; https://www.eia.gov/totalenergy/data/browser/index.php?t-bl=T11.01#/?f=A&start=1973&end=2021&charted=14

Amazing but true, beginning in 2010, CO_2 emissions began a steady decline—even while the economy grew—thanks in large part to natural gas replacing coal as the electricity-generation fuel of choice. Natural gas remains the fastest and most economical way to reduce emissions.

Global Cooling

In a 1971 article in *Parade* magazine titled "New Ice Age?" the author made the following cold case:

Since World War II, our winters have been growing colder and longer, world meteorologists point out. According to Dr. Murray J. Mitchell of the National Oceanic and Atmospheric Administration, "Generally speaking, the world warmed up by one degree Fahrenheit between the end of the 19th century and World War II. Since World War II, it has cooled off again, by one-half a degree Fahrenheit."

The cooling trend is even more apparent in Europe, where winters have been harsher and spring later since 1940. German meteorologist Dr. Martin Rodewald believes that the Continent may even be at the beginning of a new ice age. "If the present cold trend lasts longer than another two decades," Dr. Rodewald predicts, "Europe will be covered with the glaciers of a new ice age by the turn of the century."

American and Danish weather researchers in North Greenland, drilling down through 1,400 meters of ice to read the weather record of 800 years, found that cold and warm cycles run for an average of 78 to 180 years. On this basis, Dr. Rodewald does not foresee another warming trend before the year 2015. He claims an 85 percent accuracy rate in his prediction, or about the reliability of the daily weather forecast.

Many environmentalists criticize others for "ignoring the science" and lecturing us that "the science is settled." You won't find anyone more science-driven than me. But when it comes to unproven *theories* that preach scarcity, hamper growth, and lead to trillions in government mandates and higher consumer prices, you can call me a skeptic.

NEW ICE AGE? Since World War II our winters have been growing colder and longer, world meteorologists point out.

According to Dr. Murray J. Mitchell of the National Oceanic and Atmospheric Administration. "Generally speaking, the world warmed up by one degree Fahrenheit between the end of the 19th century and World War II. Since World War II, it has cooled off again, by one-half a degree Fahrenheit."

The cooling trend is even more apparent in Europe, where winters have been harsher, and spring later since 1940. German meteorologist Dr. Martin Rodewald believes that the Continent may even be at the beginning of a new ice age. "If the present cold trend lasts longer than another two decades," Dr. Rodewald predicts, "Europe will be covered with the glaciers of a new ice age by the turn of the century."

American and Danish weather researchers in North Greenland, drilling down through 1400 meters of ice to read the weather record of 800 years, found that cold and warm cycles run for an average of 78 to 180 years. On this basis, Dr. Rodewald does not foresee another warming trend before the year 2015. He claims an 65 percent accuracy rate in his prediction, or about the reliability of the daily weather forecast.

FEBRUARY WEATHER IN MAY: HEAVY SNOWFALL IN SWISS ALPS TOWN.

I keep an old copy of a book titled *The Weather Conspiracy: The Coming of the New Ice Age*, published in 1977. A subhead on the cover declares that the book "includes two CIA reports." The reports detail a bleak future where crops fail, nations starve, and winter becomes a permanent fixture on much of the planet. Like the fearmongers of today, the book is full of alarming factoids, which conveniently bolster their case. (For example: "In the Soviet Union, snow is falling further south than ever before. . . . This past winter, Buffalo, New York, lay buried under fifteen feet of snow. . . . A sustained frost destroys Florida's crops, and the entire east coast of America suffers its worst winter on record.")

What makes the book even more entertaining is the authors make oil and gas the villain—not "king coal." They were certain we were running out, thanks in part to the supposed expertise of our intelligence agencies. They quote our recoverable reserves at the time as forty billion barrels—which, by the way, is the upper end of what we believe is available today in just the Bakken.

The book is full of gloomy prognostications, but instead of warming, the catalyst for global climate terror is the return of the ice age.

And like every book, report, and speech penned by the elites, no matter what the decade, the solution is always for *you* to use less and change your lifestyle. *You* should drive a smaller car, eat less meat, and live in a smaller house while *they* buy more homes and bigger jets.

Does history repeat itself? Yet again, we have an energy crisis. Yet again, we are being told we will have to do less for the common good. Yet again, we have created scarcity when abundance is all around us.

Why do I keep a copy of the book? Because virtually everything in it turned out to be wrong. The only thing right was that, yes, weather is variable and often unpredictable and extreme. And there will always be those who live in a state of fear about the future. I will not. I refuse to. Humanity has a near-infinite ability to innovate, create, and adapt. Our progress is accelerating, our standard of living ever rising. In my seven decades, I have witnessed monumental change for the better.

Talk Is Easy

Regardless of all the noise around climate conditions and global warming, it is really all about market share and government subsidies—the primary drivers of the green movement. Seems the only cows they like are cash cows.

Occasionally someone has the courage to speak the truth, such as Akio Toyoda, of Toyota, who warned that rapid, government-mandated electrification of transportation was not advisable, not environmentally smart, and not possible without massive disruption to the economy.

"Toyota Motor Corp's leader criticized what he described as excessive hype over electric vehicles, saying advocates failed to consider the carbon emitted by generating electricity and the costs of an EV transition."

He added that if Japan is too hasty in banning gasoline-powered cars, "the current business model of the car industry is going to collapse," causing the loss of millions of jobs. He further said government regulators would make cars "a flower on a high summit," a poetic way of saying cars would be out of the price range of the average consumer.

Mr. Toyoda, this is precisely the idea of governments worldwide. Make personal transportation expensive, and the masses can be relegated and regulated into public transportation.

Don't believe me?

In May 2022, the government of Norway asked its citizens to *stop* using their electric vehicles and take the bus. Norwegian Transport Minister Jon-Ivar Nygard said, "Electric cars give us greener transport, but they also have a clear intermodal competition with public transport in urban areas. We must make it more attractive to travel by public transport, cycle, and walk."

It might be a coincidence, but it seems to me that countries that seek more control over their populations have a strange preoccupation with public transportation.

Several years ago, I joined the Giving Pledge, which is the campaign Bill Gates and Warren Buffet started to encourage individuals to contribute the majority of their wealth to philanthropic causes in their lifetime. I admired the cause. Bill Gates even joined me at Concordia College to speak to a group of students at my invitation, which is something the students and I will never forget. Sometimes friends respectfully disagree, and Bill and I certainly have different perspectives on a few things, including how to combat climate issues.

In his recent book, *How to Avoid a Climate Disaster: The Solutions We Have and the Breakthroughs We Need*, Bill admits to buying only "sustainable" jet fuel with the goal of eventually "offsetting" his family's aviation emissions. You're still cracking carbon atoms, Bill. Those jet turbines aren't going to spin otherwise. The rest of us will just have to deal with paying six or seven bucks at the pump or be taxed by the mile in the car, as some are suggesting.

He also suggested he knows of no one who has personally invested more in zero-carbon technologies—a billion or so of his own dollars—to further prove he can justify his lifestyle. Not to single out Gates, but his perspective illustrates how corporate and government elites view the solutions to energy and climate change. They are penitent at best. (For a welcome and well-reasoned balance to the climate change discussion, I suggest reading *Unsettled: What Climate Science Tells Us, What It Doesn't, and Why It Matters* by Dr. Steven E. Koonin, former undersecretary of science, U.S. Department of Energy under President Obama.)

Then there's Larry Fink at BlackRock, who—in my view—is cynically manipulating markets to add to his trillions. He and other BlackRock executives sent out an infamous letter in 2021 titled, "Net Zero: a fiduciary approach." One quote is worth mentioning, referring to climate change:

> These changes will have dramatic impacts for investors. Last year, we wrote that investors were increasingly recognizing that climate change risk is investment risk, which would drive a significant reallocation of capital. We also believe that climate transition creates a historic investment opportunity. With the world moving to net zero, BlackRock can best serve our clients by helping them be at the forefront of that transition.

It has the tone of a papal declaration. *I, Larry Fink, have interpreted the current state of climate dogma and here is what adherents must do if you want to belong in the flock, find grace among the believers, and prosper in the process.* I read it as an implicit threat. Toe the line or face the consequences.

BlackRock has gone all in on ESG, offering over one hundred mutual funds that follow ambiguous standards for "environmental, social, and governance." Coincidentally, at the time of this writing, the Labor Department is considering a rule that would force companies to offer the option of ESG funds in their 401(k) plans. President Biden's National Economic Council Chief, Brian Deese, was previously employed at BlackRock as Global Head of Sustainable Investing. Two other former BlackRock employees serve in high-ranking positions in the current administration. There is clear alignment between the Biden administration and BlackRock.

What could be more virtuous than mitigating risk while, at the same time, investing for a sustainable and utopian future where the so-called environmental experts decide about the *social* impacts of business? It also helps to be in a position to vacuum up billions of the trillions in subsidies and mandates the current administration is dispensing. The trough is open, and Larry wants to feed.

There are some folks pushing back, led by none other than Warren Buffet and Berkshire Hathaway. He's not buying the narrative Larry Fink is peddling. At his annual shareholders meeting in May 2021, Buffet offered a full-throated defense of the oil and gas industry. Here's what he had to say on his 2.5 percent stake in Chevron: "I think Chevron's benefited society in all kinds of ways, and I think it continues to do so. And I think we're going to need a lot of hydrocarbons for a long time, and we'll be very glad we've got them." Buffet acknowledged that the world is moving away from fossil fuels but added, "That could change. . . . What's happening will be adapted over time, just as we've adapted to all kinds of things."

In fact, as recently as August 2022, he received regulatory approval to purchase up to 50 percent of oil giant Occidental Petroleum. Warren is a very optimistic buyer. And who in the entire investment community is better at finding opportunity than Warren Buffet?

I happen to agree with Buffet. Technology and marketplaces adapt, always faster and more rationally than the manipulators' schemes will.

Of course, Larry Fink responded in a letter to CEOs: "Divesting from entire sectors—or simply passing carbon-intensive assets from public markets to private markets—will not get the world to net zero." Mr. Fink reserves the right to pivot when his shareholders get a tad bit nervous. It's not a full retreat, but it's certainly a more realistic view of the current energy world we find ourselves in.

Clearing the Air

What has contributed to the largest decline in CO_2 emissions in the last twenty years—the largest decline in human history? It was natural gas replacing coal as the fuel of choice when it comes to electricity generation.

Why did natural gas replace coal? Why has the air in America become so much cleaner in the last few decades?

Not because of any government intervention or mandates, as we discussed in a previous chapter. And not because multinational corporations stepped up to innovate and invest on our soil. It's because of the American Energy Renaissance and Horizontal Drilling. We can thank our intrepid domestic oil companies that went out and did the impossible, unlocking and producing vast quantities of clean-burning natural gas and light, sweet crude right in our own backyard.

Innovation and focused problem-solving can change the world. Remember the catalytic converter, a nifty piece of technology that found its way into combustion engines in the mid-seventies? In its simplest chemistry, it takes exhaust fumes and reduces them to CO_2 and water—using rare earth elements and heat. Those of you who remember *seeing* the air over Los Angeles or New York in the seventies can thank the catalytic converter for making the air far easier to endure and breathe.

And, yes, it is a smart idea to invest in "net zero" gas turbine plants. Pursuing carbon capture and underground sequestration (CCUS) makes for a cost-efficient, impactful solution. This technology could play a large role in the decarbonization of the world. From almost a zero base, the CCUS industry has many viable multibillion-dollar projects underway. What is confounding is that the most vocal detractors to this technological advancement are organizations such as the Sierra Club, whose primary purpose should be protecting the environment. Go figure.

Technology can provide rapid solutions to challenges. For example, there was pressure in the 1970s to reduce air pollution and the resulting smog. The idea of the catalytic converter had been around for years, but some talented engineers figured out how to make it small, efficient, and cheap enough to fit into a very small space under your car and rid the air of pollutants. It worked and the smog cleared out.

Imagine small, incredibly safe nuclear plants powering cities. We have the technology. Small nuclear power units have been on our aircraft carriers and submarines for decades. Additionally, about twelve thousand feet down, there's a lot of geothermal energy we can tap into—I know, because we operate there all the time. The trick is to make it economically efficient. Geothermal sources make up 66 percent of Iceland's primary energy use.

Carbon: Made in China

In 2019, China, the fastest-growing economy in the world, emitted 14.1 gigatons of carbon dioxide equivalents. That's more than triple its 1990 levels and is a 25 percent increase in the past decade. China now accounts for 27 percent of global emissions, primarily from coal, while the U.S. comes in second at 11 percent, India is next at 6.6 percent, and the twenty-seven nations of the European Union account for 6.4 percent.

You might be surprised to learn the truth about U.S. CO_2 emissions. Between 2010 and 2019, U.S. emissions dropped by 11 percent, while China's rose by 26 percent. The U.S. keeps reducing emissions—and did so while being part of the Paris Climate Accord—while other signers of the pact *increase* emissions every year. The truth is surprising only because it's the opposite of what has been proclaimed repeatedly for decades.

My friend Maynard Holt shared a story about his visit to China in 2011, when a Chinese energy executive he was meeting with asked him, "Is your country aware of what it has accomplished?" From the Chinese perspective, the U.S. had lowered energy costs on a massive scale through the shale revolution. They saw it as a huge change in the competitive landscape in the U.S. versus the rest of the world. That story has stuck with me. Sadly, many Americans *don't* realize what we have accomplished as an industry—not only for America but the entire world.

The Green New Deal & Other Doomsday Prognostications

Everything happening today can find its beginnings decades earlier—ironically, in many cases, by people who built their fortunes with fossil fuels. The Rockefellers, for example, funded some of the early environmentalist work, mainly on population control.

Anyone remember author Paul Ehrlich? He was called the "irrepressible doomster." His book *The Population Bomb* predicted a future world of starving humans. In a 1971 speech at the British Institute for Biology, Ehrlich predicted, "By the year 2000, the United Kingdom will be simply a small group of impoverished islands, inhabited by some 70 million hungry people.... If I were a gambler, I would take even money that England will not exist in the year 2000."

Funny how the predictions of the doomsters are always about what happens in twenty years if we don't act tomorrow. They never account for technology and market-inspired innovation or adaptation; they always assume the status quo. Or worse, they double down on the oldest technology of them all—windmills.

People like Ehrlich keep popping up, each with a new take on how long we've got and their urgent prescriptions for avoiding disaster. We are four years into the Green New Deal and have only eight more years until the world ends, according to AOC.

Another book was published in 1972 that heavily influenced the environmental narrative. *Limits to Growth* was released with the help of corporate interests, including Aurelio Peccei of Fiat. Maybe the corporate masters were looking for excuses to cover their poor business performance. They had become pessimists and statists, allowing the Japanese to take complete advantage of these stagnant mindsets over the next two decades and the Chinese right after them. There's no pessimism or limits to growth in their corner of the world.

The book suggested that the world was running out of natural resources at a rapid pace and called for "global equilibrium" through restrictions on growth and a "carefully controlled balance" of population and capital. In other words, the rich needed to keep what they had and screw the rest of the planet.

Because someone has to be in charge of "controlling the balance," right?

Not surprisingly, the usual suspects of the media, academia, and political circles in the Western democracies made it their mantra. Does any of this sound familiar?

One of the perverse outcomes of this kind of thinking was the previously mentioned Fuel Use Act of 1978, which then Senator Joe Biden voted for. It ensured the unbridled use of coal for power generation for the next decade in the U.S.—and to this day in many parts of the world. I realized the stupidity of the premise, but I was assigned to read the book and report on it in college in 1973 as though it was the gospel. Hopefully, *Limits to Growth*—the book and the philosophy—will be remembered as false doctrine and fake science. All their ravings in the seventies and eighties turned out to be hogwash. In fact, their prognostications were almost comically wrong. Energy demand nearly tripled, and oil production soared, resulting in the largest rise in global living standards in human history. Even life expectancy in the U.S. has increased by over 12 percent since 1960.

A recent headline from Fox News is an example of the latest cycle of doomsday reporting: "Climate Change Will Shrink 'Virtually All' Economies Around The World By 2100, Study Warns." Academia and think tanks, hungry for government and foundation funding, crank out study after study. Close to none predict a rosy future for humankind. Almost all are about us crashing into the limits of our existence, using scare tactics to try to drive their agendas. You would be hard-pressed to find a paper predicting American energy independence or the American economy benefiting from a $1 trillion swing in the balance of trade thanks to domestic energy production, even as late as 2017.

Among the many excuses for the U.S. to rejoin the Paris Climate Accord were headlines like this: "Melting Antarctic ice will raise sea levels and might cause humanity to give up New York." Ironically, a lot of people these days *are* giving up New York and moving to Texas and Florida, but not because of Arctic ice levels. The Paris Accord is all about limits imposed on us by those who know better. They form another club of climate "do-gooders" who are professional fearmongers. What is left unsaid is that China, under the terms of the accord, is free to do *whatever* until 2030. The "whatever" includes building hundreds of new coal-fired generation plants around the world. And even more alarming, China is considered a developing country by international institutions, meaning the U.S. is left footing the bill for their financial support.

In 2021, China built more than half of the world's new coal power plants, financing huge numbers of these smoke-belching plants in energy-poor countries in Asia and Africa. According to a June 2022 report, "Chinese policymakers recently greenlighted a coal mine capacity expansion of an additional 300 million metric tons in 2022—almost the annual production of the entire European Union." Not to mention China's horrific strip mining for rare earth minerals impacts the large majority of our beloved tech devices and solar panels, but that's another story altogether.

Why aren't those who proclaim to be so concerned about the environment protesting in front of the Chinese and Indian embassies and boycotting products and services from these nations? I've never heard an honest answer to this question. These people are not progressives. They are statists. What they can't see, what they never see, is that you don't have to choose between a better economy and a better environment. We can marry the best of our energy resources with a pragmatic environmental framework.

The Green Impact of Horizontal Drilling

The most important economic and environmental story of the last two decades is Horizontal Drilling and the subsequent unlocking of American energy. We went from an era of perceived energy scarcity to one of unbelievable abundance. The results were a more vibrant economy and a cleaner environment.

Our CO_2 emissions declined by 22 percent in the U.S. between 2006 and 2020, almost all as a result of generating electricity with clean-burning natural gas instead of coal, even as American oil and gas production has climbed. Natural gas is the most efficient, affordable, and reliable fuel available for power generation. Plus, it's the fastest way to clean up the air. Nothing else comes close.

The boom in U.S. shale production created millions of jobs in sectors across the economy. Energy states filled their coffers with tax dollars to pay for schools, teachers, and countless projects that made life better for all. But all our progress is at risk.

In just five years, from 2010 to 2015, the shale hydrocarbon industry drove nearly 10 percent of the increase in the country's gross domestic product, according to the authors with the Federal Reserve Bank of Dallas. And in 2018, oil and gas extraction contributed nearly $220 billion to U.S. economic output, according to the National Bureau of Economic Research.

A U.S. Chamber of Commerce study showed there would have been 4.3 million fewer American jobs, and half a trillion in GDP wiped off the books without oil and natural gas extracted from shale. What's more, from 2008 to 2018, Americans pocketed $1.1 trillion in energy savings. That's a lot of trips to the mall.

The Shale Revolution made America's air cleaner. It made Americans wealthier and more secure. And it was accomplished by entrepreneurs and scientists like me, not policymakers manipulating tax codes and granting giveaways to the connected.

Electricity Doesn't Grow on Trees

According to recent research, one of Tesla's Supercharger stations reportedly acquires 13 percent of its energy from natural gas and 27 percent from coal. In 2017, Elon Musk said that Tesla will eventually disconnect Supercharger stations from the grid. If you calculate how much land the Superchargers would occupy to be run off solar, you realize each Supercharger would need *thousands* of solar panels. What's more, Tesla doesn't publicly report its greenhouse gas emissions, so its claims cannot be authenticated. Musk's thoughts seem somewhat "Twitter-pated."

And little attention has been paid to what happened in "green" Germany in 2022, where many citizens have cut their discretionary spending to pay for their electric bills. Recently in California, electric prices were getting so high that it could have cost more to charge an electric vehicle than to pay for gasoline. But with the unnecessary doubling of gasoline prices, that threshold wasn't met. And in the summer of 2022, California Governor Gavin Newsom asked residents *not* to charge their cars during peak hours.

Where Does Electricity Come From?

Think electricity originates from an outlet on the wall? Surprise. Most electricity in the U.S. is generated using natural gas, coal, and nuclear. Today, less than 5 percent of electricity is generated by solar. Wind power produces less than 10 percent of our electric power. About 20 percent of electricity is produced by burning coal. Thankfully, in the past ten years, natural gas has replaced coal as the primary way electricity is produced.

But here's the breakdown: all those electric cars that people think are fueled by sunshine and happy thoughts are primarily fueled by hydrocarbons. On average across the country, more than half the miles driven by electric cars are powered by natural gas and coal. Same with anything we use electricity for: the Internet, our gadgets, lights, heat, air conditioning, and more only receive a small fraction of their power from wind, solar, and other renewables. Despite how hard our states are trying to end it, nuclear power still outpaces power from wind turbines and solar panels.

And as a reminder, when it's dark and when the air is still, we receive zero electricity from these renewables. Scientist Vaclav Smil, an energy historian, puts it best:

> There are no EVs. They are battery vehicles reflecting the electricity's origins. If I were to buy an EV in Manitoba, it would be a 100% hydroelectricity, truly zero carbon energy, car. In North China it is a 90% coal car, in France it is a 70% nuclear car, in Russia mostly a natural gas car and in Denmark a 50% wind car et cetera.

The Easy Path or the Difficult Path?

It's easy being green. All you need is vocal passion and good intentions. Facts and positive results are optional.

Amin H. Nasser, Saudi Aramco president and CEO, pointed out in a September 2022 speech at the Schlumberger Digital Forum:

> Instead, as this crisis has shown, the plan was just a chain of sandcastles that waves of reality have washed away. And billions around the world now face the energy access and cost of living consequences that are likely to be severe and prolonged.
>
> These are the real causes of this state of energy insecurity: under-investment in oil and gas; alternatives not ready; and no back-up plan. But you would not know that from the response so far. ... All of us have a vested

interest in climate protection. And investing U.S. conventional source, does not mean that alternative Energy sources and technologies should be ignored. But the world deserves a much better response to this crisis. . . . as the pain of the energy crisis sadly intensifies, people around the world are desperate for help. In my view, the best help that policymakers and every stakeholder can offer is to unite the world around a much more credible new transition plan.

We are doing our part not only to eliminate emissions, but we are using advanced technology to sequester carbon from other industries as well. Constant improvements in the production of all forms of energy will yield a much cleaner world than an ill-devised plan of political winners versus losers.

I'm not against renewables. I'm against dismantling the current system for another system that doesn't exist. Instead, let's make measurable changes with solutions that work. My colleagues and I prefer action over talk. Making a measurable difference is not easy—or cheap. But it's worth it.

Global Primary Energy Production by Source

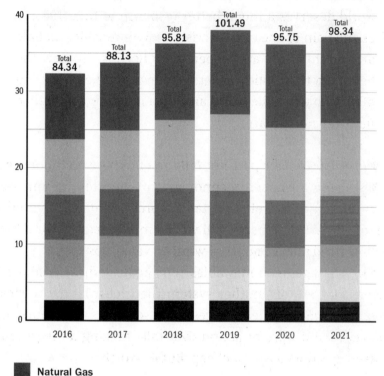

Natural Gas

Petroleum and other liquids

Total Nuclear, renewables, and other

Renewables and others

Coal

Nuclear

Source: "Primary Energy," U.S. Energy Information Administration, accessed December 22, 2022, https://www.eia.gov-/international/data/world/total-energy/total-energy-consumption?pd=44&p=004000000000000000000000000000000000000000000000000000f00o&u=2&f=A&v=mapbubble&a=-&i=none&vo=value&t=C&g=none&l=249--238&s=315532800000&e=1609459200000&ev=false&

This shows the breakdown of where most of the world's energy comes from. Natural gas continues to lead the way.

Countries with the Largest Reductions in CO_2 Emissions (Millions of Tons), 2000–2021

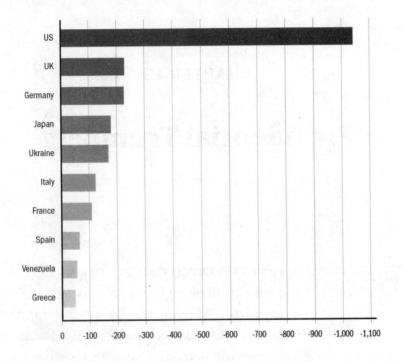

Source: "Statistical Review of World Energy," BP, June 2022, https://www.bp.com/en/global/corporate/energy-economics/statistical-review-of-world-energy.html

Here's a chart you won't see in the media or in Washington. The U.S. is leading the industrialized world in reducing emissions.

CHAPTER 13

Presidential Trumpets

BEGINNING IN 1977, I INVESTED TIME EDUCATING ELECTED officials on the benefits of oil and gas to our society and the economy. Early in my career, I'd made the decision to stand up for American oil and gas and saw it as an act of patriotism to do so. My belief was, and still is today, that without oil and gas development, America cannot sustain its global prominence.

Many across the country did not realize what the independent oil and gas producers were accomplishing with Horizontal Drilling as we tapped into the vast resources that America holds. As previously delineated, we call this the American Energy Renaissance. Around 2010, as soon as knowledge of the energy renaissance began to spread, the media began to call on me regularly to appear on their news shows. I was happy to appear in places such as CNBC, the *Wall Street Journal, Forbes, National Review, Financial Times*, NBC, Bloomberg, the *Washington Post*, MSNBC's *Morning Joe,* and Fox's *Mornings with Maria, Varney and Co., Tucker Carlson,* and *Fox & Friends*, along with many others.

I was also called on to give speeches around the country to national organizations about American energy and its impact.

In 2011, I was selected to be part of a group of energy experts charged with outlining a national energy strategy for Mitt Romney's 2012 presidential campaign. A policy memo was drawn up to plan for a new abundance of oil and natural gas—delivering energy independence to America and freeing us from foreign imports. I received many requests for various political and civic occasions to give speeches and presentations on "The Plan," as we called it.

Although Romney came up short in his bid for the White House, that wasn't the end for the energy policy we had drafted. In fact, at the Romney watch party, I met Donald Trump for the first time. And from the very beginning, he voiced his interest in what was happening in energy. He asked me if I came to New York often. My reply was that as the CEO of a publicly traded company, I regularly met with Wall Street. He invited me to come by his office on my next visit if time allowed. I agreed. A few weeks later during an energy conference break, I called him and let him know I had time to come by if he wasn't busy. He immediately invited me over.

Trump Tower, and Donald's office in particular, is unique. He has more football helmets and sports paraphernalia than I do! He even has a cookie jar made in his likeness—and the lid is a caricature of his trademark hair.

When we sat down, he got right to business, asking me to explain the American Energy Renaissance and how it had come about. I explained in detail how we were able to develop Horizontal Drilling to unleash the billions of barrels of oil and trillions of cubic feet of natural gas in the shale basins of the U.S., and how this wave of newly accessible resources could provide energy independence to America. I will never forget his response.

"Wow—this could drive the U.S. economy to a new level of prosperity." I agreed that it could, indeed, if we could get some relief from President Obama's burdensome regulations.

Trump then asked me a startling question: "Do you think I can be elected president?" My answer was, "I don't know. I've never given it any thought. Have you thought about being governor of New York?" His response was quick, "I don't want to be governor; I want to be president."

I then answered, "I don't know if you can be elected, but with your supportive view on energy for America, I will help you if you decide to run."

Energy to Run

When he did decide to run, I stepped up to help him right from the start. It wasn't easy being one of the first people to support Donald Trump. Even at Continental, some of our executives believed we would face harsh criticism. I countered that it wasn't the first time we had faced adversity for our beliefs about the right thing to do for our industry—including standing up for America. I supported the candidate's platform early on and started a growing national wave of momentum that swept the country. Here is how it began.

His enthusiasm for constructive change in America caught on quickly with Republicans and Democrats alike. On his first trip to Oklahoma, I arranged a group of business and thought leaders to meet him for a one-on-one meeting at Wiley Post Airport. Barry Switzer, the great football coach of the championship-winning Oklahoma Sooners and Super Bowl–winning Dallas Cowboys, was among those first to cross party lines to support him. During the visit, Barry told Trump that my career in drilling was analogous to poking a bunch of straws into the ground and producing oil where others had failed. Trump loved it and, to my chagrin, has retold the story dozens of times since.

Of course, I never stop seeing opportunity. Over the next few weeks, I led a group that designed a detailed leadership platform, providing candidate Trump with all the issues facing our nation in these crucial sectors: agriculture, health, national defense, energy, manufacturing, construction, technology, communication, transportation, banking, utilities, education, and financial services—headed up by ten of the top companies and individuals in each sector. I explained to many of them how the candidate's pro-business mindset could be transformative for America. Fortunately, I was able to persuade even those who were still skeptical of Trump to join the effort for our country's benefit. We had great participation in the organizational meetings and agreed to come together for a presentation in New York at Trump Tower in June 2016.

Donald Trump was somewhat taken aback when he came into the large conference room with the esteemed business and national leaders and was asked to sit and listen. Surprisingly, Trump listened attentively for the next three hours as he received information on the burdensome regulations harming each sector of the economy and what was needed to unleash American prosperity again. He engaged intently and asked questions, gathering the data that would prepare him for the campaign trail and to hit the ground running after he became president.

Many key points from those presentations still stand out to me today. For instance, representatives of both Lockheed-Martin and Boeing noted that our military was flying fighter jets that were over thirty-five years old and pointed out that the outdated technology was putting our military personnel in danger. In some circumstances, parts were being taken off museum-displayed planes to keep others in the air.

Unfortunately, this didn't come as a surprise to me.

Two years earlier, in 2014, we had lost a close family friend to the Afghan War's deadliest friendly-fire incident for American soldiers. An Air Force B-1 bomber dropped two five-hundred-pound bombs on our friend, Green Beret Staff Sergeant Scott Studenmund, and five of his fellow soldiers. Many believe the cause of the incident was an outdated aircraft that couldn't detect the soldiers' strobes, ultimately costing them their lives. The Air Force disputes this and continues to fly these outdated aircraft today.

As our summit with Trump continued, our energy representative relayed the facts about all the pipeline-delaying tactics being used to stop the oil and gas industry from getting our product to market. For example, we learned from security hired in North Dakota that Dakota Access Pipeline (DAPL) protesters were being paid upward of $19 per hour to protest, with bonuses if they were arrested. As if their uninformed disruption wasn't bad enough, the governor's office later told us it cost $38 million to police and clean up the waste and mess those folks made at the site.

The Trump Leadership Council (TLC) was very effective. He learned the solutions to the problems and was quick to respond—not only as a candidate but as president too. One of the agriculture representatives, Gene Nicholas—one of the largest landowner farmers from North Dakota—told candidate Trump that if he developed sound farm policy, rural Americans would elect him. That's exactly what happened. Trump campaign signs stood tall in every rural community. There were rallies twenty-thousand strong in communities of only ten thousand people. Voters came from all around to hear the man who sought to "Make America Great Again." Millions gave him their support, and he won a stunning victory over Hillary Clinton without the help of national media. To this day, I am convinced he was the only person who could have beaten her with all the momentum, funding, and national media coverage she had in her favor. He just never stopped fighting.

Watch Party

In November 2016, I flew to New York for the election night watch party with the unpopular conviction that he would win. There was nothing like that night in New York. At 3:30 in the morning, after most outlets had confirmed Trump's victory, I began looking for a hotel room and snagged one by 4:00 a.m. Despite the late (or early?) hour, I set my alarm clock for 6:00 a.m., waking up to shock and disbelief on the TV. My whole day was spent congratulating the supporters and TLC members and giving media interviews across the country. It was an exhilarating time.

Over the next few days, I spent some time with Trump in his office at Trump Tower, talking over plans to begin transitioning the country to his presidency. Later, I was very dismayed to learn of the eavesdropping on those conversations by Obama's agents. There was so much to do and plan. America had an unbelievable amount of pent-up demand and energy ready to be released if the regulatory burdens could be lifted. The future economic expansion would be amazing and unprecedented. My own field of energy was a prime example of what could be done.

Without a doubt, we could move America from an era of scarcity to one of abundance in a short time frame. I really wanted to be part of revolutionizing the energy policy that had limited its growth.

Later on, during the transition, I learned that Trump was considering me for an important energy post. I began to inquire about the requirements on my business ownership if I were to serve in the administration. The real stopper for me was the trust provision that would require me to place all my oil and gas holdings, including my Continental stock, in a trust over which I had no control, either now or in the future. I thought long and hard about it, but in the end and after conferring with my family, I made the difficult decision not to accept the position. It was the right decision. I had a duty to my shareholders to continue representing them well at Continental.

Instead, I began advising the president on the best cabinet-level folks to execute his policies. That counsel became more valuable to him as he faced relentless, dishonest opposition from the very beginning.

Good Policies, Good Economy

My personal Trump experience ended just like many others' did when he lost re-election in 2020. I loved his economic policies and still do and the impact that he had on the U.S. Supreme Court will last for generations to come. America thrived. We achieved energy independence and became the dominant oil and gas producer in the world, putting millions of Americans to work with good-paying jobs. Bolstering our national security saved countless American soldiers' lives, and we are still benefiting from these changes. Economically, for American consumers, it was a $1.5 trillion turnaround annually, and the prices at the pump were staggeringly low. Instead of buying and importing oil from the Middle East, we were producing it right here in America, benefiting Americans. The Trump administration found the appropriate price balance that kept the industry afloat while making consumer prices low.

American consumers enjoyed plentiful, cheap gasoline and diesel fuel. By the spring of 2020, the average price of gasoline cost Americans less than $1.70 per gallon, and diesel was just $2.50 per gallon. Inflation was 2 percent. We were admired as Americans and feared by our enemies. President Trump contained North Korea's aggressive dictator and kept Russia's Vladimir Putin and China's Chairman Xi reigned in. By shutting down aging coal plants and replacing them with clean-burning natural gas electricity generation, we cleaned up the air to the point of it being the best in the industrialized world. Abundant and cheap natural gas supplies enabled us to export clean fuel around the world and brought manufacturing plants back to America. All of this was achieved from a good policy base, some of which originated from our Trump Leadership Council discussions.

Although I held the respect of President Trump and we remained friends throughout much of his term, I saw the president become more and more distracted as he was almost overrun by many people who were only interested in *taking*.

It has been sad for me to see America slide backward in so many areas since the 2020 election. Most of these regressions were unnecessary, and all of them were harmful to the average American. I remain hopeful for the future and pray that irreversible damage doesn't befall our country before effective leadership can be restored.

People continuously ask me who could unify our great country once again and set us on a path to prosperity. As an American patriot, I always couch my answer like this: the next president must not be divisive. Stop the nonsense that rips the country apart and provide the leadership to get everyone pulling on the same rope again, instead of pitting one against the other politically. He or she must be electable by the people and have a good grasp of foreign policy to return our credibility as the world leader.

I get asked a lot about my support for former President Trump running again. Although many of his policies were sound and helped our nation prosper, he simply did not stand with many of those who stood with him.

My strong belief is there are better qualified candidates who can unite the country in the next election to lead America back to an era of energy abundance. What we are seeing in the Biden administration today—such as draining the Strategic Petroleum Reserve, limiting development on federal land, and punitive regulations—work together for self-imposed scarcity of American energy. What is necessary for our country is American energy security and independence, which supplies affordable, reliable energy that Americans want.

The Short List

I will recommend to whoever is considering leading our country today the same policies I've told numerous administrations. Here's a short list of the basics needed to secure economic prosperity and national security for all Americans:

- Don't become dependent on foreign regimes. We see what happens when a country doesn't have oil and gas reserves. Just look at Europe today.
- Provide a free market for all forms of energy. Take the government out of the business of picking winners and losers through market-distorting subsidies.
- Return to common-sense regulatory policy by repealing and rescinding crippling and punitive regulations.
- Provide for a pipeline infrastructure system under the Federal Energy Regulatory Commission using interstate commerce protection for the safe movement of all energy, including oil and natural gas.
- Streamline the permitting process for oil and natural gas drilling and completion on federal lands, which will

result in $20 trillion in unrealized energy wealth for America.

Remember, the U.S. has the largest oil and natural gas reserves in the world and is the largest producer of both. What does this mean for you? Based on my calculations, if America regains its position of prominence, we will generate over $20 trillion in economic activity by opening federal lands to energy development. It will lead to the creation of 2.7 million new jobs, generating over $5 trillion in wages. It will result in almost $4 trillion in new federal tax revenues and almost $2 trillion in state and local tax revenues.

As for who should lead our country, I keep a short list of those who display the integrity and leadership necessary for the office. Even with the current political turmoil, I am optimistic about America's bright future.

CHAPTER 14

Power Failures: How to Ensure They Don't Happen

**Energy density of oil and natural gas
compared to solar and wind.**
Solar: 0.0000015 joules per cubic meter
Wind at 10 mph: 7 joules per cubic meter
Natural gas: 40,000,000 joules per cubic meter
Oil: 45,000,000,000 joules per cubic meter

THE DOWNSIDE RISKS OF TOO QUICKLY "GREENING" ELEC-tricity generation are huge and growing. Just ask Texas.

In February 2021, Texas and parts of the Southwest suffered catastrophic power failures when a blast of polar air crashed the grid. Millions went without power; homes and business were without heat and light; and other vital utilities, such as water delivery, collapsed. Some estimate that at least two hundred and forty-five people lost their lives as a direct result of the crisis. The state's power grid was "seconds and minutes away from" complete failure when partial grid shutdowns were implemented, according to the Electric Reliability Council of Texas (ERCOT).

On the very first day of subfreezing weather, ERCOT instituted rolling blackouts, initially saying they would last for less than forty-five minutes. Unfortunately, they stretched for hours, and, in some cases, days. Because of the bitter cold, energy demand soared to record levels despite the blackouts.

As the windmills froze and the clouds blocked the sun, the "powers that be" started shutting off the very resource that was supplying that backup power generation: oil and natural gas fields. It was just one fiasco after the other.

Imagine what would happen to the people in an entire state if power simply stopped for weeks. Think about a sector as vital as health care. Hospitals would have to move patients to facilities in other states! But how could they do so if buses and airplanes could not fill up on gasoline from electric-powered pumps? Instead of hundreds of lives lost, we would have seen thousands needlessly die and millions suffer.

The irony, apparent to just about everyone, is Texas ranks as America's number one producer of energy. Yet the state, when faced with adverse weather, performed worse than even California in a disaster situation. Why?

For years, politicians and regulatory authorities incentivized the power utilities to invest in renewables. Texas is in a wind corridor, so thousands of windmills popped up across the state. To a lesser degree, incentives also drove solar-farm construction. The market incentives *did not include* backup infrastructure. Coal plants were shut down, removing resiliency for the grid. If a cleaner option was desired, the plants could have been converted to run on natural gas, ensuring resiliency. (As you know, I'm all for shutting down coal, but these plants should have been converted to run on natural gas.)

More and more of the Texas grid was relying on intermittent and unreliable renewables. The table was being set for disaster. In less than a decade, Texas had nearly tripled its commitment to wind and expanded its solar capacity by a factor of more than 260, but it wasn't enough to keep the lights on. Reliability of the power grid was sacrificed for intermittent renewables.

Solar's contribution during the extreme weather event was close to zero—and was zero at night. No surprise there. Wind power—partly because turbine blades weren't winterized and partly because of lack of wind—fell by 93 percent. At the same time, natural gas increased by 450 percent (according to the EIA). During the storm, wind went from near 40 percent of the total power for electricity generation to an average of just 8 percent.

That's right: natural gas saved the day. It's what kept Texas from an even more hellish nightmare. And in Oklahoma, the reliability of natural gas unquestionably saved lives.

Because of Continental's work in North Dakota, we know how to deal with frigid weather. Our Continental team went to work twenty-four hours a day to keep energy flowing, but we came very close to losing power as well. At one point during the storm, the utilities threatened to curtail electricity to the facilities in our natural gas fields that were feeding the gas to power-generating plants. Thankfully, we had a great relationship with the governor of Oklahoma's office, and he stopped them from making this fatal error. Texas was not as fortunate. Utilities curtailed power to a portion of the huge Permian oilfield, which furthered the crisis.

Renewables have their place. But we cannot depend on them as the primary source of power for the grid. What happened in Texas should be a clear wake-up call for policymakers, power executives, and politicians. As we all know, the sun doesn't always shine, and the wind doesn't always blow.

The question every American should be asking is, "Why are we risking lives, hurting the economy, and threatening our energy security to pretend this works?"

The Stupid before the Storm

My company and I had been warning about this scenario for years, on many fronts.

In Oklahoma, we warned the Corporation Commission that the grid relied on too much intermittent power. Some listened, and some did not. If those who didn't listen would have been as zealous about serving their citizens as they were about scoring green points, these problems would not have happened.

Another factor that still needs to be addressed is building more natural gas storage for the grid. This also relates to how power is bought and sold on the "spot" market. We can use the orange juice analogy here. Instead of juice distributors buying and storing large quantities of their product with long-term contracts, they buy what they think they need, sometimes on a daily basis, known as the spot market. This daily market can be pushed by unusual "demand" measures to extraordinarily high levels.

When a freeze in Florida wipes out the orange groves, buyers are left with no source of juice and are forced to pay much higher prices for the few oranges that are left. Scarcity and higher prices are passed on to consumers. The same thing happens with electricity producers.

These utilities, in my view, are not being good buyers in terms of looking out for their customers. They can do better. Many utilities are invested heavily in wind and solar, so perhaps their vision is clouded by their own press releases. They have the buying power and obligation to take responsibility for reliability and affordability.

Most Texans don't know it, but they will be paying for the high costs of this needless crisis with higher monthly utility bills and taxes for many years. One might expect this in California, but not in Texas or Oklahoma.

Will Texas and the rest of the world learn a lesson from this? Well, on July 12, 2022, a *Texas Monthly* story touted a headline: "Solar Power Is Bailing Texas Out This Summer" with the subhead, "Enjoying that AC? Thank the mighty power of the sun and the renewable energy source keeping the grid afloat."

The very next day, ABC News posted this story: "Texas power grid faces limited solar energy supply," and the article reported, "The Texas power grid's operator has asked consumers to use less energy as clouds threaten access to essential solar power." Tesla owners also received this message on their in-car screens: "The grid operator recommends to avoid charging during peak hours between 3pm and 8pm, if possible, to help statewide efforts to manage demand." (Many U.S. households are receiving similar messages on their "smart" thermostats. A sign of things to come?)

Speaking of California

Let's start with the good news. If California were its own country, it would have the fifth-largest economy in the world. It's blessed with an extraordinarily temperate climate and miles of spectacular coastline. Nearly forty million people live there, and that's just the "official" number.

What makes California fascinating to me is its energy history. Back in the day, it competed with Oklahoma for the rank of number one oil-producing state in the union. California oil was even credited by historians as critical to the Allied victory in World War I. But those days are long gone.

Another bit of shared history: In the Dust Bowl years of the Great Depression, Oklahoma experienced a net population loss of 440,000 through migration. Most took Route 66, looking for more fertile land and the possibility of work. The term *Okie* was not a compliment but rather a derogatory word used to label the impoverished vagabonds who desperately flooded California at this time (many of whom were not actually from Oklahoma). To quote Oklahoma's favorite son, Will Rogers, "It raised the IQ of both states!"

Today, California remains the nation's top agricultural state, producing more than a third of the country's vegetables and three-quarters of its fruits and nuts. In 2021, California's farms and ranches generated over $50 billion in agricultural cash receipts.

But there is another story to the Golden State, one that has implications for all of us. To some, California is a failed experiment gone off the rails—a progressive la-la land where every bad idea is being put in place. Not satisfied with running grand experiments involving its own citizens, the folks that manage the state insist that we should all join in. But people are voting with their moving vans—many of them to Texas and Oklahoma. For the past few years, California has lost population, and, as a result, is losing a congressional seat. But I digress. Let's talk energy.

Gas and electricity are more expensive in California. The state inflicts the highest gasoline taxes in the country. These taxes are regressive and hurt those who can least afford it.

Electricity in the Bay Area (the hotbed of progressive thinking) costs up to 70 percent more than the "flyover states," such as Oklahoma and Texas. Again, the burden falls heaviest on those with lower incomes. No one in charge in California talks about lowering energy costs; the story is always about everyone paying more for the greater good and the millions of jobs created in a green economy.

In 2022, California took the lead in energy prices again, with some gas stations charging more than $8 and even $9 a gallon. Those in charge expressed concern but were secretly smiling—thinking this would accelerate the electrification of transportation. It will do no such thing. It will only make the economic pain worse.

In August 2022, days after the state passed a law banning the sale of new gas-powered vehicles, California also asked electric-car owners to scale back charging their vehicles in a "voluntary energy conservation" notice. Again, it might be funny if it wasn't so ridiculous.

Way back in 2006, then Republican Governor Arnold Schwarzenegger began his term by signing legislation that empowered the California Air Resources Board (CARB) to "regulate" CO_2 emissions. The goal was to reduce CO_2 levels to 1990 levels by 2020. Subsequently, there has been a relentless parade of additional bills regularly flowing from the governor's office and the legislature.

Among the most egregious initiatives began in 2020: all new residential construction in the state must be NZE or "net zero energy." New commercial construction must do the same by 2030, including half of existing structures by the same date.

Governor Gavin Newsom also ordered CARB to implement the phaseout of new gas-powered cars and light trucks within fifteen years. Why is that important? California comes in first in new car and truck registrations every year at around 2 million units. There are 30 million registered vehicles on their roads. If you're a carmaker, what choices do you have if you hope to stay in business or want Wall Street to value your stock favorably? You stop investing in more-efficient gas engines and go all in on EVs. The bonus is that taxpayers pay for subsidies and incentives because most Americans won't pay $10,000–$20,000 more for a vehicle.

Climate alarmists are happy to ride the white horse of planet saving, no matter how inefficient or quixotic the quest. A clear-thinking fellow named Francis Menton made the case mathematically: "California's CO_2 emissions are about 1% of the world's annual total, and its electricity sector accounts for about 15% of those emissions, so we're talking here about approximately 0.15% of world emissions—an amount whose elimination, as you can easily see, will rapidly transform the world's climate." Thank you, Francis. Sarcasm noted.

Instead of making the necessary public investments in energy, water, and transportation, the strategy of those alarmists seems to be making owning a car too expensive, crushing new housing builds, and forcing the rationing of electricity by making it more expensive.

Two hundred years ago, there weren't forty million people taking showers and washing cars and recharging their phones in the land we now call California. The land was thinly populated because there was hardly any water. Humans didn't have the technology to create and store lakes of water or the fuels to support mega-cities. Human ingenuity made California habitable and a mecca for the world. You would think, given the state's role in game-changing technology and innovation, they would celebrate their blessings and possibly turn their own attention to desalinization plants along their long coast to deal with their water needs. The people in Israel, with a similar climate and coastline, have used their technology to design and install practical and economic facilities to even reclaim former desert lands and convert them to highly productive agricultural areas.

Up in Flames

Everything you need to know about California's approach to energy is wrapped up in the state's largest utility, Pacific Gas and Electric (PG&E). In and out of bankruptcy over the past couple of decades, it's everyone's favorite punching bag. We see PG&E blamed for everything wrong with electricity delivery and generation. Government-imposed mandates have made it a capital-poor, unmanageable enterprise with a revolving door of CEOs in recent years. Some 125,000 miles of PG&E transmission lines crisscross the state, often through forests.

For decades, foresters and timber harvesters knew trouble was brewing. Thanks to California-based groups such as the Sierra Club, any attempts to harvest timber or use controlled burns were met with lobbyists and/or litigation. In less than thirty years, annual harvests declined from roughly 6 billion board feet of timber to less than 1.5 billion.

This helped turn the state into a massive tinderbox. Tree and shrub density went from a healthy level to overly crowded, and a lot of fuel accumulated at ground level. When a perfect firestorm meets a couple of dry seasons—which is utterly normal in California—PG&E's unscientific policies become the ignition switch.

The scenes coming from California every year are avoidable. Ironically, the vast majority of the fires start or grow on federally "managed" land. Michael Schellenberger, author of *Apocalypse Never: Why Environmental Alarmism Hurts Us All*, said the 2021 wildfires were "100 percent" preventable if burns and trimming around PG&E power lines had been done properly by state and federal authorities.

Illustrative of the problem, Governor Newsom cut his state's budget for wildfire and resource management by 40 percent, from $355 million in 2019 to $203 million in 2020. So-called environmentalists let the scorching go on, allowing another million acres to go up in atmosphere-choking smoke. They vote for people who make catastrophically bad decisions, watch another $10 billion in property burn, and then tell every kid in America it's because of climate change. Point is, they aren't taking responsibility for their own decisions. Their primary interest is telling the rest of the nation how to live instead of taking the lead to manage their own issues.

California consumes far more energy than it produces. On any given day, it imports up to a quarter of the electricity it needs from bordering states, where more rational energy policies prevail. And to make matters even worse, California in 2020 imported 24 percent of its oil from Ecuador, 22 percent from Saudi Arabia, and 20 percent from Iraq.

Battery Backup?

Europe also keeps marching around like the bunny in the battery commercials—they *keep going and going*—beating the drum about renewables. But they've also experienced a shock, as journalist Bjorn Lomborg recently reported:

> For decades, the EU has claimed that renewables can deliver energy security because this can be produced at home and does not need to be imported. But the key renewables, solar and wind, are unreliable because they work only when the sun is shining or the wind is blowing. To achieve reliable power 24/7, solar and wind need

backup, provided by burning gas. Thus, the EU's green energy policy contributes to it paying Russia more than half a billion dollars each day, mostly for fossil fuels and especially gas, to provide a backstop for European solar and win.

Solar and wind campaigners claim batteries can be game changers when the sun isn't shining and wind isn't blowing. In truth, all the batteries in Europe can store power for just one minute and 21 seconds of the continent's average electricity demand—after that we're back to relying mostly on fossil fuel backup.

—Bjorn Lomborg, "Sensible alternatives to Russian oil and gas required," *Business Day*, March 17, 2022

And as of now, Russia has turned off the tap to the EU. Germany and its neighbors are running out of options. In August 2022, Google searches for *firewood* (*brennholz* in German) among Germans increased exponentially. Maybe that will light a fire under some politicians there. Meanwhile, many rare earth minerals used in battery production are imperiled by the war in Ukraine—a country rich in such elements. It's no wonder Putin is so interested in this country.

Power On

Call me pragmatic, but I believe innovation happens best when people and companies have reliable electricity and affordable fuel for heating and cooling. You can also call me an environmentalist, if by that you mean someone who appreciates our natural world and takes action to protect it. So I suppose I'm a pragmatic environmentalist. I've never been someone who covets other people's market share, which is the basis for much of the growth of the subsidized energy alternatives, even those recent adherents who would like to ban the American family's gas stove that they rely on to cook their food. They even want to regulate how American families prepare their food. I can't wait to see how this unfolds!

What my company—and other oil and natural gas producers—have done eclipses all the solar and wind farms in the world. Not only that, but Continental also takes care to extract hydrocarbons with minimal disruptions. And we do it cleanly, affordably, and responsibly.

Unlike some environmentalists, I also appreciate our way of life in America. We can have a healthy planet *and* an industrialized society. It's possible—by continuing to *grow*, not shrink, our expectations.

CHAPTER 15

Market Changer: How and Why We Fixed Global Oil Markets

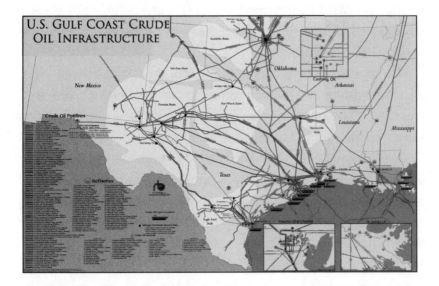

U.S. GULF COAST CRUDE OIL INFRASTRUCTURE

APRIL 20, 2020: THE DAY THE PRICE OF CRUDE OIL WENT negative. It bottomed out at *negative* $37.63 a barrel. Yes, you could buy oil for negative dollars on the West Texas Intermediate (WTI) exchange, effectively making money. And, for a day, we were *selling* it for negative dollars. To the layperson, it made no sense. To many in the oil business, it made even less sense.

At the same time, the benchmark price of Brent crude (European oil) was nearly $20 a barrel. Why was there a $57 differential between American oil and the rest of the world?

Smart people were scratching their heads. *How does something like oil suddenly have a negative value? Will the gas station pay you to fill up your pickup?* It was just another in a series of unprecedented shocks to the system that 2020 delivered with each passing week.

There were several factors in play, not the least of which was the unprecedented crash on demand caused by COVID-19. Governments across the world were locking down their citizens and their borders. Transportation networks slowed to a trickle, and with it, the need for fuels. Consumption of oil and gas decreased by a record 30 percent in mere days, the largest decline in history.

There were alleged capacity and storage issues as well. After all, where do you put all the production when there's no demand? (Storage is the name of the game, and the industry has many solutions, including tankers and storing oil underground.)

I got more than a tad worked up. I knew in my bones the market had been manipulated, and I was sure the usual bad players smelled blood in the water. Never underestimate people's capacity to become raving "capitalists" even when they are fervent nonbelievers.

Millions of jobs were at stake, and American energy independence was too. I tirelessly pointed out that when we became a net exporter in 2019, we were no longer at the mercy of rogue regimes and unreliable partners for our energy needs. Hundreds of billions of dollars stayed home. A long-standing and flawed argument for foreign intervention was put on the shelf. President Trump—and particularly Secretary of State Mike Pompeo—grasped the significance of energy independence. Our approach to geopolitics changed from one of weakness to one of strength.

But on April 20, all the progress we had made seemed to be in jeopardy. In fact, it looked like our whole energy world was about to implode, due first to COVID-19 followed by plummeting demand, then OPEC and Russia opening the taps, and finally, negative oil.

The story that quickly made the rounds and became the conventional wisdom was that this moment in time was an anomaly. Demand for oil had plummeted. The world was awash in petroleum, and some thinly traded May futures contracts based on the benchmark WTI temporarily went negative. (West Texas Intermediate is a global benchmark that's been used for decades to price oil.)

According to the Chicago Mercantile Exchange, on April 20, there was no place to put the oil because the terminals in Cushing, Oklahoma, were overflowing. Their story was twisted, like so many stories told these days. It had an element of truth; storage space *would* be a growing concern. This was just enough to create a shock in the marketplace and let some clever people take advantage of an anomaly in the market.

Commodities and Futures 101

As much as I like to think crude oil is quite a special resource, it is a commodity. There's lots of it all over the globe. There are three major categories of commodities: agriculture, metals, and energy.

Trading commodities involves buying and selling, most often in the form of *futures* contracts, in which a trader offers to buy a raw material at a certain price, agreeing to take delivery and pay for it on a certain future date. It can be a risky game but also highly profitable.

If you're an orange farmer, your crop takes months to come to fruition. You want to make sure you can sell your product at a good price when it's harvested, so you might agree to sell a futures contract for a set price in four months. If prices tank, you're smiling because you have a contract at a certain price. If the market goes up, you'll smile less.

If the prevailing prices do go up, the investor who bought a futures contract for less than the current price is smiling, because they can now sell the contract for a profit.

Geopolitical disruptions, big weather events, and changing economies can also play a part in the game. Traders are basically betting on the future. But so are producers of these commodities.

Markets vs. Reality

In the real world, not the world of electronic digits flying back and forth, you are supposed to take delivery of your oil on the date your purchase contract expires—or sell it.

"The owners of the oil have no place to put it!" clucked all the Chicken Littles. So the traders in the marketplace said, "Tough luck. Now you can pay me to take it off your hands."

Reality check: traders aren't interested in taking delivery of anything. Traders deal in "digital oil," not real oil. They want to make money off buying and selling the contracts. There's nothing wrong or illegal about that, and sometimes traders take advantage of those market "anomalies" and disruptions to make even more money.

As you might imagine, some astute traders made money on April 20—particularly a handful connected to the Chicago Mercantile Exchange where WTI was traded. While traders made money, domestic oil producers lost money.

Twenty-four hours later, oil was no longer negative. But the disruption had roiled the interconnected world of energy. It's an annual market worth $4 trillion that affects everything we depend on, from the gas in our cars to the electricity that flows into our homes, the cost of food, and the products we use every day.

The Commodity Futures Trading Commission (CFTC) chairman at the time, Heath Tarbert, said it seemed to be a simple case of "fundamental supply and demand." There was nothing fundamental about it. The lies started piling up, and I got angry. There was a fundamental flaw in the system, and I decided to do something about it.

The April event exposed the archaic nature of U.S. oil pricing. The benchmark WTI price was tied to the terminals and pipelines in Cushing, Oklahoma—a landlocked relic of the century-old oil boom that didn't remotely reflect the advanced infrastructure of U.S. energy.

In the past thirty years, huge investments have been made along the Gulf of Mexico, primarily in Texas and Louisiana. America's energy bounty flowed through the Gulf. Cushing was still important, but what was happening along the coast was game-changing. The huge reservoirs of oil and natural gas being tapped in the Permian Basin flowed directly to the refineries and terminals in the Gulf of Mexico.

Houston and Corpus Christi were becoming export hubs. Before COVID-19, we were exporting nearly four million barrels a day to the global markets. I knew there was almost unlimited storage capacity along the Gulf, between the terminals and tankers. Like Brent in the North Atlantic, it was a truly global, waterborne marketplace. *So why the hell was U.S. oil being priced based on the limited Cushing storage capacity? And why were traders being allowed to manipulate the market based on perception instead of reality?*

Transparent Oil?

The market needed more transparency. A handful of traders manipulated the market in a time of crisis, and, in my view, the Chicago Mercantile Exchange (CME), and regulatory bodies failed to meet their obligations to maintain a fair and equitable marketplace.

The quote that really riled me from the CME was, "The market worked the way the market was supposed to work." Their view was that no manipulation had occurred—the markets operated as designed. I was astounded by their ambivalence. I booked an appearance on one of the financial news programs to counter their silliness. The markets were *not* doing what they were supposed to do when they allowed prices to go negative.

The regulatory Commodities Futures Trading Commission (CFTC) promised to look into the whole mess. For some of us, CFTC stood for "Can't Find the Crime." *Nothing to see here. But we will investigate*, they promised. Fat chance they would call anyone on the carpet.

Let me clarify an important point. I have nothing against traders. They serve a valuable role in the marketplace by lining up buyers and sellers. But sometimes they get greedy and intentionally manipulate the market, allowing them to pocket what I consider ill-gotten gains.

According to Bloomberg, a group of traders in Britain managed to make over $660 million in a matter of hours that day—from the comfort of their homes. As the price plunged, they bought futures contracts betting oil wouldn't stay negative. One was reminded of the movie *Trading Places*, in which Eddie Murphy and Dan Aykroyd played traders who outsmart the insufferable Duke brothers in the frozen orange juice trades. Except this wasn't a screwball comedy. It was real. These traders messed with every energy company in the world—and every consumer. Something had to change.

American Gulf Coast Select (AGS) and HOU

I enjoy taking long walks. It's often where I work things out in my head. After one such walk following the pricing event, I hijacked the agenda of our weekly exploration and production reviews. I was single-minded about correcting flaws in pricing for domestic oil. I started with the obvious:

"This makes no sense," I said. "We have a perfectly functioning waterborne infrastructure in the Gulf. Cushing is the past. Besides, turns out they still had 20 percent capacity, so something's not adding up. We need to change this *now*."

The oil and gas marketing folks in the room nodded, but some were hesitant to make the leap. *Does Harold really think he can upend global pricing markers?*

Damn right I did.

What were the obstacles? How fast could we get it done? Did we care what the CME might think? Who did we need to talk to in Washington?

"We'll create a new benchmark, one based on the realities of American energy," I exclaimed as I started scribbling on a whiteboard, drawing from memory the various pipelines and nodes along the gulf. The more I drew, the more animated I got.

"We are the global power, not Europe or the Brent market. America is the largest energy producer in the world. Brent is a declining asset."

More heads started nodding.

"We need to name it. Create our own brand, something that will stick in people's heads like WTI."

The group quickly got caught up in the exercise.

"It would be good to have the word *American*."

"We need to designate it more precisely, geographically, like the word *Gulf.*"

Now words were scribbled on several large whiteboards in the room.

"Maybe we should suggest a grade of the product," was another comment.

About ninety minutes later, the consensus was the new benchmark brand would be American Gulf Coast Select, or AGS. The next day, we had a logo and a plan.

The exercise was indicative of the way I like to do things. Get some really smart people in the room, throw out a disruptive idea, and give everyone the opportunity to punch holes in the thinking and add even better ideas. In a typical company, months of calendar time and man-hours would have been frittered away, committees would have formed, subcommittees would have spawned, and everything would have been handed over to expensive consultants and branding experts for the final burnishing.

Instead, we mapped out a potential future in five hours. But there were still enormous hurdles to overcome.

Could we get the major players such as Marathon, Phillips Petroleum, ConocoPhillips, and Shell to play? Would the terminal operators like Magellan and Enterprise jump aboard? How would the market and traders react—and did we even care?

But AGS was a thing. From our perspective, it was a competitive standard that would more accurately reflect the fair market value of American-produced barrels in the global markets. It would bring stability and transparency to what had become a murky market. Any market needs to be representative of the true value of its products, without artificial influences on the pricing—particularly manipulation.

Two of the largest trading platforms in the world, Platts and Argus, saw the wisdom of our ways and signed on by giving us a marker for AGS. Our legitimacy was then recognized by other important players in our industry.

When it came to discussing AGS with our peers, we knew we needed most of the bigger players to buy in. We formed an organization called Best Practices to facilitate these sensitive discussions, and we had an antitrust attorney present in every meeting to make sure there was not even a whiff of unethical outcomes on pricing.

As you might imagine, discussing this new trading market with competitors could have gone in any number of directions, many of them not good. Some of the crucial parties were even in legal disputes with each other at the time. But the need for change was obvious to everyone. It was time for more efficiency and less congestion in supply. Stability, liquidity, transparency, and efficiency were all things AGS supplied.

As collaboration progressed, we agreed that the name needed one exact location to market where the exchange is made. The obvious choice was Houston, Texas. Thus, AGS became HOU. Where is HOU traded today? Not on the Chicago Mercantile Exchange, and that's no accident. HOU is traded on the New York Mercantile Exchange (NYMEX) known as the Intercontinental Exchange (ICE).

ICE Midland WTI American Gulf Coast Futures

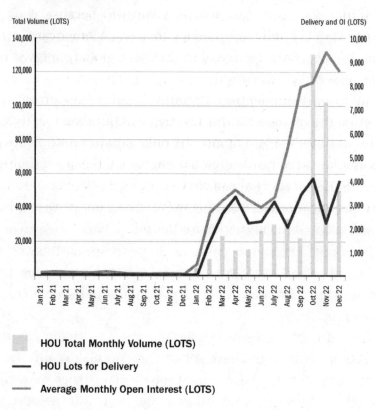

Total Volume (LOTS) | Delivery and OI (LOTS)

HOU Total Monthly Volume (LOTS)

— HOU Lots for Delivery

— Average Monthly Open Interest (LOTS)

Source: IntercontinentalExchange Services, Inc.

Here's a dramatic depiction of how important the Gulf Coast
has become to America's economic and energy future.

I keep a picture on my wall of the HOU infrastructure map, which you saw at the beginning of this chapter. It took a little over a year to establish the market, and I'm proud of that timeline. Everyone involved put blood, sweat, and tears into making this a reality. I hope this story inspires you. If the status quo stinks, you can do something to make things better. It may take time and effort, but it is always worth it.

A Win-Win for All

Anything that's good for the energy industry is good for the consumer. It's clear that HOU is a win-win because it offers greater stability and transparency to average Americans. Most of all, it recognizes the role of the U.S. as a global energy super-power essential to the world.

It's gaining momentum. Recently, I had the opportunity to check on the volumes flowing through HOU and was told they're increasing every single month. It's only a matter of time before this marker becomes the global energy market for crude oil. Today, HOU is trading ahead of WTI at Cushing primarily due to the transportation difference. However, as it gains in momentum it will become a major market for U.S. oil.

CHAPTER 16

ESG:
Horizontal Drilling
Delivers Again

THE GREATEST THING TO HAPPEN TO ESG IS HORIZONTAL Drilling. Small footprint, abundant, clean oil and natural gas.

The following graphs show how energy consumption in the U.S. has been declining even though our population has been growing. The reason? Efficiency and innovation on the part of producers.

It's all the rage—restructuring businesses and national economies. A new "industry" has been birthed to deal with it. Every board of every publicly held company must wrestle with it, because it has become the ultimate virtue signal. Every CEO needs to develop their strategy to make sure their ESG story will attract investors and ward off regulators and legislators.

But most Americans have never heard of it. I'm talking about ESG—an acronym for Environmental, Social, and Governance.

(We touched on it briefly in chapter 12's discussion of BlackRock.) Although these subjective factors are nonfinancial, more and more investors try to measure them and apply their judgments to investments. In short, ESG is kind of a beauty pageant for businesses seeking capital. Instead of financial performance, they compete in how their business impacts the environment, social causes, and how they "govern."

BP Primary Energy Consumption
(GJ per capita)

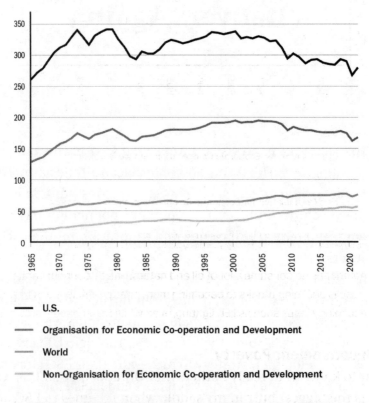

— U.S.

— Organisation for Economic Co-operation and Development

— World

— Non-Organisation for Economic Co-operation and Development

Source: "Statistical Review of World Energy," BP, accessed December 21, 2022, https://www.bp.com/en/global/corporate/energy-economics/statistical-review-of-world-energy.html

Petroleum Liquids Consumed per Capita
(gal/d)

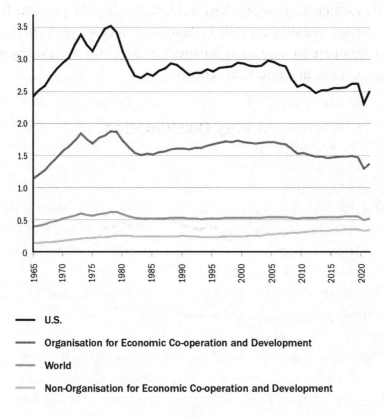

—— U.S.

~~~~ Organisation for Economic Co-operation and Development

~~~~ World

~~~~ Non-Organisation for Economic Co-operation and Development

Source: "Statistical Review of World Energy," BP, accessed December 21, 2022,
https://www.bp.com/en/global/corporate/energy-economics/statistical-review-of-world-energy.html

Americans do consume a lot of oil and natural gas, but our per capita
use is declining thanks to becoming more energy-efficient and to
technology leaps such as LED lighting, even while the economy grows.

An Inconvenient Poverty

Want to know what really bothers me? Untapped potential. And
this is the biggest burr in my saddle when it comes to ESG and
other unscientific do-gooding.

I've been to almost every continent and have seen so much potential—in human beings and in energy. There's a scientific connection between expanding human potential and the availability of reliable, affordable energy to power our lives.

Many scientists believe much of the African deserts were once full of lush vegetation, but thousands of years of humans cutting and burning wood destroyed those ecosystems by causing desert creep. Half of the people in sub-Saharan Africa do not have access to electricity and cook with wood, charcoal, kerosene, coal, and even dung. (Wood chips, dung, and ethanol are considered "renewables" by some but are far more dangerous to the environment—and people—than hydrocarbons.) As a result, disease is rampant, and their way of life remains a challenge. This breaks my heart because globally, billions of lives could be so much better with reliable, affordable access to clean energy, water, and sanitation.

To illustrate the level of hypocritical ignorance the "experts" routinely tout, consider these two quotes.

> "We have to increase tree cover five times faster. It means we have to ramp up renewable energy six times faster. It means we have to transition to electric vehicles at a rate twenty-two times faster."
>
> —JOHN KERRY, SPECIAL PRESIDENTIAL ENVOY FOR CLIMATE, AT THE 1 WORLD ECONOMIC FORUM, IN DAVOS, SWITZERLAND

> "Around 2.4 billion people cook using polluting open fires or simple stoves fueled by kerosene, biomass (wood, animal dung and crop waste) and coal. Each year, over three million people die prematurely from illness attributable to household air pollution from inefficient

cooking practices using polluting stoves paired with solid fuels and kerosene."

—2021 WORLD HEALTH ORGANIZATION REPORT

Are they saying that people who have no option but to burn these fuels should simply drive an electric car? What makes me furious is the fact that the poverty caused by energy inaccessibility is not the fault of the millions who live in sub-Saharan Africa; it's the fault of leaders in their countries and leaders in the Western world who claim to care about poverty but turn a blind eye to human suffering that could be solved with sensible energy policies. They oppose oil and natural gas in the name of saving the environment but ignore the fact that people are tearing down forests and burning heavily polluting fuels just to cook and stay warm.

This brings me to a term you may not have heard if you're reading this in the U.S.: *energy poverty*.

The World Economic Forum defines *energy poverty* as the lack of access to sustainable, modern energy services and products. The International Energy Agency (IEA) claims that nearly 800 million people on this planet live without any access to electricity, and more than 2.5 *billion* (yes, *billion* with a *b*) people do not have access to clean cooking facilities. What is wrong with our world when billions of human beings live without sanitary methods of cooking food for their families?

Take one country in sub-Saharan Africa, for example: the Democratic Republic of the Congo. Of the roughly one hundred million people living there, only 9 percent have access to electricity. Nine out of ten people there depend on wood for their basic energy needs. Yes, wood does grow on trees, but it takes a long time to grow a new one.

There is a better way. The U.S. has plenty of capacity to export Liquified Natural Gas (LNG) to any country on the planet—and this can be a game changer for billions of people. Skeptical? The U.S. is exporting fourteen billion cubic feet (BCF) of LNG per day and heading to twenty BCF by 2025. Much of this product is currently destined to Europe to ease the energy crisis perpetrated by Russia. Many national gas experts believe the U.S. has the potential supply to triple that number by 2035. Stay tuned. We are exporting a cleaner fuel to the rest of the world.

Where there is no electricity, there is no light, no access to the tools that power business, and only limited access to modern health care or education.

Energy Poverty Is Personal

My home didn't have electricity when I was a young boy—or indoor plumbing, but that's another matter. As a five-year-old, I still remember the magical sight of the Rural Electrical Association's utility crews drilling holes and popping in massive highline poles as the power lines slowly approached our rural Oklahoma home.

Up to that point, we used kerosene lamps for light and an icebox—with an actual block of ice we bought in town weekly—to cool our fresh food and milk. Electricity transformed our lives, and soon after we were connected to the grid, we got propane gas for cooking. When I visit a developing country, I instantly recall my struggles as a child. Maybe that's why energy poverty upsets me so: it's completely unnecessary and destroys the ecosystem surrounding it.

As a boy in rural Oklahoma, I couldn't imagine the technology we now take for granted. Most people alive today have no idea how much energy poverty there was in rural America right up until the 1960s. Electrification, like the interstate highway system, changed America for the better, driving huge gains in economic growth and quality of life.

Poverty can be soul-crushing and nation-crushing. Growing up, I saw all the collateral effects of poverty—broken marriages, alcoholism, and depression, to name a few. But I also saw people rise above it. My family did. They made choices, and in some cases, very brave choices and sacrifices to make ends meet as they contended with harsh economic times.

Poverty should make everyone angry—or at the very least, impatient to fix the problem. Some blame capitalism and free enterprise, wishing instead for socialism. If they paid attention to the last century of human existence, they would realize socialism causes insurmountable challenges, and it is not the answer to their problems.

Socialists love the word *fair*. "It's not fair that some people have more than others." Socialism solves that by making everyone equal—*equally poor*, that is. Except, of course, for the crooks in charge of all the "fairness."

My family was rich in love but poor in money. Life wasn't "fair" for us when I was a kid. But this is one of the few countries that allows people like you and me to rise above poverty and make a big difference in the world through hard work and perseverance.

Using our immense U.S. energy supply, I believe we have an opportunity to lift the rest of the world out of energy poverty as fast as possible. I also believe the only way to do it quickly and responsibly is with a reliable oil and natural gas supply.

Hydrocarbons changed our standard of living exponentially in a century. And we haven't scratched the surface of untapped potential. Imagine how the lives of fellow humans in countries without reliable access to electricity and other forms of energy could change in this generation with fact-based energy policies.

Lowering the Cost of Prosperity

Did you know the amount of energy needed to produce one unit of prosperity in the Western world has decreased by 1 percent a year for over one hundred and fifty years? And as a result, our air is cleaner, our water is pure, and our environment is healthier than at any time in our modern history, even with the bad coal-promoting policies in the Fuel Use Act of 1978.

Our progress came through harnessing hydrocarbons. This cheap, reliable, abundant source of energy enabled the inventors, innovators, and big thinkers to step up their game and change the world.

We seem to lose all track of just how far we've come and how quickly we've gotten here. The electrification of America expanded opportunity for every citizen. In the scope of human history, air travel, personal transportation, communications, refrigeration, space travel, computing, and countless other modern miracles appeared in the blink of an eye. In all of recorded history, only the last four generations have experienced massive declines in mortality rates.

What was the game changer? You guessed it: our oil and natural gas—not only as an energy source but as an essential ingredient in medicines, plastics, sanitation, and infrastructure.

Humankind has made extraordinary progress, but these gains are continually obscured by those who think our future is likely to be a foreboding place. When you recognize the simple truth that energy demand is going up and our need for cheap, reliable energy will not slow down, oil and clean-burning natural gas have to lead the way.

Even at our current rate of consumption, by my calculation, in one hundred and fifty years, we'll have used a mere 15 percent of what's under our feet. Yes, oil and natural gas are a finite resource, but they are also the path to new technology. Decisions we make should be based on doing the most "good" for the least amount of harm.

The most "good" would be ridding the world of energy poverty. The least harm would be doing it with American-produced natural gas. Moving from coal to natural gas cleaned up America's environment in a big way.

We can all agree that there's nothing more environmentally unfriendly than the mass burning of wood, charcoal, and coal. Would those in undeveloped nations without clean cooking fuel appreciate natural gas with which to cook? Would they be as excited as I was when I saw those power lines coming over the horizon? The answer is obvious to you and me.

A Warped Measuring Stick for Business

Imagine being an oil and gas company in the age of ESG. Some believe we shouldn't even be allowed to use the letters in our business. Others use it as a velvet hammer to suggest we can never measure up. But almost none believe we are worthy of praise for the benefits we provide to the environment and society.

There are all kinds of scorecards out there, and as with government regulations, there's no cap on how many freshly printed rules they can manufacture. I should know. We are squarely in the middle of the maelstrom. But having dealt with all three parts of ESG very effectively for the past fifty-five years, I do not have any concern about how it affects our company. We have worked diligently to perfect all three aspects of ESG. Over the entire life of our company, I have personally witnessed a never-ending evolution within our industry to improve our environmental performance.

Right now, subjective scoring on a company's "environmental, social, and governance" has not been legislated. There are no laws passed by our elected representatives on the topic.

But certainly, the regulatory edicts and peer pressure are endless with the threat of being "canceled." We continue to holistically make changes and improvements.

A Nonscientific Way to Measure Investments

Somehow, our financial system has gotten to the point where climate risk is investment risk—a mantra now repeated by many of the institutional capital organizations (that is, the large lenders and investment firms). You can visit any number of websites and learn how to create a net-zero carbon portfolio and play a huge role in accelerating the transition to a low-carbon economy. There are algorithms that purport to optimize portfolios across risk, return, and carbon.

The real risk with ESG is KJR—*knee-jerk reactions*. If lenders and investors decide they don't like the "feel" of oil or the "smell" of natural gas, they will make it almost impossible for us to provide the energy America needs to remain strong and secure. Reserve-Based Lending, the common way for oil and gas companies to borrow against their producing properties, has been trending downward in recent years. More and more establishment experts have believed it is virtuous to strangle domestic oil and gas production. The pressure they have exerted on decision-makers in the capital markets, including big banks, is tremendous. This has hurt independent energy producers, consumers, and our national security. Only recently has there been some pushback against those heavy-handed measures.

ESG is inherently weighted against the oil and natural gas industry, effectively producing a sector bias away from energy. When investors allocate capital away from oil and gas, it makes it that much harder to decarbonize and produce more, as the Biden administration demands. Some energy-producing states are pushing back. As I write this, there are reports that at least fifteen states are proposing policies to limit dealings with banks that are hostile to fossil fuel lending.

There are only two "on demand" and reliable sources of energy available to humankind. The first is my business: hydrocarbons. The second is nuclear. Nuclear, for the most part, is shrinking rapidly. Investment dollars are nowhere to be found—another casualty of the current hypocrisy of "responsible investing." You can thank the so-called environmentalists for putting a stake in the core of nuclear energy—despite the fact (yes, *fact*) that nothing is safer and gets you to zero emissions faster.

I would argue the biggest risk the planet faces is the energy transition being implemented at a faster rate than new technologies can develop, without a backup plan. Energy demand is growing in every part of the globe. We can cover the planet in solar panels and windmills and still not satisfy the global appetite for energy. A sensible low-carbon fuel plan would substitute coal-generated power with a reliable fuel such as natural gas.

The investment houses are happy to tell you that if you want to bet your family's financial future on windmills, solar panels, and green subsidies, you now have that choice. But like most green-intentioned schemes, this can lead to all kinds of unintended consequences.

You probably didn't know that Europe imports megatons of wood chips from the forests of the southern U.S. Because wood somehow makes the ESG scorecard as a renewable resource, they are favoring wood chips over fossil fuels. But lumber is still carbon, its carbon footprint is Sasquatch-sized, and it's not energy-dense. That doesn't stop entrepreneurs from taking advantage of what I'd call a ridiculous loophole in the ESG movement.

We have always operated our company in a way that respects the environment, is socially responsible, and practices good governance. You don't stay in business for decades if you don't. Every public company is already scrutinized by a myriad of regulatory bodies and investment analysts.

We imported ESG from Europe, and unlike French wine or German cars, there's not as much to admire. The American version (or *perversion*) of ESG comes with a "market" view. In other words, we Americans can make the market more virtuous by scoring a company's ESG efforts. By identifying those companies that don't measure up to the ever-changing standards and opinions of "experts," and by diverting capital to those that win their favor, winners and losers are chosen despite their financial performance.

A free market that creates products and services to improve lives used to be the engine that drove our economy—and the economies of every developed nation. Simpler times for sure. But now companies must live up to someone else's subjective benchmarks of virtue.

Shine the Light

Truth be told, I don't mind telling our ESG story. In our category, we are doing everything right, and we make the case in all of our materials at Continental. Bill Berry, our former CEO, put it this way: "We believe domestic oil and natural gas is fundamental to the well-being and security of our nation and the world. We also believe working to secure American energy independence is an essential goal for our business."

In a pragmatic world, these words should be a clarion call to those who value the American way of life. And yes, we still have a good number of folks who connect the dots and support what we do and why. The problem is those who believe otherwise. And no ESG report from an oil and gas company is going to change their minds. In their view, we are in the way of decarbonization and net zero. They have labeled us evil, and our extinction is their goal. (Ironically, their efforts are powered by the standard of living that oil and natural gas made possible.)

When our company talks about ESG, we quote President John F. Kennedy, "We all inhabit this small planet. We all breathe the same air. We all cherish our children's future. And we are all mortal." Those words were spoken almost sixty years ago, but they remain true today. In the early 1960s, America was a nation of 180 million souls. In this decade, we are somewhere north of 330 million. The world's population was around 3 billion, and today it's over 8 billion. Global energy consumption has increased by over 300 percent in the same period.

We went from perceived energy and food scarcity to one of abundance, and hydrocarbons played a critical role in delivering this to the modern world. No other energy source has had a more dramatic impact on the well-being and wealth of our global society. The food we eat, the way we heat and cool our homes, the clothes we wear, the medicines that keep us healthy, our electricity grids, our transportation and logistics networks—virtually everything we rely on to power modern life is dependent on hydrocarbons. It will be that way for decades to come.

What could be more virtuous than that? Who can claim a more beneficial societal impact, not just today but over the past hundred years?

The S of ESG

Continental Resources would not be in business today if we didn't do our best to take care of our Environment, the *E* of ESG. As you've read, we spend tens of millions of dollars each year to explore efficiently, using Horizontal Drilling to lessen our footprint and environmental impact. The technologies we have pioneered (and patented) are used throughout our industry and have benefited our land in measurable ways. In addition, we have, along with Summit Carbon Solutions, initiated the first of its kind CO_2 collection system over a five-state area of the Mid-Continent to gather and sequester CO_2 from ethanol producers' plants and fertilizer manufacturing facilities.

Now, let's talk about the *S,* Social. What is our industry's impact on society? With respect, I'd say the folks fixated on ESG might benefit from stepping back and imagining what life would be like without oil and natural gas. Does anyone want to return to the standards of living our ancestors endured two hundred years ago? I don't see many people choosing to live that way.

When it comes to our global food supply, like it or not, man-made fertilizer has been a game changer for ever-increasing production of affordable food. Many nitrogen fertilizers are made with natural gas. And friends of President Biden have a unique perspective on the current crisis. According to U.S. Agency for International Development (USAID) Chief Samantha Power:

> Fertilizer shortages are real now because Russia is a big exporter of fertilizer. Even though fertilizer is not sanctioned, less fertilizer is coming out of Russia. As a result, we're working with countries to think about natural solutions like manure and compost, and this may hasten transitions that would have been in the interest of farmers to make eventually anyway. So never let a crisis go to waste.

With all due respect, Ms. Power, the most cost-effective and efficient way to combat this food crisis is to support domestic energy production.

How about the *G,* the Governance aspect of ESG? When I think of governance, I think of how this country has been managed. Why not measure the effects of the Biden administration's management of the economy and our energy policies? Maybe those who wish to impose ESG standards on private industry could do us all a favor and point their spotlight on our government.

If you believe I'm a little biased as to the lack of scientific data applied to ESG, here's a case in point. In May 2022, the S&P 500 ESG Index (which describes itself as "broad-based, market-cap-weighted indices designed to measure the performance of securities meeting sustainability criteria, while maintaining similar overall industry group weights as their underlying benchmark") took Tesla off its list. Yes, a company that only manufactures electric cars and trucks was removed. The explanation? In part, there were two claims alleging racial bias in the workplace.

What if we took a more rational approach for the ideas of ESG and worked to measure what I consider society's highest calling: to dramatically reduce poverty by ending *energy* poverty? In the process, we can continue to expand our decarbonization efforts in measurable ways.

Backward Thinking

The first time I went to Beijing, in 2004, I noticed the sun was blotted out by gray clouds when I stepped out of my hotel. After a few difficult breaths, I realized the air was full of smog. When I returned home, it took a couple of weeks for my breathing to improve. And in case you imagine that all this pollution came from their billion citizens driving automobiles, let me tell you, there were relatively few automobiles or paved roads in China in 2004, outside of their largest cities.

China became the world's largest emitter of carbon dioxide in 2006 and now contributes over 30 percent of global CO_2

emissions. What caused almost all that choking pollution? Coal-burning power plants.

Today, it's even worse in China, which uses more coal than every other country combined. And they continue to bring new coal-fired plants online. The number two economy in the world continues to subject its citizens to toxic pollution. And all of that pollution blows over the Pacific to its neighbors, including you and me.

What's my takeaway from this whole ESG discussion? Let's break it down:
- Wrong thinking about energy causes wrong believing.
- Wrong believing causes wrong policy decisions.
- Wrong policy decisions cause energy poverty.
- Energy poverty causes and perpetuates financial poverty.
- Financial poverty causes significant adverse environmental impact, intensifies human suffering, and limits our potential.

Bottom line: we need to base our thinking on facts. And what are the facts?

Our nation has spent over $25 *trillion* since President Lyndon Johnson declared the War on Poverty in 1964. Fifty years after Johnson's announcement, we spent sixteen times more (adjusting for inflation) on means-tested welfare or anti-poverty programs than when the initiative began. Yet despite the huge increase in spending, the percentage of Americans living in poverty has remained consistent (between about 11 and 15 percent) since the mid- to late-1960s.

During our all-too-brief period of complete energy independence two years ago, wages went up and unemployment went down to levels not seen in decades. I wonder if the "experts" have drawn any conclusions from these facts. We can regain energy independence in America if we're given a fighting chance by policymakers.

There is no reason to beg despotic regimes for more oil just so they can line their pockets and fund invasions of other nations. And it's way past time to stop demonizing an industry that's the backbone of our economy and national security. Oil and natural gas aren't the "bad guys." These resources are our ticket to a prosperous future. Energy policy directly impacts the standard of living for people in every country. Come hell or high water, that's why I am so vocal about our energy possibilities.

Standing Up for Energy

As soon as I started to make a little money in the early days of the business, I had a rude awakening about the corruption in my beloved state of Oklahoma. Put more bluntly, government officials who oversaw the oil and natural gas industry not only accepted bribes but *expected* them. If they didn't receive envelopes full of cash, they'd stop by your house to collect them.

These officials had the power to make life miserable for business owners, and evidently, many chose to pay the fee. When one of these birds came by my humble home in Ringwood, I suppose a combination of shock and moral outrage caused me to say, "No way. I am *not* paying anybody to be in business." I decided to take my lumps and be able to look at myself in the mirror with a clear conscience. Corruption and bad policy happen when people don't take a stand and speak up.

Eventually, a fine man by the name of Charles Nesbitt, whose reputation has remained stellar, cleaned house at the Oklahoma Corporation Commission with the help of other upstanding men and women. The feds were even brought in for the cleanup. When you add lots of new oil money to the Wild West, bad stuff can happen. But courage from just a few good men and women can rout them out.

I never wanted to be a voice for our industry; I was drafted into the trenches at an early age. During the energy crisis in the winter of 1977, it became necessary for a number of America's oil and gas producers to step up and testify before various committees in Congress and at industry events to detail the enormous natural gas supplies that would be available if the regulatory burden was lifted. Artificial price regulations had distorted the market and dried up natural gas supplies. As a young geologist, I believed natural gas was ubiquitous, and there for the taking in our country, if artificial price controls were lifted. Instead, as we all know, the Carter administration chose the wrong path and mandated 100 percent use of coal and boiler fuels with a few limited exceptions. From that point forward, I never stopped speaking up. I saw the huge amount of damage a misdirected government policy could cause and sought to alleviate others to the best of my ability.

I've spoken before the U.S. Senate, House of Representatives, House Energy Action Team, and all kinds of national and international events when called on over the past forty-five years. Too many company leaders are slow to speak up. Recently, I talked to a gentleman in the private equity arena who owns large stakes in oil and natural gas companies. "We could use your help with what we're doing in energy advocacy," I said.

He replied, "I don't get involved. I just keep my head down." In other words, he was just a taker. There are too many takers; we need more *givers* and *doers*. It is sad to see so many folks who have benefited from this industry lack the courage to stand up for it and be counted whenever it is under attack. Don't get me wrong; I've made countless friends in this industry who are strong advocates. But we need more.

If you are interested in the well-being of our society, you have the responsibility to be an advocate for this industry. You must be willing to give your time and your resources, because those who oppose domestic energy production are certainly committed. George Soros is a good example—he has financial interest in the oil and natural gas sector, yet he tries to curry favor with environmental extremists in social circles. Seems a bit hypocritical.

Another example is Tom Steyer, a self-proclaimed "activist" who ran for president a few years ago. Even though he made a fortune from hydrocarbons, he was a thorn in the side of our efforts. In my work promoting American energy exports, I kept hearing his name and thought, *I need to meet this guy face-to-face, just to size him up and find out why he's doing this.*

After I returned from the meeting, a colleague asked me what I thought of Tom. I said, "His campaign won't last. He's in this for himself and will never be elected." Sure enough, he spent untold millions of his own money and garnered a small fraction of the votes. He never showed up on my radar again.

I am happy to take time to meet with so-called activists if it can help our fellow citizens. But we need people to stand up for our industry on every level of government, from local to state and national. Without our involvement, corruption will reign, and consumers will be stuck with the bills.

Fighting the Good Fight

I dislike meetings, especially those in D.C., but when you're passionate about a cause, a person will tolerate almost anything—even the smell of the swamp.

Advocacy is not for the weak-stomached. But we must oppose bad policy and recommend solutions that bring results. If we're shocked at the legislation we do see, imagine how bad the stuff is that we *don't* see. Trade groups have their place but can never replace the voices of individuals who are willing to stand up for what's right and speak truth to power.

Things have changed since the days the commissioners drove around picking up cash from business owners.

For example, *why would any elected representatives want to import oil instead of producing it here?* I asked myself that same question many times on our quest to lift the export ban and still wonder about it today. When the Biden administration was panicking about gasoline prices, did they call me? No. They called Maduro in Venezuela, flew to Saudi Arabia, sent a fax to Iran, and forwarded a purchase order to Putin. They would rather talk to an ayatollah in Iran than to Harold Hamm, American oil and gas producer. Frankly, much of it seems very unpatriotic.

It's one thing to be critical of a policy or administration; it's quite another to do something about it. As soon as President Biden's team came into power, I started trying to set up an appointment with John Kerry. Between March and June of 2021, I made numerous attempts to discuss energy policy and help them navigate a tightening market to avoid the energy crisis we're currently in. As was published in my interview with the *Financial Times*, published January 7, 2022, I "requested a meeting with John Kerry, Biden's international climate czar, but had no response."

I'm an eternal optimist and probably still pretty naive. I just had to believe that, perhaps with all the facts, we could sit down and talk about the situation, and maybe they would change their plans and take their foot off the neck of this industry.

Within a few days of that publication, we received a call from his office. Soon after, Blu Hulsey and I traveled to D.C. and met John Kerry and a couple of gentlemen from his staff at the State Department. We shared what the industry was doing with carbon capture and why the practice needed to grow. We talked to him about oil and natural gas production and how the administration's policies—particularly bans on federal leases—were hurting the industry and would result in shortages and higher prices. I pled our case to convert coal-burning plants to natural gas for the sake of our environment.

He was attentive and genuine. On some points, however, he got it wrong. As an example, he repeated the rhetoric about how our industry was subsidized. I probably was a bit animated when I replied, "I can tell you right now, I've drilled more dry holes than anybody alive today. And nobody ever paid me a nickel." With the billions in subsidies that have been flushed down the green toilet, that false narrative gets me riled. But it was a pleasant conversation otherwise, and in my optimistic view, it was a productive one. I hope he thinks the same. So far though, nothing has come of it.

I offered my time and my staff's expertise as a resource, and we exchanged contact information. He asked if I'd spoken with anyone else in the administration. I replied, "No. We can't get through."

That meeting was January 19, 2022, and I haven't heard back from anyone since. But we keep reaching out.

Will I stop standing up and speaking up for our industry and for the American consumer? Never. And I hope you'll join me in whatever sphere of influence you inhabit.

CHAPTER 17

EQ vs. IQ: Which Will Guide Your Energy Future?

MY TEAM KNOWS I OFTEN BEGIN A MEETING BY ASKING, "What are we trying to solve?" If you start there, the path to the right answer usually reveals itself. It may not be an easy path, but once you define what you're trying to fix or figure out, you can line up the right questions and start finding answers.

For example, if the problem we are trying to solve is reducing CO_2 emissions and thus mitigating climate change, why not celebrate—and support—the measurable, game-changing steps the oil and natural gas industry has taken to reduce these emissions?

I am not a climate denier, although I'm sure many people would label me as such. I'm a pragmatic, solutions-oriented scientist. I've always been someone who looks at the whole story, forms opinions, and makes decisions based on hard facts.

There's a song by a fellow named Michael Martin Murphey titled "Cowboy Logic." I happen to be partial to the song and the idea behind it for reasons that don't need a lot of explanation. Don't ask me to sing it, but here's my paraphrase: *Simple solutions are usually the best solutions.*

We need to apply a tanker load of cowboy logic to the debate about our energy future and our path to get there. I think most would agree what our energy future needs to be one hundred years from now. We all want sustainable, affordable, reliable energy, and we want this for all humans. The real debate is about how we get from here to there.

I believe there's a simple solution to just about anything, especially when it comes to energy. But it begins with understanding the facts and asking the right questions.

EQ or IQ?
One of my observations on the current energy debate is the tension between "emotional quotient" versus "intelligence quotient," or EQ versus IQ.

As I've demonstrated in this book, IQ can produce game-changing results, such as Horizontal Drilling, which propelled America's energy renaissance from five million barrels of oil per day to thirteen million barrels of oil per day in less than two decades, giving us the equivalent of natural gas for the next hundred years.

On the other hand, there's EQ—and, in my opinion, far too much of what we read and hear in the energy debate is way out on the far end of the EQ scale. One example is Greta Thunberg, the Swedish teen-turned-global-activist who became famous for yelling, "How dare you?!" to world leaders. I have no problem with her or anyone else speaking their mind and heart. Greta is not the problem. The problem is that all the "adults" in the room simply put on a remorseful face and nodded at her speech. They are using her to prop up their own shallowness, cowardice, and intentional ignorance.

Those leaders did nothing to honestly address the concerns and offer real solutions. By placating emotional expression, activists are left to believe that more yelling is the solution. Their lack of problem-solving leadership *is* the problem. Instead, the leaders are incompetent cowards, afraid to engage in real debate and to arrive at a simple action plan.

Of course, much of this is politically expedient—use emotion to cloud the debate or cut it off entirely. After all, EQ and IQ both motivate people's votes. And when you're convinced that we have ten years (or three years, or twenty-three and a half years) to save ourselves and the planet from extinction, no tactics are off the table. Millions of young, emotionally engaged voters, clamoring for their very survival, make a powerful political force. The irony is they are the most energy-consumptive generation in human history. Their entire lifestyle is predicated on access to the energy-gobbling grid.

Let's be honest. Trillions of dollars are at stake. Big bets are in play. There is money to be made by channeling all that emotion. I recently heard it said that Tesla isn't so much a car company as a subsidy company. Public utilities want their share of tax incentives. That's understandable; if the federal government is going to throw money at you, why not learn how to play catch? This is one of the reasons why so many companies become wards of the federal government. After all, they have a fiduciary responsibility to their shareholders. It's a cynical cycle of bad thinking and bad investment that leads to bad, hard-to-get-rid-of policies such as wind and solar subsidies.

Billions of dollars are being poured into the coffers of the climate groups such as the Sierra Club that rile up voters and convert the unconverted. If environmental nonprofits spent as much time and money on forestry and water management as they do on scaring the crud out of people, we could make some real progress.

When emotions run wild, silly and counterproductive things happen—such as the Fuel Use Act of 1978 that mandated burning coal in power plants and excluded burning clean natural gas as a boiler fuel. If you ban federal leasing based strictly on emotion, you reduce the supply of domestic oil and natural gas, increase the price of everything tied to energy (which is everything), create inflation, limit coal alternatives, and kill jobs along with the economy.

The Texas power failure I mentioned in chapter 14 was set up by emotional policies—flying too close to the sun and overlooking the need for stable backup. Ban leasing and permitting? More pressure on the cost of energy. Who suffers the most? Not the globe-hopping climate preachers or political elite. Rather, those among us who live paycheck to paycheck pay the price. Intelligent debate would make these consequences clear. And while we're spinning our windmills, nothing is solved—because there's no intelligent strategy and no realistic plan based on facts.

That's what gets me. Policies, pronouncements, and speeches are not strategy. Let's quit pretending we have an energy strategy. "No more fossil fuels" sure isn't one. The energy transition and the use of oil and natural gas are not mutually exclusive.

Considerations

Current energy policies revive the very regimes that are out to do us in. Crush domestic production, and we give the Russians, Venezuelans, and Iranians a green light to increase the world's dependence on OPEC+. Almost half of Russia's state revenue comes from oil and gas sales. Some estimate that almost a third of Iran's comes from hydrocarbons. Do we really want to prop up bad actors and recharge their treasuries so they can make our lives more difficult while they try to kill their enemies?

Greta doesn't remember the seventies; she wasn't there. I was. I could get emotional about how ineffective our nation's policies were then. And we are about to repeat the mistakes all over again. Signing an accord in Paris that limits U.S. emissions while tolerating and paying the Chinese government to pollute the globe does little to solve the problem people are screaming about. We need to wring the emotion out of the debate and start dealing with the facts. I want clean air, clean water, and a sustainable future for all. But until we deal with real global solutions—such as curbing China's and India's appetites for coal—all the emotional venting is for naught. And as I've pointed out, U.S. carbon emissions have been falling for a long time and not because of a speech or an accord. It's because of American ingenuity and the fact that we all want to treat our planet with care.

I'm not the government. I can't negotiate with the Chinese when it comes to climate behavior. As we have discussed, there are over six thousand coal-burning units in the world. China generates over half of the world's coal-fired power, and I'm told they are building three hundred new units a year while helping energy-poor nations around the world build even more. Chinese banks are responsible for financing over 70 percent of the new coal-fired electricity-generation plants in the world.

Here's what's getting lost: hydrocarbons have changed the world for the better. On the game-changing scale for humanity, nothing comes close. None of humankind's immense progress in the last sixteen decades would have happened if we hadn't unlocked energy-dense hydrocarbons.

At this moment, no matter how hard we wish and protest, there is no large-scale substitute on the horizon. Energy demand is on the rise everywhere. Yes, there are capital-efficient measures we can take to reduce our carbon emissions, but we have to be smart about them. We can ration energy or we can share the bounty and enrich lives across the globe.

Results Matter

As David Harsanyi pointed out in his June 2022 *Federalist* article, while Germany had good intentions about its energy policy, let's look at the results today.

In recent years, Germany dismantled most of its nuclear power plants and went all-in on "decarbonization," even though nuclear is carbon-friendly. They import, and therefore depend, on oil and natural gas from Russia. German households face the second-highest electricity prices in the world, following Denmark. And in a flailing effort to regain some energy stability, German leaders have reverted to burning more coal.

Germany is weaker—and polluting more—as a result of emotionally driven policies. "At least they tried," some might say. But of what value is an emotional response to failed plans?

Do we want good feelings or good results? If we want to solve a problem, we need strategy based on intelligence and not emotion.

Changing the Future

To recap Germany's failed plan, even with an all-in approach to "green" energy, they are on track to need huge quantities of hydrocarbons for heating and electricity production in 2050. So why are some people calling for the elimination of fossil fuels in ten years?

Could it be emotions?

We need a hundred-year energy strategy in this country—one that other nations will admire and emulate because it produces results and transcends government's whims. Every advance in the human standard of living came about when free enterprise created wealth to invest in innovation.

Why has the U.S. excelled in elevating living conditions for its citizens? Because of free enterprise and abundant energy in the form of oil and natural gas. Sure, you may say China has advanced technology, but has the standard of living and quality of life for average citizens improved?

So-called renewables are decades away from replacing a significant percentage of energy produced from oil and natural gas. I hope everyone involved in the energy debate chews on this reality and presents ideas accordingly. The U.S. can have an energy policy that fuels prosperity and innovation—or we can become green martyrs and slow our progress. Consider all of the preceding without picking winners and losers through wasteful subsidies. Renewable energy is indeed innovation, but as you've read in these pages, innovation is alive and well in the oil and natural gas industry. My point is this: if we believe new technology is the answer to our energy challenges, why not do all we can to foster innovation by unleashing our current, primary energy sources?

Yes, there is a finite amount of oil. That's a fact. (Although there's a lot more than anyone thought just twenty years ago!) But there is no limit to our potential if we don't restrict our possibilities.

If wind and solar power generation could replace oil and natural gas tomorrow, I'd be in that business. But it can't. It can't do it tomorrow, and it can't do it in a century of tomorrows. So what do we do?

What if Americans had always assumed life would stay as it was: subsistence farming, the Pony Express, horsepower from actual horses, and iceboxes with actual ice?

What do we do about today's—and tomorrow's—challenges? We believe there's a better way. We see ourselves as a nation of possibilities. We leverage our strengths.

Energy transitions have been going on since humankind began. We are in the midst of yet another, one in which hydrocarbons will be essential and irreplaceable but technological innovation is needed. Let's not make every decision emotionally. Let's make them rationally—together.

Mythbuster

Back in 2007, I decided to run a newspaper ad. It was my first real attempt to dip my toes into the political swamp and address the myths that were shaping energy policy. Our nation was on the precipice of an economic meltdown caused by a bunch of bad bets.

A few people were beginning to take notice of Continental Resources. We were finding lots of oil in the lower forty-eight states. Yet a Republican administration—one that traditionally would have supported domestic energy production—kept us at arm's length. I suppose some of George W. Bush's political advisers were telling him to put some distance between us and his administration because it might not be in his political interest, since he came from a family in the oil and gas business in Midland, Texas. But the solution was there for anyone to see. When supply is crimped, prices go up. Basic economic principles like supply and demand are always ignored when politics intrude.

My dander was up. We checked the rates for a full-page ad in the *New York Times*. Its six-figure price tag frustrated me even more. So we instead ran a full-page ad in the number one newspaper in Enid, Oklahoma, (I was angry, not stupid). The advantage of the Enid paper was the sheer number of oil and gas people who read it. They needed a shot in the arm, and I needed to get a few things off my chest and clear the proverbial air.

The headline was simple and direct: "Myths about America's energy industry are threatening the U.S. economic recovery." These myths were deceptive then, and they're still around today, as you'll see. Funny how that works.

Myth #1: We have an energy crisis—we're running out of crude oil and natural gas.

I told anyone who would listen at the time that the U.S. could become energy independent. Our reserves were immense and growing every year, which was the opposite of what the "experts" said. Spoiler alert: we proved them wrong.

Myth #2: The U.S. consumes 25 percent of the world's crude oil but has only 3 percent of its reserves.

Let's simply look at some facts, which are literally and politically buried.

This misleading chart (please see the next page) perpetuates the narrative that America is running out of oil. This is simply untrue. Due to a political Securities and Exchange Commission (SEC) rule barring the inclusion of proven reserves of oil and gas beyond five years, U.S. reserves are artificially and grossly understated compared to the reserves of any other country in the world. Case in point, according to this EIA chart, the U.S. would run out of proved oil with today's usage (approximately 4.38 billion barrels of oil annual usage) within ten years. We know this isn't rational or realistic.

Technically recoverable U.S. crude oil resources as of January 1, 2020

REGION	Proved reserves, billion barrels	Unproved reserves, billion barrels	Total technically recoverable resources, billion barrels
Lower 48 states onshore	**38.8**	**229.1**	**267.9**
East	0.9	5.1	6.0
Gulf Coast	5.9	36.5	42.4
Midcontinent	2.9	7.3	10.2
Southwest	17.8	126.9	144.7
Rocky Mountain	3.1	28.8	31.9
Northern Great Plains	6.2	21.4	27.6
West Coast	2.0	3.0	5.0
Lower 48 states offshore	**5.6**	**54.9**	**60.5**
Gulf (currently available for leasing)	5.3	37.2	42.5
Eastern/Central Gulf (unavailable for leasing until 2023)	0.0	3.7	3.7
Pacific	0.3	10.0	10.3
Atlantic	0.0	4.0	4.0
Alaska (onshore and offshore)	**2.7**	**42.0**	**44.7**
Total United States	**47.1**	**326.0**	**373.1**

Source: Lower 48 states onshore and offshore–U.S. Energy Information Administration; Alaska–U.S. Geological Survey; federal (Outer Continental Shelf) offshore–Bureau of Ocean Energy Management; proved reserves–EIA. Table values reflect removal of intervening reserves additions between the date of the latest available assessment and January 1, 2020.

Note: Crude oil resources include lease condensates but do not include natural gas plant liquids or kerogen (oil shale). Resources in areas where drilling is officially prohibited are not included in this table. The estimate of 7.3 billion barrels of crude oil resources in the Northern Atlantic, Northern and Central Pacific, and within a 50-mile buffer off the Mid- and Southern Atlantic Outer Continental Shelf (OCS) is also excluded from the technically recoverable volumes because leasing is not expected in these areas.

We have huge reserves of oil and natural gas, but thanks to the quirky way our regulatory bodies like to report "proven reserves" it appears we are going to run out. We're not; check out the third column.

**Myth #3: The U.S. imports 70 percent of its
crude oil from unstable, hostile countries.**
Our country did a lot of business with the Saudis back then,
so this claim wasn't completely false. The numbers were a
bit off, however. We're still importing too much from some
of those countries. What needed to be set straight was the
false conclusion that to eliminate reliance on these regimes,
we had to abandon domestic oil and natural gas exploration
(see Myth #1) and somehow flip a magical switch to solar and
wind power.

Because so many people falsely believed we had puny
reserves, their sentiments, policies, and *subsidies* followed suit.
But my fellow geologists knew differently.

Where should we look to supply our energy needs through
the twenty-first century and beyond?

Instead of sending our dollars to Kazakhstan, Turkmenistan,
and Uzbekistan, why not buy from right here—a place I endear-
ingly refer to as "Cowboyistan"? A place where Horizontal Drilling
innovation brought about an entirely new type of productive
reservoir to exploit "tight rock."

The Biden administration got a crude awakening in June
2022, courtesy of French President Emmanuel Macron. "I had a
call with MBZ," Macron told our president at the G7 summit. "He
told me two things. I'm at a maximum, maximum [oil production capacity]. This is what he claims. And then he said Saudis
can increase by 150 [thousand barrels per day]. Maybe a little bit
more, but they don't have huge capacities."

I'm glad to inform these presidents, and any other world
leader, that the US has *huge capacities* of oil and natural gas, and
the Saudis have never proved they were able to increase production by as much as they promised world leaders. The remaining
excess production capacity in the world is right here in the U.S.A.

Myth #4: The U.S. energy industry is really just "Big Oil."
This lie really chapped my hide. Yeah, we're both in the same business, but we shared little else. We spent our toil and treasure developing domestic energy. Meanwhile, "Big Oil" was investing across the globe. They were tied to foreign governments, some unsavory and some outright awful. But we all got painted by the same broad

brush. We still are. If there was ever "Big Oil," it was the refiners and marketers of this industry, many of whom were multinationals. The independent producers like Continental are the explorers and developers who drill 90 percent of the wells in America.

When I go to Washington, D.C., I still have to explain the difference between a multinational and a company like Continental Resources. Most Americans have no idea that independent oil and gas producers have taken the vast majority of the financial risks to unlock our domestic energy riches. Vertically integrated companies make money by refining and distributing. They are in the "margin" business. We, the independent producers, are in the oil and gas development and production business.

For a time, Big Oil set its sights offshore and overseas while we followed the science and innovated onshore. Independent producers and millions of their hardworking employees made the difference for this county. And we haven't stopped.

If I were writing this today, I would debunk the following additional myths:

Modern Myth #1: There are plenty of federal drilling permits.
The Biden administration has relentlessly pushed the story that there are nine thousand unused federal permits. "You don't need any more than you already have," they say. Half are awaiting approval by the Biden administration's Bureau of Land Management, and thousands are tied up in some form of litigation, which has made those areas impossible to drill in.

A related myth that government would like to push is on the topic of rising gasoline prices:

Oil companies and Vladimir Putin caused it!

Wrong.

Imagine if the government restricted the amount of land that could be used to grow oranges. Would the price of orange juice go up? The Biden administration took about a quarter of the landmass off the table in some of the most productive lands in America.

It boggles my mind that I need to state this fact, but I know you'll understand: America is far better off when our energy is

U.S. Greenhouse Gas Emissions, 2006–2019
(million metric tons of carbon dioxide equivalents)

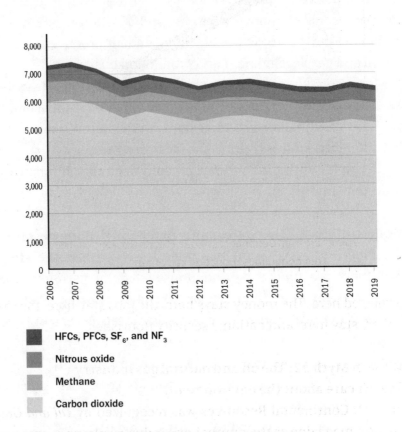

Source: "Climate Change Indicators in the United States," U.S. Environmental Protection Agency, www.epa.gov/climate-indicators

Here's another example of how technology and industry initiatives are making huge strides in reducing methane emissions.

Methane Intensity Reduction

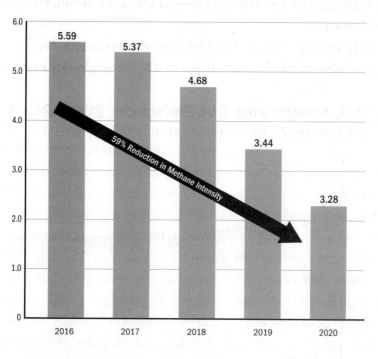

Source: Continental Resources 2021 ESG Report.

This chart from Continental's 2021 ESG Report demonstrates
our continuous reduction in methane intensity.

produced here. The money stays here, the jobs stay here, the tax
dollars stay here, and national security flourishes.

Modern Myth #2: The oil and natural gas industry doesn't care about the environment.

In 2021, Continental Resources was recognized by *Oil and Gas
Investor* magazine as the number one industry player in environmental, societal, and governance work, also known as the aforementioned ESG. We had once learned how to drill up to twelve
wells on a single pad site, which greatly reduces the footprint

of our operations. Today, we are drilling up to thirty-six wells on a single pad site. Our greenhouse gas emissions have gone down down by 28 percent, and methane emissions have been lowered by 34 percent from 2019 levels. Why did we implement these improvements? Not because of government mandates but because it's the right thing to do.

Our company was focused on ESG before it was called ESG. And it wasn't an emotional decision.

You probably have not heard about what many in the oil and natural gas industry are doing to reduce carbon emissions, but do you know *why* you haven't heard? One of the biggest myths about energy producers is that we don't care about the environment. Well, if you measured caring in dollars—not speeches at rallies—you'd see we care a lot.

When I first heard about a company working with a technology that captured CO_2 from ethanol plants and stored carbon within reservoirs better than a mile deep underground I was interested. I will talk with almost anyone who has an opinion about energy, no matter what side of the argument they're on. We immediately scheduled a face-to-face meeting with the company leading the innovation, and I was impressed. They are good folks from Iowa who care about agriculture, energy, and the environment. We were in.

It made sense to utilize a new tool to reduce emissions, even if it cost billions of dollars. We will soon capture tens of millions of tons of carbon and safely place it underground. Does it offset the CO_2 outputs of China and its allies? Probably not, but it's the right thing to do. Thankfully more and more are following our lead.

Right now, up to twelve million tons of carbon will be captured yearly in North Dakota alone, and over forty million tons of carbon are being captured every year by other forward-thinking energy producers worldwide.

Modern Myth #3: The oil industry is full of dinosaurs.
We may be extracting the remains of plant and animal life from the Mesozoic Era, but independent oil producers have always looked to the future. Our company uses an increasing amount of new technology throughout our operations, including solar panels, drones, continuous methane sensors, aerial surveys, and artificial intelligence (not to be confused with *genuine* intelligence from our teams) to reduce fuel consumption and provide secure operations.

We can't force so-called renewable resources into existence, and no amount of government subsidies can advance technology overnight. As I discussed earlier, there are good applications for solar panels in our operations. However, they are a piece of the puzzle, not the whole puzzle.

Whether you knew it or not, your tax dollars were part of a half-billion-dollar investment the Obama administration made in a solar company named Solyndra. Was it a good bet? No. The company went bankrupt two years later in 2011. This was a very heavily subsidized solar project funded by the government, in which many so-called green companies benefited at the expense of taxpayers to the tune of hundreds of millions of dollars. We can build energy policies that are friendly to the environment—and our economy—so the free market can grow new technologies from a position of economic strength.

Are you more or less likely to invest in new, efficient technology when you're worried about the economy and your utility bills? Common sense always busts the myths. My article with myth-busting facts went across the nation and hopefully changed some minds.

In the years since I ran that ad, more myths have surfaced that are just as hard to dispel, threatening our way of life and harmful to people in developing countries without reliable access to electricity and fuels.

Literally trillions of dollars are being thrown at projects that aren't making a dent in the growth of energy demand or making any measurable difference when it comes to reducing CO_2 emissions.

I owe you the truth. We'll keep running ads, writing op-eds, presenting to Congress, talking with unelected and elected officials alike, and getting up early in the morning to go on CNBC or *Mornings with Maria* to tell it like it is.

I'm all about myth-busting, and I'm not about to stop now.

CHAPTER 18

Culture of the Possible from a Wildcatter's Mentality

I'M A WILDCATTER AT HEART.
Wildcatter is a term originally used in our business to describe oil finders from the late nineteenth century who were willing to drill exploratory wells in territories not known to contain oil. That "Wildcatter Mentality" has set us apart and has led to big discoveries.

To have the "Wildcatter Mentality" is to have a natural curiosity and the willingness to take risks to explore the possibilities. Exploration is always at the heart of discovering something new and requires a willingness to see the world in a way it hasn't been seen before.

Being a wildcatter has always come naturally to me. I have always been a prudent risk taker. When looking at a new prospect, I want to know all the risks involved. It's so important to have the wisdom and knowledge to properly assess the geological, mechanical, and economic risk prior to commencement.

It's a skill set of its own. It comes with making sure you're really facing the risk head-on and estimating it as best you can.

Once that risk is assessed, the key is being unafraid. You can't be afraid of failure. It's being an eternal optimist–always seeing the glass half full.

All of this culminates in doing what you do for the greater good of others. It's a mentality and a mission to take bold steps forward to change the world in the face of adversity.

My Two Cents

In May 2021, I was asked to give the commencement address to my old high school. I've given many speeches around the world, but I probably spent as much time preparing for this presentation as I did for meetings with presidents or heads of state.

When I told my daughter Hilary about the opportunity, she wondered about my ability to connect with those young people. What could I possibly tell them about life that might resonate in the modern world of smartphones and instant gratification?

"Dad, you grew up before all that stuff, the world is really different. People have access to all the information in the world in their pockets."

Yes, I did, and yes, they do. But I believe there are always "universals" worth passing down.

Lexington High is still a small-town school, forty-five minutes south of Oklahoma City. Back when I was there, Lexington was a rural community across the Canadian River from Purcell. Not much has changed. It wasn't a big crowd—sixty-two kids in the graduating class—and a bunch of people who were related to me in one way or the other (my daughter once had to create an extended family tree for a school project and found out she had ninety-six first cousins!).

Even decades after my own graduation from high school, I am certain some students in the audience also faced major challenges, including the same type of severe economic hardships that I experienced as a child. Lexington is a town of hardworking people with grit and determination, but it is not opulent. Graduation was held on the football field, even with the threat of rain, because the auditorium was too small to accommodate the crowd.

The story I shared with them centered on two main points.

First, find your passion in life. *Passion is always much more important than privilege.* Take your time to discover what truly captures your imagination, and once you find it, go all in.

Second, embrace the fact that learning never ends—not just academic learning, but learning in the school of life. Stay curious, stay passionate, and stay engaged. Life's more rewarding as a lifelong student. Here's a synopsis of what I shared.

Painful and Priceless Lessons

I told the kids about my former high school teacher James E. Hunter. He taught at Lexington for thirty-two years following World War II. If you've read the book or seen the movie *Unbroken* about the Olympic athlete who spent much of the war in a Japanese prison camp, James's story is eerily similar. Like so many young people who went to war and survived, his life was never the same.

James made it safely through eight aerial missions before his life was forever changed on mission number nine. On the way to the German city of Cologne, his B-17 was hit by flack between the first and second engines. His plane, the "Oh Natural," disintegrated. Miraculously, he was thrown from his waist-gunner position into the icy slipstream at thirty thousand feet over enemy territory. Because the temperature at that altitude was forty degrees below zero, his wounds froze before he could bleed out. After initially being knocked out from the explosion, he somehow regained consciousness as he fell though the thin air and pulled his parachute's ripcord. James was one of only two survivors. Seven of his crewmates perished.

He was captured by angry German civilians and turned over to Nazi soldiers. For the next six months, he was a prisoner of war, shunted from camp to camp, starved, tortured, and exposed to the elements, never knowing if his next day would be his last. But he kept his faith and marshaled what little strength he had so he could get back to his beloved Oklahoma. On April 29, 1945, his prayers we answered by the sounds of Patton's tanks roaring through Germany.

Years later, James Hunter wrote a book, *Ice Cream in My Freezer*, to pay homage to his fellow airmen who never made it back—and to tell others how he relied on his faith to see him through the terrible journey. I keep a copy of the book in my office. The title comes from a vow he made upon his return: he would always keep some ice cream in his freezer to remind him of the simple pleasures of life and never let go of his passion for helping others.

He taught generations of kids at Lexington, yet very few knew his life story. His passion was teaching, and he was extraordinary. He mixed book learning with life lessons and the principles it took to succeed. There are not enough Mr. Hunters around these days. Before he passed away, I was fortunate to have the opportunity to tell him how grateful I was for all he shared with me and for the inspiration he was to me.

I told the graduates, "When it comes to discovering your passion, give yourself some time. Don't get locked inside your own limited sphere. Put down those cell phones for a minute and absorb some of the world around you."

I told them how my breakout moment in high school came when I wrote a thesis about the oil and gas industry—the same paper I've quoted in this book. The passion started to build from that day forward. Once I discovered my passion, learning became energizing. But after high school, I had to earn a living—doing a lot of learning outside the classroom.

Thinking outside the Sandbox

I hope those graduates understood these points from my talk:

- Use your passion to step outside of your limited sphere.
- Challenge conventional wisdom.
- Surround yourself with people who help you find a better way of doing things.

For years, I've carried a Garth Brooks lyric around in my head reminding me not to miss the dance. That's my message to you. Make sure you don't miss the dance. Oil and gas has been my waltz, jitterbug, twist, and every move imaginable. I'm still dancing, and my hat is off to those other daring dancers who helped me pioneer Horizontal Drilling, which has unlocked untold riches for Americans.

Together, we helped the U.S. become the largest producer of energy in the world again after a four-decade decline. We reversed our import dependency and ended the energy export ban. Thanks to all the natural gas we found, our nation became an *exporter* of clean-burning fuel while reducing CO_2 emissions by the largest amount in the industrialized world. And together we will provide the nation with an abundance of oil and gas to fuel a clean, growing, and robust future.

I've had the privilege of advising four U.S. presidents on energy policy. Some listened better than others. My road from the cotton fields to the Oval Office could not have happened in any other nation. Don't believe what you hear in the mainstream media or in some classrooms—this country still offers more opportunity to pursue your passions than any other nation in the world. Here, plenty of folks still believe in free enterprise and individual freedom. Be glad you live here.

Many years ago, I came back to Lexington for a class reunion. At the evening banquet, one of my classmates leaned across the table and said, "Harold, you're lucky. You escaped and got out of this place." But for me, life was never about escaping or getting out. It was all about finding my passion and pursuing it—wherever it led me.

As I wondered how to respond to my classmate, I saw an older gentleman sitting at another table. It was my former teacher, James Hunter, at ninety-five years old. He was still invested in his students, sharp as a tack, and still dispensing wisdom and hard-earned life lessons. *Now there's a lucky man*, I thought.

I closed my address to the students with these words:

"I hope each and every one of you finds your passion. Selfishly, I would love for you to be the brains behind the next generation of my industry. Find something that brings you fulfillment and joy. Take your passions to the ends of the earth. And change the world for the better."

My Big Thoughts

I'm always scribbling down thoughts and notions. I can't count how many yellow pads I've covered with musings, memories, and "big" thoughts. Occasionally, I dig them out and see if anything sticks or is worth revisiting.

Here's the output from one pad I believe is worth sharing. Call it "My Whys"—truisms that have guided me on this journey. I hope they also bring clarity to your exploration of life, business, and your passions.

It's never about the money. My "why" is always about so much more than money. More than fifty years ago, I left one of the best-paying union jobs with a major oil company (Champlin Petroleum Co.) to start a one-man, one-truck oilfield service company. I had what felt like a ton of debt—and what felt like a ton of ambition too. Yet I was fueled by an inner voice that told me I had a destiny. All I needed to do was trust myself and keep my pedal to the metal. Yes, money is a way to keep score and survive, but it has never been my reason for being. There are better ways to keep score. Maintaining purpose in life, an abundance of close friends, and a wonderful family tops the scorecard.

Reputation is the foundation for success. And like an oil tank, the reserve is built one drop at a time. Mr. Potter, the owner of the truck stop where I worked in high school, helped me secure my first business loan. There was plenty I didn't love about that high school job, but I'm sure glad I showed up and brought my best. You never know how past relationships can make or break future relationships.

Be allergic to debt. Of course, there are opportunities for which using other people's money to advance the cause is smart. I seized my first opportunity with that first truck when I assumed the payments. But my plan from the very start was to extinguish the debt as soon as possible. I did it in ninety days. It's a lesson I've never unlearned.

A combination of our Cedar Hills assets, corporate debt, and proceeds from a successful IPO made it possible to secure a majority-ownership position in the huge Bakken resource, which has proven to be an invaluable holding for Continental. In my fifty years, I've seen too many instances when too much debt rendered companies helpless and hopeless. The burden of excessive debt and interest load has crushed many a company—especially in a commodity business where price swings are the norm.

Lead by example. Never expect anyone to do a job you wouldn't do yourself. I'm always the first one in and the last one out. I'm always willing to roll up my sleeves and dive in. Whether we like it or not, we all serve as examples to those around us. For too long, I played too hard. I was not as good of an example as I could have been. I regret that. So I work a little harder every day at being a better example to others.

Advocate for your interests and your industry. Stand up for what you believe in. Don't expect someone else to carry your load or represent your view. Trade associations have their place. Elected officials *say* they are in office to represent you, but it's your responsibility to speak up for your interests. You can't outsource advocacy.

Act with integrity. Never sacrifice integrity, and never be silent when others do. Tell the truth even when it hurts. Be transparent and honest to a fault. Integrity must occupy the center of your corporate culture and be ingrained into every employee and associate. Avoid those outside of your organization who don't have it.

Keep it simple. Start with your own life, including the way you structure your company and execute your business. When it comes to making deals—if you can't write the details down on a dinner napkin in plain English, walk away.

Decide daily your "main thing." Brush fires and dust storms occur all the time and often obscure the primary mission. Don't get distracted. Solve challenges or delegate personnel to correct them and move on to the job at hand. Stay relentlessly focused on your "main thing," and you'll be amazed at your productivity and satisfaction.

Be happy. It's contagious to all those around you. Stay clear of bad apples. Or make sure they go out with the evening's trash.

Have some fun! Enjoy the adventure. You only get to play one round.

Exercise daily and be healthy. Eat the foods that are good for you. Drink in moderation. (And please don't smoke unless it's an occasional celebratory cigar.)

Persevere. "Rome wasn't built in a day" and, as many of my fellow travelers know, it's still under construction. Sometimes meaningful change takes years to accomplish. Never surrender to the naysayers. If it's worth doing, keep trying until you find a way. After drilling seventeen dry holes in a row looking for the larger prize, we found the Cedar Hills field, Ames Hole, and the monstrous Bakken. Horizontal Drilling was a pipe dream (pun intended), and making it work took years and untold millions. It took me nearly two years to reverse the export ban. American energy independence was considered an impossibility, but it happened in less than a decade.

Pick good friends and associates. Become an expert listener. You will gain in intelligence, wisdom, and the ability to grow. And always remember that you can learn some valuable things from—as Garth would say—"friends in low places." Never forget where you came from.

Enjoy working hard. Nothing supplants the willingness to give it your all. You must put in the time to get the job done, but it should never be a grind. If there isn't fun and fulfillment in your work, it will become a grind, and *you* will grind to a halt.

Identify the "doers." Not everyone is motivated, and some can't "get 'er done." Surround yourself with people who want to take the next hill. Nurture the stars. Ditch the asteroids. Do it quickly and compassionately, then go out and find more stars.

Additional principle-driven values I endeavor to live by:

- Be fair
- Do no harm
- Always do the right thing
- Written or not, stick to a deal

- Adhere to the realm of the possible
- Reputation is all you have in the oil business—protect it

When I think about my first jobs and first businesses, I realize there were many game changers in motion. If you'll permit me, here are some takeaways I hope are encouraging for *your* life and career:

There's a line in an old movie that says half of life is "showing up." You probably noticed that a surprising number of people have a hard time doing even that. Showing up is a simple signal, a sign of respect to those around you. How many people do you know who show up? If you answered "not enough," then maybe you should look for some new people to hang around with—or work with.

For me, that's where it starts. I set an example by showing up. I love what I do and the people I work with, so showing up has become the easy part. As you get more successful and your business grows, you have to surround yourself with more folks who will show up. No business succeeds otherwise. When I was working in the field every day, show-up time was 7 a.m. Period. Didn't matter if I had been up all night, if I felt awful, or if the weather was atrocious. I showed up when others didn't. My customers trusted me to get the job done, and, consequently, awarded me more business. Maybe I learned that from my mom. She showed up for her thirteen kids every day.

Unconventional thinking has always been a driver for me. But sometimes, unconventional is just trying a little harder—or simply asking more questions—than other folks. For example, searching for oil while others are chasing natural gas plays can be a form of unconventional. Conventional wisdom is often a barrier to success. Herd thinking has always given me a rash. Our business is infected with it. That's why, in the late eighties, when everyone was moving to natural gas, we bet on oil in the U.S. Rocky Mountains and the out-of-favor Williston Basin.

Another trait that seems to be innate to successful people is impatience. I've heard people in my company joke, "There's a clock, and then there's Hamm time." Yes, I like to move quickly. Tomorrow misses today's possibilities.

Ask questions and ask for help. I don't know where I'd be today if not for the true generosity of mentors and colleagues. Give help when asked. When someone asks me for information or advice, I try to remember the twenty-one-year-old me.

You can be good to everyone you work with, but you don't have to compromise your standards or your dreams. Pay the bills but don't sell your potential for a paycheck.

Listen to your muse. Mine mostly speaks to me when I'm walking my dog. Then check those ideas with all the smart people you've hired. I encourage everyone to speak their mind. If you're in the room, and you have something to say, then say it. Sometimes I'm the only person in the room who thinks a course of action or a decision is right. But having people who can argue the other side is so valuable and can eliminate a lot of second-guessing.

I try not to screw up. But if I do, then I make it right. Don't let people talk you out of doing what's right with excuses such as, "It will cost too much," or, "It's really not our fault," or, my favorite, "The whole thing will go away if we just ignore it." I have found that fixing what's wrong has a very high ROI.

If you're straightforward about what you want and how much you're willing to invest, deals naturally fall into place. Don't play games. Don't create drama. Don't think because you won a few bucks at a poker table that you're a master negotiator or smarter than the average bear.

There are a lot of people walking around trying to prove how smart they are. I have met very few *truly* smart people. They're not easy to find, because they're usually the humble ones. And I hire them when I can. I'm fortunate to be surrounded by some of the smartest people in the industry. They prove it every day. But they do it the right way, without bombast or hubris. I dream big. I always have and always will. But I also try to adhere to the realm of the possible.

Core Values

A few years back, I asked my team to try to put some of my scribblings into a one-pager we call our core values. Whether leaders know it or not, every company has core principles, which they show by their behaviors. The trick is to articulate those values, live by them, and build a culture that's consistent with what you believe. Here's Continental Resources' statement:

> *Continental is a culture of the possible. You are free to change the world. In order to be an A-Class company, you must be willing to change the world for the better.*
>
> *Everyone in the company is empowered to become doers, to be leaders, to improve every aspect of our business. This is why we routinely make the impossible possible. We are a no-blame company. It is expected to experience failure during times of great achievement.*

Our offices are littered with awards and accolades for the innovation, exploration, bit records, depth records, and lateral length records our teams have set across our areas of operation. With unique exploration finds such as Ames Hole and cutting-edge geologic concepts, along with our expertise for drilling and development, Continental has become known for being a low-cost, best-in-class explorer and operator that can get the job done.

Today, we are proud to be the number one producer of oil and of natural gas in Oklahoma, the number one producer of oil and of natural gas in North Dakota, the second-largest lease-holder in the Powder River Basin of Wyoming, and a top ten oil and natural gas producer in the nation. We are among the top five most active drillers and explorers in the U.S.—all driven by a deep, abiding sense of optimism. This is our *Culture of the Possible*. Our innovation and geologic expertise is ongoing as we participate in the development of the first-of-its-kind carbon capture project, which, once operational, will be the largest such project in the world.

One of the aspects of Continental that I'm proudest of is the fact that we're a *possibility company*. Even when the business was just one truck and me, it was a possibility company. What does this mean? Every person and every business faces challenges. Heck, just staying in business is difficult. But when a team discusses a new challenge, *impossible* is not considered as an outcome.

I suppose it's faith in some form, but it's also a choice. *There is always a way*. The way might be tough, expensive, or quite different from what we considered, but there is always a solution. It's amazing how a possibility culture keeps things moving forward.

If a company can choose this mindset and achieve great things, what about an entire country? What if a country articulated its core values and endeavored to live them? It has been done. Yes, I'm talking about the U.S.

This nation was born with challenges, and many of them were, and still are, self-inflicted ones—specifically in the area of civil rights. But our core principles, written in our founding documents, gave us the resolve to solve them—at great cost, I might add.

For example, one of our core values is found in the second paragraph of the Declaration of Independence: "We hold these truths to be self-evident, that all men are created equal, that they are endowed by their Creator with certain unalienable Rights, that among these are Life, Liberty and the pursuit of Happiness." This belief ultimately led to the righting of terrible wrongs. Another example is that belief in the value of free expression led to the creation of the First Amendment.

A culture of possibility is powerful and unstoppable.

If our national values helped us make such progress in these two and a half centuries, it should be a simple matter to create an energy policy that most would agree on, right?

Imagine if Americans came together and decided on some basic energy values. I'll start with these because they seem self-evident to me.

- We need to move away from coal because it literally tarnishes our world.
- Our country is better off when we produce our own energy. So let's stop punishing the resource we need to survive.
- When we keep our energy dollars here, our economy benefits. Thriving, stable economies foster innovation. Let free enterprise continue to surprise us with breakthroughs.
- Renewables are in their infancy. While they crawl and learn to walk, we need oil and natural gas. Not everyone needs to like this fact, but we can agree it is a fact today,

nonetheless. This is an example of policy planning based on intellectual honesty, not emotion.
- The U.S. should sell its oil, natural gas, and products to help friendly nations break free of coal and have an alternative to buying from hostile nations. As a side benefit, this will bolster our economy and help keep prices affordable. It's a smart national security agenda item.
- We believe it's possible to have energy stability for the next hundred years or longer with resources under U.S. soil. And at the same time, we can continue to improve our environment

Think all this is impossible? Let's review these facts:

The State of American Energy Today
- The U.S. has the largest recoverable oil reserves in the world and can produce more oil and natural gas than any other country.
- There is a vast supply of American-made energy resources with the capability of supplying the U.S. market for decades to come.
- American innovation and ingenuity have reduced green-house gas emissions and pollutants dramatically while demonstrating it is possible to grow the economy at the same time.
- America is a leader and we will export our ingenuity to the rest of the world to clean up their emissions too. If allowed, we will employ our carbon capture technology globally.

The Future of American Energy Prosperity

AFFORDABILITY

The U.S. Economy Depends on the Affordability of Domestic Energy

- America has an energy-driven economy (GDP growth requires cheap energy abundance).
- America's ability to compete globally is dependent on domestic energy affordability.
- National debt can be eliminated by expanded production and export infrastructure as a result.

Personal Financial Security Depends on Affordable and Reliable Energy

- Gasoline and electricity bills are lower when domestic energy production is expanded.
- This allows Americans to spend hard-earned money on other priorities and save for the future.

Expensive Energy Is Dangerous and Hurts the Poor the Worst

- Countless lives are lost due to extreme weather events. Resilient and reliable energy systems save lives during these events.
- Anti-fossil fuel policies like the "Green New Deal" and carbon taxes are regressive—they dispro-portionately impact those who have the least. Lower-income families spend significantly more (as a percentage of income) on energy than other Americans.

SECURITY

America Is an Energy Superpower

- Horizontal Drilling has given us another type of reservoir that is predominant in North America known as "tight rock" and a century or more of clean-burning natural gas and oil.
- This nation's abundance of resources is critical to the geopolitical security of America and our allies.

American Energy Has Fundamentally Shifted the Global Geopolitical Balance

- Americans are no longer required to import energy to have affordable and reliable energy. We should never sacrifice our energy independence again by allowing U.S. oil and gas production to fall below our consumption level. We have the resources.
- Plentiful American oil and natural gas reserves disarmed despotic dictators and enemies of our country.
- American energy exports are improving the energy security of our allies because they can access American, as opposed to Russian, Venezuelan, or Middle Eastern energy.

Americans Should Not Have to Police the World to Secure Foreign Energy

- Conflicts throughout history have been driven in large part by the need for nations to secure the development of and access to resources.
- We have expended significant financial and human resources in the past to secure energy.

ENVIRONMENTAL LEADERSHIP

We Lead the World in Innovation and Environmental Achievement

- We now enjoy the cleanest and safest environment of any economic power in modern history.
- In the U.S. oil and gas industry, we achieve environmental standards that are more stringent than our global competitors.

We Need to Stop Exporting Jobs and Importing Pollution

- World public health suffers because our competitors emit pollutants we know hurt humans.
- Trade imbalances result from competitors not being subject to adequate environmental laws.

American Fuels and Technology Can Reduce Energy Poverty and Improve Health

- Too much of the world's population live in energy poverty, with approximately eight hundred million people having no access to electricity whatsoever—shortening life and limiting freedom and opportunity. (That's approaching the current population of both North and South America living in energy poverty, not unlike conditions in this country in the early 1800s.)
- Widespread access to affordable electricity would help the developing world to access clean water, refrigerate food, produce life-saving medicines, and stop burning wood and dung for indoor heating and cooking.
- American light, sweet crude and clean-burning natural gas can accelerate global access to affordable electricity for billions of people in energy poverty worldwide.

The Path Forward: Practical Steps for a Strong Nation

Here are some specific ideas our nation should adopt.

1. Improve Vital U.S. Infrastructure

Pipelines: More pipelines are needed to reduce pollution and meet demand. Pipelines are the safest, most efficient way to transport hydrocarbons. Think of them as the interstate highway for energy.

Refineries: Stop converting existing refineries to get credits for biomass and renewable diesels. *Crack spreads* (the profit margin of refiners) are now at historic highs. Pipelines are the safest, most efficient way to transport hydrocarbons. We haven't built a new refinery anywhere in the U.S since the 1970s. Despite shouts from the White House to increase supply, they are at capacity. But no one's going to invest in something labeled as an archenemy of civilization.

- Streamline permitting processes
- Reform regulatory burdens

2. End Punitive Regulations

The June 2022 ruling by the U.S. Supreme Court was a step in the right direction. The majority ruled that the executive branch of government does not have the authority to mandate sweeping energy regulations—such as the Obama administration's 2015 Clean Power Plan. In the majority opinion, Chief Justice John Roberts wrote, "A decision of such magnitude and consequence rests with Congress itself, or an agency acting pursuant to a clear delegation from that representative body." In other words, *elected representatives* should debate and create legislation to address energy transitions. Hopefully the tide can turn away from presidents and unelected officials punishing private industry. As noted earlier in the book, Congress, including then Senator Joe Biden, enabled President Carter to create the biggest environmental and energy blunder of all time by picking coal over natural gas.

3. Create an International Agreement to Reduce Particulate Matter and Mercury

Coal plants in Asia pump out millions of tons of pollutants that float across the Pacific. For those of us old enough to remember Los Angeles in the seventies prior to the invention of catalytic converters, the sky was a dull yellow—like Shanghai today.

4. Paris Climate Accord

Individuals and companies can't do anything about other countries' actions. Our government must act responsibly to accomplish change.

As a country, we can bring about change through restraint of trade and sanctions on polluting countries instead of signing on to a meaningless promise that does nothing to stop the world's number one polluter. Again, climate activists should be protesting in front of the Chinese embassy if they really wanted to highlight a major cause of environmental damage.

- Develop and utliize domestic assets
- Use free markets for all forms of energy

It's time to stop yelling about what we *can't* do and talk about what we *can* do. Adopt the *culture of possibility.*

Change in the Air in South Korea

Because of Horizontal Drilling and recent discoveries of new reserves, the U.S. has plenty of natural gas for the next century, including enough to export to growing, energy-hungry countries such as South Korea. When I first visited South Korea, I was surprised by the thick, smoky haze in the air—something I had experienced decades earlier in China. I soon learned that some of the pollution was coming from coal-burning power plants in China *and* from coal-burning facilities in South Korea. The country is ranked as the eighth largest in the world for coal operational capacity.

This was surprising in a modernized nation with beautiful new buildings. Even more surprising was the fact that they were building more and more coal-fired plants to keep up with demand. *That's just wrong*, I thought. I wanted to learn why they hadn't made the switch to a lower-carbon fuel, like natural gas.

My team and I met with South Korea's utility commission and various other players over several months in 2012. Long story short, after multiple visits to their country and hosting their teams many times, we created a win-win joint venture. They knew they had a problem with energy production in terms of keeping up with demand and being good stewards of the environment. The solution was to import liquified natural gas (LNG).

We came to an agreement in 2014, and because they were such good partners to us, we expanded it in 2017. Here's a portion of the press release on the venture.

Oct. 27, 2014 — Continental Resources, Inc. announced today it has formed a joint venture with a wholly owned U.S. subsidiary of SK E&S Co. Ltd ("SK") to jointly develop a significant portion of Continental's Northwest Cana Woodford natural gas assets, primarily in Blaine and

Dewey counties, Oklahoma. SK E&S is a subsidiary of SK Group, one of the largest conglomerates in South Korea and part of SK Holdings, a Fortune Global 100 company. . . . J. J. Yu, President and Chief Executive Officer of SK E&S, said, "SK E&S is pleased to join with Continental Resources, a proven leader in developing U.S. unconventional resource plays, in what we expect will be a long-term strategic relationship in energy production.

In January 2022, South Korea announced it was retiring its two oldest coal-fired generation plants and replacing them with units using LNG. As I write this, they are importing about two trillion cubic feet of LNG per year. Guess where much of this resource is coming from? Yes, from the U.S.

What we quietly helped accomplish in this case—*with a possibility attitude*—has done more to clean up our air than countless protests and conferences.

Can an energy company from Oklahoma really help a major industrialized nation change the way it generates electricity and clean up the air? Yes. Our partnership was a game changer. And we're just getting started.

CHAPTER 19

Giving Back

IBELIEVE WE HAVE A RESPONSIBILITY TO MAKE SURE WE don't leave anyone behind, or at least make sure folks get an opportunity to rise. For me, this is simple. I started this life with very little, other than a big family who loved me. Everyone pitched in for everyone else. We shared what we had with each other and our neighbors. It's just the way it was in rural Oklahoma. Giving was a way of life.

I'll never forget the first pair of sandals—hand-me-downs—I got when I was six or seven years old. Didn't matter that they began their life on someone else's feet; they kept mine off the hot summer sand. I had a new spring in my step because someone paid it forward for me.

So when I started accumulating some means, I wanted to make sure I was putting sandals on someone else's feet.

I started as a one-man, one-pump truck operation inspired by those who came before me. Frank and Jane Phillips gave away every dime of their huge oil and gas fortune. Countless universities, museums, and medical centers have been the beneficiaries of the wealth created by the giants who have gone before me, such as the Phillips, Noble, Champlin, and Skelly families, to name just a few. All were full of energy and incredibly generous; the list is long, and their legacies even longer. Every one of their stories inspired me to be as passionate and as giving.

I believe strongly in giving to areas that mean something to you. For me, those areas are health, education, and energy literacy—what I call my guiding pillars.

The Giving Pledge

In 2010, I joined Bill Gates, Warren Buffet, and forty others in the inaugural group of the Giving Pledge. Politics didn't matter; philanthropy did. The idea of the Giving Pledge was simple: By joining, we publicly committed to give the majority of our wealth in our lifetime to address some of society's most pressing problems. This giving philosophy raised the bar and set a new standard for giving, in perfect keeping with my guiding pillars.

This was attractive to me because I wanted to share the blessings I had received after a lifetime of hard work. This country gave me great opportunity. I was able to lift myself out of poverty, create wealth for a great many people around me, and use my money to change the world in many ways, small and large, for the betterment of mankind.

When you sign up, they ask you to post a letter explaining why you joined and the causes that motivate you. Here's a small part of what I shared:

> We live in an amazing country. Because of our capitalistic society and free enterprise system, I was able to work my way out of poverty. . . . I hope to continue the legacy of encouraging others to commit their time and resources

to worthy causes that will enable people with ambition and tenacity to achieve their goals.

I'm an unabashed believer in the American experiment. No other system in the world comes close. What a blessing to be born here.

My Friend Nate

I had a friend a few years back, a gentleman named Nate Waters. When he was nineteen, he was beaten and suffered a severed spinal cord and permanent paralysis. I heard about him through some associates, and we got to know each other.

Nate was an inspiration. There was nothing in Nate's way. Not the wheelchair, not his paralysis, not the terrible fate life handed him. He just needed a little help, and he would do the rest. Nate had a huge heart and knew his role was to give back as best he could. We were able to purchase and retrofit a home for him for his specific needs. He had earned his GED and secured transportation, ultimately earning his physical therapy degree. Nate became an integral part of the Tulsa community, his smile lighting up the downtown clinic every day. He made a difference and deeply touched all who knew him.

Nate passed away a few years ago, tragically, because of his injuries. But from the moment of the fight until his passing, he gave back with everything he had. His friends raised a bunch of money and built the Nate Waters Physical Therapy Clinic on Cincinnati Street in Tulsa. I think of Nate often. There are those special people God places in your life over time who change you; Nate was one of those people. Getting to know Nate was a reminder that it is not always about money—sometimes giving back is about a life well lived.

My Personal Game Changer

At the age of fifty, I was diagnosed with type 2 diabetes. Like many of us who find ourselves facing the realities of diabetes, if you continue on your current path, risks for more serious illness will increase dramatically—terrible things such as heart disease, stroke, kidney failure, blindness, and even lower limb amputation.

It got my attention.

I became one of the millions of people with diabetes. Since I was diagnosed, the number of my fellow Americans with diabetes has doubled. The numbers are devastating—thirty-seven million people have some form of the disease in our country, and experts project ninety-six million adults have pre-diabetes. In other words, their lifestyles and genetics are pointing them to full-blown diabetes unless they take the necessary steps to prevent it.

Diabetes is a pandemic, and I believe we should have the same urgency treating diabetes as any other pandemic we may face. This disease fuels so many afflictions and is ravaging populations across the globe. My form, type 2, means the body doesn't use insulin very well and can't keep blood sugar levels where they should be.

You can adopt lifestyle changes that can make a difference, like eating healthier and getting more active. I'm in my mid-seventies now, and I walk five miles every day. I maintain my weight, and I pass on the local favorites like Oklahoma fried onion burgers with a pile of fries.

In 2007, I had an epiphany, another "get 'er done" moment. I was with my friend David Boren, who was president of the University of Oklahoma at the time. He had previously served as Oklahoma's governor and then three terms in the U.S. Senate. David wanted to make OU a world-class research center. Like me, he has that "game changer" mindset. As we talked, we realized diabetes wasn't getting much attention, or at least not the attention it deserved, and it was time to put the medical center on the map.

I wanted to make a game-changing gift to the university and establish a diabetes center for research, patient care, and education. But I wanted to do it privately. David encouraged me to put my name on the mission so we could compel others to come along. He was right. In addition to the $65 million put forth, we've managed to garner over $100 million in grants for research since the center's inception.

We also established the Harold Hamm International Biomedical Research in Diabetes Award, which grants $250,000 to a deserving researcher every year—the largest prize of its kind. We are rewarding the best and brightest minds with their cutting-edge innovations on the path to a cure. And we are making progress. But while we are on the path to a cure, we need to do everything we can to help people with diabetes to develop the skills they need to manage the disease.

I think in terms of what is possible. I learned insulin was far too expensive and becoming more expensive with each passing year due to some loopholes in patent law and how some of the pharmaceutical companies were exploiting those regulations. While I am not personally on insulin, I could not stand the thought of people having to ration the insulin required for them to live.

Those who were dependent on insulin were facing larger and larger bills to the tune of $1,000 per month. The absurdity of this grows when you learn that a century ago, the inventors who discovered insulin believed it was unethical for a doctor to profit from a discovery that would save lives. They put their money where their mouths were, too, selling the patent to the University of Toronto for just one dollar each. More and more people are self-rationing their insulin because they can no longer afford the drug, and this practice can be life-threatening. I decided it was time to find a better way.

Our team made numerous trips to Washington to discuss the cost of insulin with legislators and even the White House. Everyone agreed it was a problem, but no one seemed to be able to find a solution. We met with one person in particular who became a champion of this cause, a fellow diabetic, Mike Kelly. He is a U.S. Congressman from Pennsylvania and took this mission on personally. At the same time, I learned about a highly successful businessman named Mark Cuban who had decided his other passion, besides technology and basketball, was founding a company whose purpose was to lower the cost of prescription drugs for all Americans.

We reached out to Mark to see if he would be interested in partnering in some way to focus on insulin. We made the trip down I-35 to Dallas and listened to Mark and his colleagues—a bunch of brilliant medical folks who were fellow game changers. We found out he was already on the path to affordable insulin. We offered to jump in and sponsor necessary trials to achieve what no one thought possible: affordable insulin for anyone who needs it.

His new, state-of-the-art manufacturing facility will soon be up and running, producing affordable prescription drugs. This story continues to play out as it looks like the existing pharmaceutical companies may be coming in line to make a private-label insulin for Mark's company. Sometimes when you start a project the path can change, and that's OK, as long as the result is affordable insulin for those who need it. As of this writing, we have just received confirmation of the pharmaceutical company's first shipments!

While there is still more work to be done, the world's three largest makers of insulin are finally giving in to mounting pressure to reduce costs for consumers. This is one of those instances where the impossible just took a little longer. Eli Lilly announced in March 2023 it would cut its insulin price by 70 percent, capping patient costs at $35 per month. Just days after, Novo Nordisk followed in line lowering insulin prices by 75 percent and then Sanofi doing the same, lowering prices by 78 percent. There really is no reason it should have taken this long to get to this point—and there is no excuse for watching Americans ration their life-saving insulin use, when the initial discoverers sold the patent for just $1 each. But this is a step in the right direction and will certainly be a relief to diabetics across the country.

I am proud of our efforts to combat the pandemic of diabetes and will continue to lead in this area until we have found a cure. I believe it can be done and will do everything I can to ensure this happens in our lifetime.

If you'd like to learn more about Cost Plus Drugs, check out Mark's website at costplusdrugs.com. You can learn more about our work with the Harold Hamm Diabetes Center at ouhealth.com/harold-hamm-diabetes-center/.

Education Unlocks Opportunity

One of my early forays into bigger philanthropic work happened when our company was still headquartered in Enid. Due to some mismanagement, Phillips University found itself in serious financial trouble. In fact, the university was insolvent and faced closing its doors. But it was the only institution of higher learning for miles around. Kids in and around Enid, especially those who came from backgrounds like mine, would have to travel hundreds of miles or just not go to college.

Phillips had a storied past. The Haymakers were an athletic powerhouse in the early part of the twentieth century, with football victories over Texas and Oklahoma, even becoming part of the original Southwest Conference after World War I. But in April 1998, Phillips declared bankruptcy and closed its doors.

I had a soft spot in my heart for Phillips. I had attended the college back in the seventies as part of my more formal education, which supplemented my out of the classroom schooling. For example, I still remember a fellow by the name of Don Longdon who worked for the Western Company. I have fond memories of Don sitting on the hood of his car, his shoes off, his white socks on display for all to see. He'd lean back, take a draw on his Camel non-filter, and regale me with his latest techniques in well-stim work. I can't tell you how many hours I spent with guys like Don.

I can't really say which learning is more valuable, street or book. But in 1977, I was deep into the book learning at Phillips. I helped the school create a forum, the "Winter of 1977 Energy Congress." We brought in energy experts from thirty states to little old Enid. Lee White, former Chairman of the Federal Power Commission, debated Dr. Phil Gramm, then an economist from Texas A&M University and soon to be a Texas senator. The topic was deregulation of natural gas. Phil and most of the energy executives were in the camp of deregulating, that there would be more supply if pricing controls were lifted. Sadly, despite reams of evidence presented during the forum, the Carter administration decided to impose the Natural Gas Policy Act of 1978, expanding regulations and controls on interstate and intrastate gas, guaranteeing government-mandated scarcity for years to come. I never forgot the forum, the folks I met there, or the role Phillips played in my development as an oil and gas entrepreneur.

Fast-forward twenty years, and I knew we had to do something fast. Phillips was on the ropes, so I gathered people from business, government, and academia, and we quickly put together a task force and raised some money. It wasn't easy and is probably a whole book by itself. But in the end, we "got 'er done." Phillips became part of Northern Oklahoma College in June 1999, and the students of the Enid area again had a local educational resource. I learned from the experience that good people with a common goal can make great things happen.

I love sparking young minds and giving young people the tools and resources to take on their passions and the world. I have endowed a bunch of scholarships at every school in Oklahoma. I'm glad to do it. There's now a Harold Hamm School of Geology and Geological Engineering at the University of North Dakota and a Hamm School of Engineering at the University of Mary in Bismarck. The mission is to inspire and train the next generation of oil and gas leaders—we are going to need them if we are to remain energy independent and continue to produce hydrocarbons abundantly, affordably, and responsibly.

Most recently, I had the opportunity to give back by donating $50 million to the Theodore Roosevelt Presidential Library being built in Medora, North Dakota. Many remember the impact that Teddy Roosevelt had on North Dakota but may not realize the impact and transformation that North Dakota had on him. I see North Dakota having also transformed me in a similar way. North Dakota helped expand my vision that America could be energy independent.

I believe in investing in big ideas that are built to last. This is an opportunity to memorialize one of our country's great presidents. This library will inspire Americans for centuries, not just decades. It's an ambitious vision that has been easy to get behind because it will perpetuate Teddy's legacy and bring visitors from around the world to the Badlands for generations to come.

If you want to donate to the library, you can visit https://www.trlibrary.com/.

Pass It On

Speaking of generations, one of the most rewarding parts of giving has been watching my own children embrace the causes we support and discover causes that fuel their own passions. All my kids have found organizations and nonprofits to get involved with over the years, and I hope my philosophy on philanthropy has had a little bit to do with that.

There's no shortage of worthy causes, big or small. You don't have to be a billionaire to give back. My friend Nate did his thing, just like Warren Buffet is doing his. For the world to be a better place, we should all invest in our own way. Find the causes that you are passionate about and give back to them, whether it be financially or volunteering your time. The returns are extraordinary.

CHAPTER 20

Powering the Future

TOWARD THE END OF 2020, I DECIDED TO ADD ANOTHER project to my list of "Get 'er dones." For some time, I believed the energy industry needed a place where the best and the brightest could come together and figure out the future for the betterment of humankind.

Sure, there are a bunch of trade associations, lobbying organizations, and the like. But nowhere is there a center for innovation and intellectual capital whose ideas can be shared with the world. That's the first aspect of my mission.

The other goal is to help the next generation get fired up about making a difference in the energy industry. Even in Oklahoma, it's increasingly difficult to inspire young people to pursue a career tied to energy, especially oil and natural gas exploration and production. I bet you can guess why. From grade school, kids are fed a daily diet of—forgive me—*propaganda* demonizing everything related to these resources. Wind and solar might sound like they're on the side of angels, but the technology is

U.S. 2019 Energy Consumption by Type
(% Share)

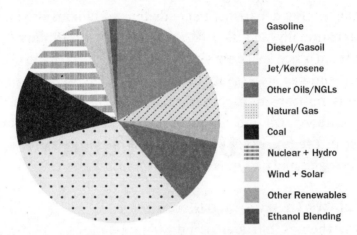

Gasoline
Diesel/Gasoil
Jet/Kerosene
Other Oils/NGLs
Natural Gas
Coal
Nuclear + Hydro
Wind + Solar
Other Renewables
Ethanol Blending

World 2019 Energy Consumption by Type
(% Share)

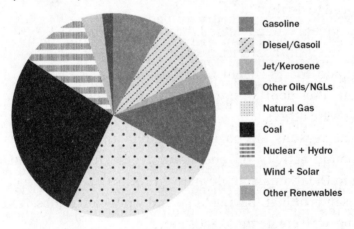

Gasoline
Diesel/Gasoil
Jet/Kerosene
Other Oils/NGLs
Natural Gas
Coal
Nuclear + Hydro
Wind + Solar
Other Renewables

Source: "Statistical Review of World Energy," BP, https://www.bp.com/en/global/corporate/energy-econom-
ics/stat-istical-review-of-world-energy.html; "Short Term Energy Outlook, May 2021," U.S. Energy Information
Administration, https://www.eia.gov/outlooks/steo/

Hydrocarbons still rule and will for decades to come. Wind and
solar, while growing, will not keep pace with the increase in
demand or even come close to contributing 10 percent of the mix,
no matter how much money is thrown at these renewables.

limited by the realities of physics and chemistry. No amount of wishful thinking is going to change the math.

Our energy department spends tens of billions of your tax dollars annually, and its accomplishments since Jimmy Carter gave them office space are skinny at best. We need to do better.

Oil and gas are essential to our future. As we have proven, there is no transition path without huge contributions from hydrocarbons. Oil and natural gas can literally fuel us into a better future, so why take our foot off the accelerator to new technologies and better living conditions for the world?

Possibility Thinking on a Global Scale

Kristin Thomas, our media and public relations dynamo, first brought the idea of an institute to my attention in a staff meeting a couple of years ago. As always, she was prepared and persuasive: "The industry needs a hub for ideas, and so does the world. We need to do this!"

I agreed. When I floated the idea by our then CEO, Bill Berry, he jumped on board immediately. So did our governor, Kevin Stitt, and the president of Oklahoma State University, Kayse Shrum. President Shrum and OSU were proud to partner with us, as were others.

The reasons are obvious. The billions in tax dollars and economic activity oil and natural gas create are indispensable to Oklahoma and ultimately to America. We have created thousands of high-paying blue- and white-collar jobs. And God willing, we'll create thousands more.

At the Hamm Institute, we believe in a world where every person has access to the reliable, affordable, and sustainable energy they need to thrive.

We opened the Hamm Institute for American Energy in Oklahoma City in December 2021. Our announcement stated,

"Our vision is to develop the energy leaders of tomorrow by engaging industry and academia in developing practical, global, science-based solutions through collaboration, research, and development. We promote scholastic excellence in the field of energy development and production to benefit the global environment and serve consumers across the world."

I can hear you thinking, *That's pretty ambitious.* Yes, it is. Intentionally so.

Energy demand continues to grow as developing nations want what we have: abundant, affordable, and reliable energy.

No one I respect has come up with a forecast predicting declining energy demand.

Our mission, our reason for being, is to help find ways to meet the growing demand. The modern-day prohibitionists are wrong. No one in the modern world can live without what we produce. So I say, let's inspire the innovators and the inventors and stir the imaginations of the next generation of energy leaders.

We need to ensure our policymakers and politicians make wise choices for our shared energy future. Why? Because our national and economic security is at stake.

Consider the choices we are making yet again. Billions to fight a war in Ukraine, sanctions on Russian oil and natural gas. How many times are we going to use this playbook? Our security and our way of life begin and end with energy. When more than 80 percent of the world's energy comes from hydrocarbons, it's time for everyone to get real.

Mike Pompeo, our former secretary of state, relayed to me that each of his meetings with foreign heads of state always started with a discussion on energy security. As you might expect, I bring a sense of urgency to this mission. I have kids, grandkids, and great-grandkids. Hopefully, I'll see some great-great-grandkids someday. I don't want them wondering why we went *back* one hundred years instead of forward.

We need all the energy we can get, which means everyone has to quickly become honest about what will work—and what won't.

What better place to headquarter our new center for energy innovation than in Oklahoma City, in the state that turned America into an energy superpower over one hundred years ago—and where the first energy visionaries came to change the world? I'm humbled to stand on the shoulders of these pioneers and encouraged that America will rise to the occasion yet again.

As I stood on the stage during the celebratory announcement, with many family members in attendance, it was my hope that the world will look to us for innovative solutions for energy stewardship, research, and education. The Hamm Institute is a game changer—a place where the best and the brightest will come together to responsibly solve energy challenges for all humanity. People from around the world will come here and take on the biggest goals—free of politics, free of biases, and free to exchange ideas. *Possibility thinking on a global scale.*

I am pleased to see my daughter Hilary has taken a special interest in the Hamm Institute's mission and vision. This is so important as future leaders will steward my legacy through the institute for generations to come.

Energy poverty hurts the quality of life for billions of our fellow human beings. We need to fix that. We need to make sure Americans will always have an abundance of reliable, affordable energy for generations to come. The world is in energy transition. We will always be in transition because we need *more* energy, not less. And it can be both produced and consumed intelligently without damaging the environment we live in.

In just one century, a massive advance in the human experience has occurred—one we often take for granted. Most Americans don't realize there were rural parts of the country that were finally being electrified post–World War II, including my little corner of Oklahoma. What happened in the 1950s in some rural communities in the U.S. is now going on across the world.

We need energy to be *accessible* and *affordable* to all, and we need to get it done in the most sustainable and environmentally sound way as possible. Anything less is unacceptable. In case you are wondering if "accessible and affordable" means government control or some form of socialism, you can forget it. As I write this, Stanford University canceled summer classes because of power outages in California. Is that the model to follow? Free enterprise brought us the highest standard of living in history, and free enterprise can work in any nation.

The future depends on the next generation of energy leaders. We need technologists, engineers, geologists, and environmentalists to figure out what's next, and we need to do it together.

After all, the stakes are high, and the risks are enormous if we don't get it right. To reframe President Carter's 1978 plea: "Failure to act will fuel inflation, erode the value of the dollar, render us vulnerable to disruptions in our oil supply, and limit our economic progress in the years to come." But unlike Jimmy Carter, we must take the *right* steps for all the right reasons, using intellect versus emotion, IQ over EQ, and truth instead of fiction.

The war on energy continues as I write this, as the Biden administration persists in trying to eliminate oil and gas companies while somehow expecting them to produce more. This administration's energy policies—including the removal of permitting, leasing, and development on all federal lands—hurt this country and exacerbated the world's energy crisis, leading to the highest fuel prices in history and the highest inflation in forty years.

The decision to eliminate oil and gas, which has been around for the past one hundred and fifty years, is just as wrong as the decision then Senator Joe Biden helped pass in 1978, mandating the use of coal and eliminating clean-burning natural gas in power generation. Those actions were punitive and aimed directly against oil and gas, and they caused the energy crisis that soon followed. Ignorant and unscientific decisions produced environmental devastation in America and set many developing countries on a quest to power their energy needs with coal.

The U.S. has always been the world leader in energy exploration and production. But this happened in spite of, not because of, global energy policy. Good private-sector leadership impacted the globe for good. Bad government leadership created hardships for billions of people.

We are nearing a breaking point in America. If policymakers don't relent and reverse hostile oil and natural gas policies, the American economy will retract just as it did under Jimmy Carter. Inflation will continue to spiral upward, and the quality of life for all Americans will be lowered. I hope they will change course before the breaking point is reached. Six dollar gas was very predictable, as I voiced in my op-ed in 2020, when then candidate Biden's policy was unveiled. A course correction away from the abyss of economic depression is also predictable if he and his advisers will simply end this internal war against energy— and American citizens.

Changing the Company—Choosing Freedom

In the past few years, it became increasingly obvious to me that Continental Resources needed once again to leave the herd.

When we took the company public in 2007, as I mentioned, the strategy was to raise capital and seize big opportunities. We did both as we developed the behemoth Bakken field across Montana and North Dakota—which quickly became the largest find in the U.S. at the time. From its inception, many critics have downplayed the Bakken. But I knew what we had discovered. The Bakken is the driver that has put Continental as the number one privately held oil and gas company in the nation, and perhaps even the world. It took stepping out of the public markets to solidify our standing.

I've never been afraid to collaborate when it made sense, and I always work for win-win partnerships. But the climate had changed for us, so to speak, as a publicly traded energy company since the downturn of 2020, following the COVID-19 outbreak. There was decreasing support from the public markets, and my team determined that the private companies have more freedom to operate and aren't limited by public-market support. Our belief was that taking Continental private would enhance our ability to maintain our competitive edge and would also enable us to be even more nimble in our efforts to create value through the drill bit.

At Continental, we are a group of earth scientists with sufficient expertise who always generate our own geologic ideas to power our growth. Positioning ourselves as a private company can allow us to take maximum advantage of our greatest strength—our strong heritage as one of the leading exploration companies in the world. We would be unhindered by Wall Street once again and free to supply the needs of the marketplace.

Don't get me wrong. I thoroughly enjoyed the time Continental was in the public eye. We entered the market in 2007 as a leader of the pack, established the lowest lease operating costs for a majority oil-producing company, and enhanced our prowess in both drilling and exploration—in basin after basin and play after play. All that time, we innovated, developing and sharing the novel idea of Horizontal Drilling from its infancy through world-changing significance. Our team did it all, from beginning to end, with peer-leading performance.

But being on the stock exchange tends to meld companies into a herd mentality, thinking only of the next quarter, instead of long-term possibilities like the next quarter century. Continental must be free to think and act independently, as we did with Horizontal Drilling, bold exploration, and the adoption of carbon capture and storage.

The recent Bloomberg headline explained it well: "Shale firebrand Harold Hamm's $4.3 billion play to win 'freedom' to drill"

Here's what the *Wall Street Journal* said about the move:

> More producers would go private to have more flexibility, oil-and-gas executives have said, but few are in a position to do so. Analysts said they didn't expect to see more publicly traded U.S. oil producers go private. Among large publicly listed producers, Mr. Hamm is unique in retaining most of the shares of the company he founded, giving him the ability to regain sole control 15 years after taking it public. The company's initial public offering brought it cash to expand drilling in the Bakken.

Through the months-long process, there was very little criticism, except for one party who must have had an urge to get some publicity out of the deal. I can't think of any other reason he would say the things he said and accuse me of lowballing an offer when the stock was nearly two times greater than it was when he began investing in Continental. I'd say he reaped the benefits quite well since being a CLR shareholder for just two years.

> **C. WILLIAM SMEAD**
>
> Harold,
>
> First off, I want to thank you for the leadership and stewardship you provided to us and our investors. You are the best capital allocator in the energy business. We saw green pastures elsewhere in the oil business, but will miss being a partner with you. If you are ever in Phoenix or I'm ever in Oklahoma, I'd love to buy you dinner to thank you.
>
> Warmest Regards,

Although the accusations caused me a lot of grief, personally, he must not have been too serious about it. Here's the note he sent me after the transaction closed.

Funny how quickly his tune changed. I may just take you up on that dinner offer, Mr. Smead.

A Company Built to Last

Succession planning is another pillar important in creating a company built to last. More than two decades ago, my family and I sat down to discuss what this would look like and began making plans toward that end. In 2020, I announced I would "step up" to the role of executive chairman at Continental and, for the first time, hand over the CEO role to someone other than myself. I called it stepping *up* because that was, in fact, what I did. Stepping up allowed me the opportunity to focus on other critical issues in the industry and beyond, such as the new pricing marker for crude and the ongoing regulatory matters you read about earlier. I am still ingrained in the day-to-day of

Continental, but what has probably made me most proud is to see my family truly live out what it means to be a family-owned business. Today there are three generations of Hamms working throughout Continental. The benefit of this is that there is a different level of engagement, energy, caring, risk management, and stakeholder engagement with a family-owned company. It truly is "personal" in all the positive senses of the word.

Continental is not just a business to us; we care deeply about this company and the individuals who make it up. We all work as hard as any of our employees to ensure its success, and we make sure that every employee is valued and appreciated. I am confident Continental will be here for decades to come because my kids and grandkids all have our shared vision and understand the impact we can continue to make on humanity by producing the energy our world needs.

Fueling Your Future

I was born with what every unconventional thinker requires: curiosity, a hunger for truth no matter where it leads, and a desire to change the world for the better.

It's been a six-decade journey, with more ups and downs than a pumpjack. As a young man, I put a million miles on my old water truck before I ever found a geologic drop of oil. As you know by now, we found quite a few drops. But I was like millions of other Americans at the time. I wanted to start my own business, control my own destiny, and maybe do things just a bit better than the guy down the road. If you share those aspirations, I believe what I've learned can make a big difference in your life.

I'm the furthest thing from an "overnight success." But I am a relentless learner who loves to change for the better. I've never been afraid of change or exploring improvements. And many people might tell you that I'm impatient, especially when something needs fixing. They're not wrong. Getting things done is my rallying cry to make things happen—most always on "Hamm time," which, in my experience, is far faster than most organizations are comfortable with. In marketing parlance, I suppose that makes me a fast mover—not a drill sergeant, but a visionary with a sense of urgency.

Somewhere along the way, I realized there was divine intervention in my life. Some may call it luck, but I have always been driven by a real sense of purpose, and I still am. God has his own timing, and it is not meant to be understood by us. He sees the big picture, and we just get the thirteen-inch view.

I have a small plaque in my house that reads, "What I am is my gift from God. What I become is my gift to God." God gave me the wonderful gift of life. My goal is to give something back just as great, and I thank God for all the opportunities and protection He has given me.

I remember driving out to my first oil prospect, the Oakdale Oswego area, and even before we were drilling, I would get goosebumps thinking about what was coming down the pike.

Through time, the industry has toughened me up. The hard knocks of this business have made me stronger and prepared me for the mission ahead. This industry has been so good to me. I still get excited thinking about our future prospects and opportunities.

Is it destiny? Part of it was, for certain. It would have been easy to sell out or retire. Instead, I want to build something that will stand the test of time for America and the world.

I want my legacy to serve as an example to young people, to those who have nothing but aspirations toward greater achievements. It can still be done right here in America.

I hope my journey of unconventional thinking, with a wild-catter's mentality, inspires you to follow your own passions and dreams. The culture of the possible teaches us that from a less-than-zero starting position, you too can be a game changer through opportunity, hard work, passion, and persistence—mixed in with destiny. This has been my dance.

As I said in my commencement address to the graduating class at Lexington High,

"Make sure you don't miss your dance."

One Daughter's Perspective

By Shelly Lambertz,
Daughter of Harold Hamm and Executive Vice President, Chief
Culture & Administrative Officer, Continental Resources

THE SMELL OF OIL INSTANTLY TAKES ME BACK TO MY CHILD-hood. My dad would come home from a long day's work with oil-stained fingers. I remember the countless wristwatches Dad would go through because oil seeped inside them. He had an unmatched work ethic, and he still does to this day. I credit a lot of that to him having kids at a young age and his drive to break the cycle of poverty in our family.

He has never been afraid to take risks. It was a risk when he picked our family up and moved us to Enid. It was a risk when he bought his first truck. But looking back, you see that it was those risks that led to his success today. I'll never forget when he bought our first home out in the country in 1982. It was a big moment of pride for him because he had worked so hard to provide for us.

We often joke as siblings that Continental is Dad's favorite child. He has always loved finding oil and gas. He knows every part of this business. No one today has that kind of experience. When you're in the business, you learn that not everybody can find oil and gas. It takes special people who have those unique skills. These aren't necessarily learned skills but rather the combination of experience and wisdom and an expertise in geology and earth mechanics that makes up the best earth scientists—Dad is one of those special people.

It's his love of people that drives what he does. He cares deeply for his employees and considers them to be extended family. I'll never forget in 1996 when the industry was facing a downturn and he was forced to lay off a few of his staff. This pained him so much that he vowed never to do it again, and through the ups and downs of the industry, he has stayed true to that commitment. It's part of what sets Continental apart.

The same "culture of the possible" I grew up in is thriving now throughout our company. I've had the opportunity to work alongside Dad these past five years as a member of the board and now as an employee at Continental. It is so special to watch him on the job.

Exploration meetings remind me of my childhood. His enthusiasm for finding oil and natural gas is contagious. One of the most rewarding opportunities is to sit in these meetings and see his face light up as he watches a young engineer or geologist make a new discovery, present a game-changing idea, or find an entirely new petroleum system using the geologic concepts we encourage here at Continental. It's rewarding to watch him develop the next generation of leaders in our company and in the industry. This collaboration has always been Continental's secret sauce. In fact, when the COVID-19 pandemic hit, a key driver for safely getting our teams back in the office was making sure we didn't lose this collaboration. In fact, I've always observed we make our greatest strides during challenging times. It's fun to see how the feedback he provides inspires the explorationist in our teams and prompts their entrepreneurial spirit. He thinks outside the box and encourages others to do the same.

Dad has always understood his purpose on this earth is greater than himself. He was raised with a strong faith, something that guides him still today. He is ultimately a producer. It's the most philanthropic thing he can do. He doesn't take lightly the responsibility he has to provide for his employees. And through the success of his business and his employees, he can have the greatest societal impact. When Dad gives back, he does so with purpose. A little contribution to everything doesn't have the same impact as does giving back to what you're passionate about.

He has made a profound impact on health and education in Oklahoma and across the country, but I think I'm most proud of what we have accomplished through the Harold Hamm Diabetes Center. Diabetes is not a popular cause, but it's a real problem. He has dedicated so much to finding opportunities for those that suffer from this disease, and he remains committed to finding a cure. I know there are great things to come through our family's philanthropic efforts.

His family roots run deep. If you've ever been to a Hamm family reunion, you'd see no fewer than 165 Hamms coming together. These reunions are one of Dad's favorite things. He has always had a deep sense of loyalty when it comes to his siblings,

308 • Game Changer

and he's built special bonds with each of them and their families all through their lives.

Dad has always been ahead of the curve. He has always believed in what is possible. I can never thank him enough for believing in me. Even at a young age, he didn't let gender stereotypes influence the drive he instilled. Instead, he pushed me to do great things. He pushed me to be all that I could be. And he has done that with all his children.

Despite the fame that has come with his career, he will always be Dad. He is still the same Harold Hamm who grew up in Lexington, Oklahoma, and envisioned a better life—a more prosperous life for his family. Dad has always been driven and never known to take the easy road. He is a risk-taker. A visionary and a doer.

Acknowledgments

INEVER WOULD HAVE THOUGHT AS I GRADUATED ENID HIGH School in 1964 that I would get to be part of such a significant time in our history. The development of Horizontal Drilling literally changed the world for the better and revolutionized everything about the American oil and gas industry, taking it from what was believed to be a dying or nearly dead industry to the leading producer of both oil and natural gas across the world.

Horizontal Drilling was a game changer. It set the many naysayers on their heels and changed the entire scope of what was possible. I don't claim to have done it alone. Within my own shop, my hat's off to Jeff Hume, Jack Stark, Bob Sandridge, Glen Cox, Jack Tarkington, Kenny Cottrell, Tom Luttrell, Ken Ainsworth, and the many other engineers, geologists, and landmen who were a part of our team in those early days.

Across the industry, I appreciate those few other adventurers who bucked the trend in the very early days of the Horizontal Drilling experiment and tried the unconventional alongside us. I am especially grateful for our team members in the field, whose ingenuity and persistence helped unlock the code of the Bakken shale and overcome many of the drilling challenges as we worked to perfect the technique. Thank you to all of Continental's employees through the years who have helped build the culture of the possible. Thanks also to those in the industry who are willing to stand up for American energy. I also want to extend my appreciation to the various teachers and educators through the years that have helped shape my eagerness to learn, including the late Alan Baharlou and Jewell Ridge.

Success has many authors, and so does this book! My thanks go out to Kristin Thomas, Lincoln Ferguson, Mike Malone, Mike Loomis, Jane Trotzuk, Hilary Hamm, and Lucy Spaay, who kept me focused and persistent in getting this book to the finish line to tell this story. This never could have been accomplished without your guidance. I will always be indebted to Lynne Hames, who transcribed and printed so many pages for me. Many thanks to the Public Relations team for laying out the expansive timeline of this story and building out the library, and to Heather Scott and the Facilities and Administration team for digitizing the library. Thanks also to our diligent researchers and Deb Richards for archiving files for me for many years.

Citations by Chapter

THIS BOOK INCLUDES DATA FROM THE U.S. ENERGY Information Administration, International Energy Agency, World Bank, U.S. Environmental Protection Agency, U.S. Geological Survey, *BP Statistical Review*, World Health Organization, Bureau of Labor Statistics, and U.S. Congress.

Note on Stock Prices

Any references to the Continental Resources (NYSE: CLR) stock price prior to 2014 do not reflect the two-for-one stock split distributed in 2014. Any references to the stock price after the distribution reflect the two-for-one-stock split.

Continental Resources. "Continental Resources Announces Two-for-One Stock Split." Press Release, August 18, 2014. https://investors.clr.com/2014-08-18-Continental-Resources-Announces-Two-For-One-Stock-Split.

Introduction

"Petroleum has been used": "Waste In Oil Regions Found To Be Serious." *Titusville Herald*, July 19, 1909. https://www.scribd.com/document/16415562/1909-July-19-Titusville-Herald-Titusville-PA-Article#from_embed.

"Al Gore predicted": James, Frank. "Al Gore Slips on Artic Ice; Misstates Scientist's Forecast." NPR, December 15, 2009. https://www.npr.org/sections/thetwo-way/2009/12/al_gore_trips_on_artic_ice_mis.html.

"Manhattan would be underwater": Bell, Larry. "Rising Tides of Terror: Will Melting Glaciers Flood Al Gore's Coastal Home?" *Forbes*, June 26, 2012. https://www.forbes.com/sites/larrybell/2012/06/26/rising-tides-of-terror-will-melting-glaciers-flood-al-gores-coastal-home/?sh=424a43594ee8.

"AOC predicted": Bowden, John. "Ocasio-Cortez: 'World will end in 12 years' if climate change not addressed." *The Hill*, January 22, 2019. https://thehill.com/policy/energy-environment/426353-ocasio-cortez-the-world-will-end-in-12-years-if-we-dont-address/.

"Myron Ebell's article": Ebell, Myron and Steven J. Milloy. "Wrong Again: 50 Years of Failed Eco-pocalyptic Predictions." Competitive Enterprise Institute, September 18, 2019. https://cei.org/blog/wrong-again-50-years-of-failed-eco-pocalyptic-predictions/.

"Courage is contagious": Thibodeaux, Wanda. "51 Quotes to Spark Unshakable Bravery and Courage." *Inc.*, April 5, 2019. https://www.inc.com/wanda-thibodeaux/51-quotes-to-remember-when-you-need-more-courage.html.

2 – Trucking and Trusting

"Ten thousand hours": Gladwell, Malcolm. *Outliers: The Story of Success.* New York: Little, Brown and Co., 2008.

"Price of oil dove": Morgan Stanley Research. "Oil Price Plunge Is So 1986..." April 2, 2015. https://www.morganstanley.com/ideas/oil-price-plunge-is-so-1986#:~:text=From%20November%20of%201985%20to,(See%20below.

3 – Whale Tales and Industrial Evolution

"Total U.S. consumption of oil in 2021": U.S. Department of Energy. Energy Information Administration. "Frequently Asked Questions: How much oil is consumed in the United States?" Updated September 19, 2022. https://www.eia.gov/tools/faqs/faq.php?id=33&t=6#:~:text=In%202021%2C%20the%20United%20States,day%20over%20consumption%20in%202020.

"Nova Scotian physician and geologist": Dalhousie University. "Abraham Gesner." Accessed July 7, 2022. https://www.dal.ca/about-dal/dalhousie-originals/abraham-gesner.html.

"In the summer of 1859": American Society of Mechanical Engineers. "The Drake Oil Well." October 21, 1979, 7. https://www.asme.org/wwwasmeorg/media/resourcefiles/aboutasme/history/landmarks/40-drakeoilwell.pdf.

"In the Oklahoma Territory": Wells, B. A. and K. L. Wells. "First Oklahoma Oil Well." American Oil & Gas Historical Society, updated April 8, 2022. https://aoghs.org/petroleum-pioneers/first-oklahoma-oil-well/.

"Tom Slick": Wells, B. A. and K. L. Wells. "Oklahoma's King of the Wildcatters." American Oil & Gas Historical Society, updated November 30, 2022. https://aoghs.org/petroleum-pioneers/wildcatter-tom-slick/.

"Frank Phillips": Wimberly, Dan B. "Phillips, Frank Freeman." Oklahoma Historical Society, accessed October 19, 2022. https://www.okhistory.org/publications/enc/entry.php?entry=PH006.

"Strange thing about money": Wallis, Michael. *Oil Man: The Story of Frank Phillips and the Birth of Phillips Petroleum* (Norman: University of Oklahoma Press, 2014), 377.

"Extreme poverty": Roser, Max. "The short history of global living conditions and why it matters that we know it." Our World in Data, accessed October 20, 2022. https://ourworldindata.org/a-history-of-global-living-conditions-in-5-charts?linkId=62571595.

"In 2018": Aguilar, R. Andres Castaneda, Aleksander Eilertsen, Tony Fujs, Christoph Lakner, Daniel Gerszon Mahler, Minh Cong Nguyen, Marta Schoch, Samuel Kofi Tetteh Baah, Martha Viveros, and Haoyu Wu. "April 2022 global poverty update from the World Bank." World Bank Blogs, April 8, 2022. https://blogs.worldbank.org/opendata/april-2022-global-poverty-update-world-bank.

4 – Setting the Stage for Terminal Oil Decline

"The oil and natural gas we rely on": Carter, Jimmy. "Address to the Nation on Energy (April 18, 1977)." The American Presidency Project, UC Santa Barbara. https://www.presidency.ucsb.edu/documents/address-the-nation-energy.

"11 percent mortgage": Freddie Mac. "30-Year-Fixed-Rate Mortgages since 1971," accessed October 18, 2022. https://www.freddiemac.com/pmms/pmms30.

"Reality in the late seventies": Rankin, Deborah. "Auto Loans of 5 Years Emerging." *New York Times*, November 24, 1978, Section D, 1. https://www.

nytimes.com/1978/11/24/archives/auto-loans-of-5-years-emerging-as-prices-climb-banks-stretch-out.html.

"First wave of mandates": Harris, Richard. "Fuel Efficiency Standards Live On after 1973 Oil Embargo." NPR, October 17, 2023. https://www.npr.org/2013/10/17/236033141/fuel-efficiency-standards-live-on-after-1973-oil-embargo.

"Reserve is the largest of its kind": U.S. Department of Energy. Office of Cybersecurity, Energy Security, and Emergency Response. "Strategic Petroleum Reserve." Accessed June 29, 2022. https://www.energy.gov/ceser/strategic-petroleum-reserve.

"Our decision about energy": Carter, Jimmy. "Address to the Nation on Energy (April 18, 1977)." The American Presidency Project, UC Santa Barbara. https://www.presidency.ucsb.edu/documents/address-the-nation-energy.

"$550 billion a year": Carter, Jimmy. "Address to the Nation on Energy (April 18, 1977)." The American Presidency Project, UC Santa Barbara. https://www.presidency.ucsb.edu/documents/address-the-nation-energy.

"Sent off to Paris": Lewis, Paul. "Schlesinger Warns West U.S. Energy Plan Is Vital." *New York Times*, October 6, 1977, 97. https://www.nytimes.com/1977/10/06/archives/schlesinger-warns-west-us-energy-plan-is-vital-program-to-ease.html.

"We need to shift to plentiful coal": Carter, Jimmy. "Address to the Nation on Energy (April 18, 1977)." The American Presidency Project, UC Santa Barbara. https://www.presidency.ucsb.edu/documents/address-the-nation-energy.

"Coal had declined": U.S. Department of Energy. Energy Information Administration. *Monthly Energy Review September 2022*, 7. https://www.eia.gov/totalenergy/data/monthly/pdf/sec1_7.pdf.

"The world now uses": Carter, Jimmy. "Address to the Nation on Energy (April 18, 1977)." The American Presidency Project, UC Santa Barbara. https://www.presidency.ucsb.edu/documents/address-the-nation-energy.

"Coal was a huge contributor to air pollution": U.S House of Representatives. Committee on Science and Technology. Subcommittee on the Environment and the Atmosphere. *Environmental Implications of the New Energy Plan*. 95th Cong., 1st sess., July 21, 1977, 425. https://play.google.com/books/reader?id=jjwrAAAAMAAJ&pg=GBS.PA425&hl=en.

"John O'Leary brushed off the concerns": Maize, K. P. "America's Coal Economy." *CQ Researcher*, April 21, 1978. http://library.cqpress.com/cqresearcher/cqresrre1978042100.

5 – *The Explorationist: Fifty Years on a Journey of Discovery*
"M. King Hubbert": Deffeyes, Kenneth S. "Overview." In *Hubbert's Peak: The Impending World Oil Shortage (New Edition),* STU-Student edition, 1–13. Princeton, NJ: Princeton University Press, 2001. http://www.jstor.org/stable/j.ctt7t9r1.5.
"Four hundred and fifty years ago": Wells, B. A. and K. L. Wells. "Ames Astrobleme Museum." American Oil & Gas Historical Society, updated August 11, 2022. https://aoghs.org/energy-education-resources/ames-astrobleme-oil-museum/.
"Publish articles on our findings": Hamm, Harold, and Rex E. Olsen. "Oklahoma Arbuckle lime exploration centered on buried astrobleme structure." *Oil & Gas Journal,* April 20, 1992, 113-16.

6 – *Horizontal Drilling: The Game Changer*
"Little two-column story": "Enid Company Drilling Long Horizontal Well." *Tulsa World*, April 21, 1991, G5.
"In the summer of 1989": Lippman, Thomas W. "The Quiet Death of Natural Gas Price Controls." *Washington Post*, June 25, 1989. https://www.washingtonpost.com/archive/business/1989/06/25/the-quiet-death-of-natural-gas-price-controls/21d0b275-cbb3-438d-8383-f2926678f146/.
"Active rig count plummeted": U.S. Department of Energy. Energy Information Administration, released February 9, 2023. https://www.eia.gov/dnav/ng/hist/e_ertrr0_xr0_nus_cm.htm.
"Saudi Arabia was producing": Mearns, Euan. "Saudi production laid bare." Oil Drum: Europe, March 19, 2007. http://theoildrum.com/node/2372.
"Biden grovels and fist-bumps": Flood, Brian. "Biden's 'shameful' fist-bump with Saudi Arabia's Mohammed bin Salman shocks Twitter, *Washington Post* CEO." Fox News, July 15, 2022. https://www.foxnews.com/media/bidens-fist-bump-saudi-arabias-mohammed-bin-salman-shocks-twitter.
"Five million barrels a day": U.S. Department of Energy. Energy Information Administration. "U.S. Field Production of Crude Oil." September 30, 2022. https://www.eia.gov/dnav/pet/hist/LeafHandler.ashx?n=pet&s=mcrfpus2&f=m.

"Thesis by Michael Ray": "An evaluation of known remaining oil resources in the United States: Project on advanced oil recovery and the states. Volume 1." United States, 1994. https://doi.org/10.2172/10193870.

"Risk is the price you pay": Weinraub, Bernard. "As Taboo Fades, Actors See Little Career Jeopardy in Playing Gay Characters." *New York Times,* September 10, 1997, Section C, 11. https://www.nytimes.com/1997/09/10/movies/as-taboo-fades-actors-see-little-career-jeopardy-in-playing-gay-characters.html.

"Dresser Industries merger": CNN Money. "Halliburton, Dresser Merge." February 26, 1998. https://money.cnn.com/1998/02/26/deals/halliburton/.

"Horizontal work": Reiff, Nathan. "Top 3 Companies Owned by Halliburton." Investopedia, January 23, 2022. https://www.investopedia.com/articles/company-insights/090216/top-3-companies-owned-halliburton-hal.asp.

"Drilled horizontally": Baker Hughes. "North America Rotary Rig Count (Jan 2000–Current)," accessed August 18, 2022. https://rigcount.baker-hughes.com/static-files/90780957-4e13-42d5-81d8-47c7c2c8591f.

"Total field recovery": Nehring, Richard. "Giant Oil Fields and World Oil Resources." RAND. R-2284-CIA, June 1978, vi. https://www.rand.org/content/dam/rand/pubs/reports/2006/R2284.pdf/.

7 – Shale Yes! Cracking the Code of the Bakken

"Harold Hamm": Moore, Stephen. "How North Dakota Became Saudi Arabia." *Wall Street Journal,* October 1, 2011. https://www.wsj.com/articles/SB10001424052970204226204576602524023932438.

"Henry Bakken": "Son of Bakken formation namesake remains reserved." Associated Press, December 3, 2012. https://journalrecord.com/2012/12/03/son-of-bakken-formation-namesake-remains-reserved-energy/.

"The Bice 1-29H flowed": Continental Resources. "Continental Resources Reports Completion Results on Its First Well in the Three Forks/Sanish Formation in North Dakota Bakken Area." Press Release, May 20, 2008. https://investors.clr.com/2008-05-20-Continental-Resources-Reports-Completion-Results-on-Its-First-Well-in-the-Three-Forks-Sanish-Formation-in-North-Dakota-Bakken-Area.

"U.S. Geological Survey": U.S. Department of the Interior. "Bakken Formation Oil Assessment in North Dakota, Montana will be updated by U.S. Geological Survey." Press Release, updated September 5, 2019. https://www.doi.gov/news/pressreleases/

Bakken-Formation-Oil-Assessment-in-North-Dakota-Montana-will-be-
updated-by-US-Geological-Survey.

"Top fields in the world": North Dakota Petroleum Foundation. "2022
ND Oil and Natural Gas Production Infographic." March 23, 2022. https://
ndpetroleumfoundation.org/2022-nd-oil-and-natural-gas-production-
infographic/.

"Diesel prices": U.S. Department of Energy. Energy Information Adminis-
tration. "Weekly U.S. No 2 Diesel Ultra Low Sulfur (0-15 ppm) Retail Prices."
February 13, 2023. https://www.eia.gov/dnav/pet/hist/LeafHandler.ashx?n=-
PET&s=EMD_EPD2DXL0_PTE_NUS_DPG&f=W.

8 – *The Renaissance: America Achieves Energy Independence*

"Largest energy producer": U.S. Department of Energy. Energy Information
Administration. "The United States is now the largest global crude oil
producer." September 12, 2018. https://www.eia.gov/todayinenergy/detail.
php?id=37053.

"101 billion cubic feet of natural gas": Dobbs, Kevin. "November Natural
Gas Futures Fall Following Second Straight Triple-Digit Storage Injection."
Natural Gas Intel, September 29, 2022. https://www.naturalgasintel.com/
november-natural-gas-futures-fall-following-second-straight-triple-digit-
storage-injection/.

"11 billion cubic feet of natural gas": U.S. Department of Energy. Energy
Information Administration. "U.S. LNG export capacity to grow as three
additional projects begin construction." September 6, 2022. https://www.eia.
gov/todayinenergy/detail.php?id=53719#.

"$6,000 in income": Trump White House. "Trump Administration
Accomplishments." January 2021. https://trumpwhitehouse.archives.gov/
trump-administration-accomplishments/#:~:text=Before%20the%20
China%20Virus%20invaded,during%20the%20entire%20previous%20
administration.

"6 million barrels a day": U.S. Department of Energy. Energy Information
Administration. "U.S. Field Production of Crude Oil." November 30, 2022.
https://www.eia.gov/dnav/pet/hist/LeafHandler.ashx?n=PET&s=CRF-
PUS2&f=M.

"13 million barrels per day": U.S. Department of Energy. Energy Information
Administration. "U.S. Field Production of Crude Oil." November 30, 2022. https://
www.eia.gov/dnav/pet/hist/LeafHandler.ashx?n=PET&s=MCRFPUS2&f=M.

"Over 10 million jobs": Pritchard, Edd. "Study: Oil and gas industry supports more than 11 million jobs nationwide." *Repository*, July 20, 2021. https://www.cantonrep.com/story/news/2021/07/20/study-says-oil-and-gas-industry-supports-11-million-jobs-nationwide/8020371002/.

"7 percent": Baker, Andrew. "Natural Gas, Oil Found to Support Sizeable Chunk of U.S. GDP, Including Pennsylvania." Natural Gas Intel, July 28, 2021. https://www.naturalgasintel.com/natural-gas-oil-found-to-support-sizeable-chunk-of-u-s-gdp-including-pennsylvania/.

"Upward of 30 percent": American Petroleum Institute. "New Analysis: Oklahoma-Made Natural Gas and Oil Drives U.S. Economic Recovery, Strengthens All Industries." Press Release, July 20, 2021. https://www.api.org/news-policy-and-issues/news/2021/07/20/oklahoma-pwc.

9 – The Triple Whammy of Extreme Volatility

"Price discounts": Ma, Richie Ruchuan, Tao Xiong, and Yukun Bao. "The Russia-Saudi Arabia oil price war during the COVID-19 pandemic." *Energy Economics* 102 (2021): 105517. https://doi.org/10.1016/j.eneco.2021.105517.

"Negative $37.63": "U.S. oil prices turn negative as demand dries up." BBC News, April 21, 2020. https://www.bbc.com/news/business-52350082.

"Price of gasoline": U.S. Department of Energy. Energy Information Administration. "Gasoline and Diesel Fuel Update." October 17, 2022. https://www.eia.gov/petroleum/gasdiesel/.

"$3.61 per gallon": AAA. "Higher Pump Prices Reflect War's Dark Uncertainties." February 28, 2022. https://gasprices.aaa.com/higher-pump-prices-reflect-wars-dark-uncertainties/.

"$5.00 per gallon": Edmonds, Ellen. "National Average Hits New All-Time High at $5 Per Gallon." June 13, 2022. https://newsroom.aaa.com/2022/06/national-average-hits-new-all-time-high-at-5-per-gallon/#:~:text=WASHINGTON%2C%20D.C.%20(June%2013%2C,summer%20driving%20season%20ramps%20up.

"Here's the situation": Sabes, Adam. "President Biden seems to praise high gas prices as 'incredible transition' Americans must go through." Fox News, May 24, 2022. https://www.foxnews.com/politics/president-biden-incredible-transition-high-gas-prices.

"Record-high levels of coal use": International Energy Agency. "The world's coal consumption is set to reach a new high in 2022 as the energy crisis shakes markets." December 16, 2022. https://www.iea.org/news/

the-world-s-coal-consumption-is-set-to-reach-a-new-high-in-2022-as-the-energy-crisis-shakes-markets.

"Endure high gasoline prices": Keene, Houston. "Buttigieg latest Biden official to push green transition as gas prices soar." Fox Business, April 4, 2022. https://www.foxbusiness.com/politics/buttigieg-latest-biden-official-to-push-green-transition-as-gas-prices-soar.

"Granholm said high gas prices": Keene, Houston. "Buttigieg latest Biden official to push green transition as gas prices soar." Fox Business, April 4, 2022. https://www.foxbusiness.com/politics/buttigieg-latest-biden-official-to-push-green-transition-as-gas-prices-soar.

"90 percent built": Mountain Valley Pipeline. "MVP Total Project Work 90% Completed by Year-End." News Release, October 22, 2019. https://www.mountainvalleypipeline.info/wp-content/uploads/2019/10/2019-Project-Recap-and-Cost-Schedule-Update-FINAL2.pdf.

"Stalled by special interest groups": Weber, Maya. "Groups seek stay to prevent Mountain Valley pipeline construction." S&P Global Market Intelligence, January 5, 2022. https://www.spglobal.com/marketintelligence/en/news-insights/latest-news-headlines/groups-seek-stay-to-prevent-mountain-valley-pipeline-construction-68303230.

"Stop digging": Gormley, Ken. *The Death of American Virtue: Clinton vs. Starr.* (New York: Crown, 2010), 246.

"Almost $120 a barrel": U.S. Department of Energy. Energy Information Administration. "Cushing, OK TWI Spot Price FOB." December 21, 2022. https://www.eia.gov/dnav/pet/hist/LeafHandler.ashx?n=PET&s=RWTC&f=M.

"Natural gas reached $10": "U.S. Natural Gas Jumps to $10 for the First Time since 2008." OilPrice.com, August 23, 2022. https://finance.yahoo.com/finance/news/u-natural-gas-jumps-10-132000090.html.

"We would make sure it's eliminated": CNN. "Transcripts—Second Night of Democratic Debates." July 31, 2019. https://transcripts.cnn.com/show/se/date/2019-07-31/segment/02.

"Holding them liable": Sky News Australia. "Biden suggests fossil fuel executives should be jailed." YouTube Video, 0:42. Filmed December 29, 2019. https://www.youtube.com/watch?v=49x01nQAJGk.

"Stopping new pipeline infrastructure": Griffith, Rep. Morgan. "Pres. Biden cannot shirk blame for higher energy prices." *Roanoke Star*, April 12, 2022. https://theroanokestar.com/2022/04/12/pres-biden-cannot-shirk-blame-for-high-energy-prices/.

"Get rid of fossil fuels:" Griffith, Rep. Morgan. "Pres. Biden cannot shirk blame for higher energy prices." *Roanoke Star*, April 12, 2022. https://theroanokestar.com/2022/04/12/pres-biden-cannot-shirk-blame-for-high-energy-prices/.

"No more drilling on federal lands": CNN. "Transcripts—CNN Democratic Presidential Primary Debate." March 15, 2020. https://transcripts.cnn.com/show/se/date/2020-03-15/segment/03.

"Replaced by renewable energy": *USA TODAY*. "Debate transcript: Trump, Biden final presidential debate moderated by Kristen Welker." October 23, 2020. https://www.usatoday.com/story/news/politics/elections/2020/10/23/debate-transcript-trump-biden-final-presidential-debate-nashville/3740152001/.

"No fracking or oil on federal land": *USA TODAY*. "Debate transcript: Trump, Biden final presidential debate moderated by Kristen Welker." October 23, 2020. https://www.usatoday.com/story/news/politics/elections/2020/10/23/debate-transcript-trump-biden-final-presidential-debate-nashville/3740152001/.

"Biden revoked approval": Lefebvre, Ben, and Lauren Gardner. "Biden kills Keystone XL permit, again." *Politico*, January 20, 2021. https://www.politico.com/news/2021/01/20/joe-biden-kills-keystone-xl-pipeline-permit-460555.

"Moratorium on oil and gas leasing": Rott, Nathan, Scott Detrow, and Alana Wise. "Biden Hits 'Pause' on Oil and Gas Leasing on Public Lands and Waters." NPR, January 27, 2021. https://www.npr.org/sections/president-biden-takes-office/2021/01/27/960941799/biden-to-pause-oil-and-gas-leasing-on-public-lands-and-waters.

"Social cost of carbon": Woellert, Lorraine, and Zack Colman. "Biden hikes cost of carbon, easing path of new climate rules." *Politico*, February 26, 2021. https://www.politico.com/news/2021/02/26/biden-carbon-price-climate-change-471787.

"Production on federal land": Volcovici, Valerie. "House Democrats seek reform of federal lands drilling program." Reuters, March 2021. https://www.reuters.com/business/sustainable-business/house-democrats-seek-reform-federal-lands-drilling-program-2021-03-02/.

"Prohibitively expensive": C-SPAN. "Oil Executives Testify on High Gas Prices." April 6, 2022. https://www.c-span.org/video/?519140-1/oil-executives-testify-high-gas-prices.

"National energy tax": C-SPAN. "Oil Executives Testify on High Gas Prices." April 6, 2022. https://www.c-span.org/video/?519140-1/oil-executives-testify-high-gas-prices.

"Increase taxes on energy producers": Frazin, Rachel. "Biden budget aims to raise $35B from cutting fossil fuel tax benefits." *The Hill*, May 28, 2021. https://thehill.com/policy/energy-environment/556031-biden-budget-aims-to-raise-35b-from-cutting-fossil-tax-benefits/.

"Biden asked foreign operators": Hunnicutt, Trevor, and Jeff Mason. "U.S. calls on OPEC and its allies to pump more oil." Reuters, August 11, 2021. https://www.reuters.com/world/middle-east/us-call-opec-its-allies-increase-oil-production-cnbc-2021-08-11/.

"Methane fee": "Democrats float new methane fee in spending bill." Reuters, October 28, 2021. https://www.reuters.com/world/us/democrats-float-new-methane-fee-spending-bill-2021-10-29/.

"Investigation into oil and gas companies": Woellert, Lorraine. "Biden asks FTC to investigate oil and gas companies." *Politico*, November 17, 2021. https://www.politico.com/news/2021/11/17/biden-ftc-investigate-oil-gas-companies-522804.

"FERC Chairman pushed through changes": Willson, Miranda. "FERC issues 'historic' overhaul of pipeline approvals." E&E News, February 18, 2022. https://www.eenews.net/articles/ferc-issues-historic-overhaul-of-pipeline-approvals/.

"Massive new tax": Stech Ferek, Katy. "Democrats Propose Tax on Large Oil Companies' Profits." *Wall Street Journal*, March 11, 2022. https://www.wsj.com/livecoverage/russia-ukraine-latest-news-2022-03-11/card/democrats-propose-tax-on-large-oil-companies-profits-LGIlAAwuIUF2onWRFZZ1.

"Rule change": Woellert, Lorraine, and Zack Colman. "SEC proposes landmark climate rule." *Politico*, March 21, 2022. https://www.politico.com/news/2022/03/21/sec-outlines-climate-disclosure-rules-for-businesses-00018849.

"$45 billion tax increase": Lenton, Christopher. "Biden Administration's 2023 Budget Doubles Down on Energy Transition." Natural Gas Intel, March 29, 2022. https://www.naturalgasintel.com/biden-administrations-2023-budget-doubles-down-on-energy-transition/.

"Safety of the financial sector": Federal Deposit Insurance Corporation (FDIC). "Statement by Martin J. Gruenberg, Acting Chairman, FDIC Board of Directors on the Request for Comment on the Statement of Principles for Climate-Related Financial Risk Management for Large Financial Institutions." March 30, 2022. https://www.fdic.gov/news/speeches/2022/spmar3022.html.

"Saudi government released": Turak, Natasha. "Biden administration asked Saudi Arabia to postpone OPEC decision by a month, Saudis say." CNBC, October 13, 2022. https://www.cnbc.com/2022/10/13/biden-admin-asked-saudi-arabia-to-postpone-opec-cut-by-a-month-saudis-say.html.

"Consumer prices increased": U.S. Department of Labor. Bureau of Labor Statistics. "Consumer prices up 8.6 percent over year ended May 2022." June 14, 2022. https://www.bls.gov/opub/ted/2022/consumer-prices-up-8-6-percent-over-year-ended-may-2022.htm.

"I wrote an op-ed": Hamm, Harold. "Biden's War on Oil Hits Consumers." *Wall Street Journal*, March 13, 2022. https://www.wsj.com/articles/bidens-war-on-oil-hits-consumers-gas-prices-producer-exporter-energy-drilling-federal-land-11647179341.

"Future of the liberal world order": Parks, Kristine. "High gas prices worth it for 'future of liberal world order,' White House economics adviser tells CNN." Fox News, July 1, 2022. https://www.foxnews.com/media/high-gas-prices-worth-future-liberal-world-order-white-house-economics-adviser-tells-cnn.

"My message": Biden, Joseph R. Twitter post. July 2, 2022, 11:00 AM CT. https://twitter.com/potus/status/1543263229006254080.

"Ouch. Inflation is far too important": Bezos, Jeff. Twitter post. July 2, 2022, 8:42 PM CT. https://twitter.com/JeffBezos/status/1543409762867494912.

"What we're saying": "Transcripts—New Day: Jennifer Granholm Is Interviewed about Oil Supplies; Election Lies Becoming Big Business." CNN, June 15, 2022. https://transcripts.cnn.com/show/nday/date/2022-06-15/segment/06.

"Comments from Treasury Secretary Janet Yellen": Chasmar, Jessica. "Treasury Sec. Yellen says only way to fix energy crisis is to 'move to renewables.'" Fox Business, June 19, 2022. https://www.foxbusiness.com/politics/treasury-sec-yellen-says-only-way-fix-energy-crisis-move-renewables.

"Secretary Yellen is tasked with": U.S. Department of the Treasury. "Duties and Functions FAQs." Accessed July 19, 2022. https://home.treasury.gov/subfooter/faqs/duties-and-functions-faqs#:~:text=The%20Secretary%20of%20the%20Treasury%20is%20responsible%20for%20formulating%20and,and%20managing%20the%20public%20debt.

"U.S. GNP": Macrotrends.net. "U.S. GNP 1962–2022." Based on World Bank, accessed July 20, 2022. https://www.macrotrends.net/countries/USA/united-states/gnp-gross-national-product.

"Total Primary Energy Consumption": U.S. Department of Energy. Energy Information Administration. *March 2022—Monthly Energy Review*, March 29, 2022, 19. https://www.eia.gov/totalenergy/data/monthly/archive/00352203.pdf.

"Tens of thousands of farmers": Colton, Emma. "Dutch farmers form 'freedom convoys' to protest government's strict environmental rules." Fox News, July 10, 2022. https://www.foxnews.com/world/dutch-farmers-form-freedom-convoys-protest-governments-strict-environmental-rules.

"Not all farmers can continue": Corder, Mike. "EXPLAINER: Why are Dutch farmers protesting over emissions?" Associated Press, June 28, 2022. https://apnews.com/article/netherlands-wildlife-the-hague-a0809b0fb37e8923ac9184b86325d2e3.

"Ban on agrochemicals": Priyadarshana, Tharaka S. "Sri Lanka's hasty agrochemical ban." *Science* 374, no. 6752 (December 2021): 1209. https://doi.org/10.1126/science.abm9186.

"Rice crops dropped": Swenson, Shea. "Sri Lanka's Organic Experiment Went Very, Very Wrong." *Modern Farmer*, March 26, 2022. https://modernfarmer.com/2022/03/sri-lanka-organic-experiment/.

"Agricultural production will decrease": Jayasinghe, Uditha. "Sri Lanka appeals for farmers to plant more rice as food shortage looms." Reuters, May 31, 2022. https://www.reuters.com/markets/commodities/sri-lanka-appeals-farmers-plant-more-rice-food-shortage-looms-2022-05-31/.

"Destroy the American economy": Hanson, Victor Davis. "Biden and Oil: Destroy America in Order to Save It." American Greatness, June 21, 2022. https://amgreatness.com/2022/06/21/biden-and-oil-destroy-america-in-order-to-save-it/.

11 – Pipelines of Power

"Just say thank you, please": Richardson, Valerie. "Obama takes credit for U.S. oil-and-gas boom: 'That was me, people.'" *Washington Times*, November 28, 2018. https://www.washingtontimes.com/news/2018/nov/28/obama-takes-credit-us-oil-and-gas-boom-was-me-peop/.

"Miles of pipes": Energy Infrastructure. "Why Pipelines?" Accessed October 23, 2022. https://www.energyinfrastructure.org/pipeline/why-pipelines.

"Two million dekatherms": Mountain Valley Pipeline. "Overview." Accessed October 23, 2022. https://www.mountainvalleypipeline.info/overview/.

"We're going to end fossil fuel": Phippen, Thomas. "Biden keeping his promise to 'end fossil fuel' increased gas prices, RSC memo shows." Fox Business, March 28, 2022. https://www.foxbusiness.com/politics/biden-fossil-fuel-gas-prices-promise-republican-study-comittee-memo.

"I am in favor of banning fracking": Cawthorne, Cameron. "Harris: 'There Is No Question I'm in Favor of Banning Fracking.'" *Washington Free Beacon*, September 4, 2019. https://freebeacon.com/politics/harris-there-is-no-question-im-in-favor-of-banning-fracking.

"No more, no new fracking": "Transcripts—CNN Democratic Presidential Primary Debate." CNN, March 15, 2020. https://transcripts.cnn.com/show/se/date/2020-03-15/segment/03.

"I am not banning fracking": German, Ben. "Biden: 'I am not banning fracking.'" Axios, August 31, 2020. https://www.axios.com/2020/08/31/joe-biden-fracking-not-banning.

"Biden will not end fracking": Allassan, Fadel. "Kamala Harris: 'Joe Biden will not ban fracking. That is a fact.'" Axios, October 7, 2020. https://www.axios.com/2020/10/08/kamala-harris-biden-ban-fracking.

"Joe Biden will not ban fracking": Harris, Kamala. Twitter post. October 7, 2020, 8:46 PM CT. https://twitter.com/kamalaharris/status/1314019248344305664.

"Joe Biden has been clear": Block, Eliana. "VERIFY: Did Joe Biden say he would ban fracking?" WUSA9, October 9, 2020. https://www.wusa9.com/article/news/verify/verify-does-joe-biden-want-to-end-fracking/65-1595c0c6-a90f-4e1b-ab55-5c516fa28240.

"I have met allies who can report": Harvey, Fiona. "Russia 'secretly working with environmentalists to oppose fracking.'" *The Guardian*, June 19, 2014. https://www.theguardian.com/environment/2014/jun/19/russia-secretly-working-with-environmentalists-to-oppose-fracking.

"Phony environmental groups": U.S. House of Representatives. Committee on Science, Space, and Technology. *Russian Attempts to Influence U.S. Domestic Energy Markets by Exploiting Social Media*, March 1, 2018, 6. https://republicans-science.house.gov/_cache/files/f/d/fd019c96-dd07-466e-bd46-33a430d05288/A0504DB9367098664CAE6FC6EF9EC854.sst-staff-report---russian-attempts-to-influence-u.s.-domestic-energy-markets-by-exploiting-social-media-03.01.18.pdf.

"Where is the U.S. gonna go?": Silverstein, Joe. "Citadel CEO says energy policy in the U.S. and Europe is a 'train wreck.'" Fox News, May 25, 2022. https://www.foxnews.com/media/citadel-ceo-energy-policy-in-the-u-s-and-europe-is-a-train-wreck.

12 – It's Easy Being Green

"New Ice Age?": "Vintage Scan #36: *Parade* (March 21, 1971)." RetroSpace, July 11, 2015. https://www.retrospace.org/2015/07/vintage-scan-36-parade-march-21-1971.html.

"Copy of a book": Impact Team. *The Weather Conspiracy: The Coming of the New Ice Age.* New York: Ballantine Books, 1977.

"Toyota Motor Corp's leader": Landers, Peter. "Toyota's Chief Says Electric Vehicles Are Overhyped." *Wall Street Journal,* December 17, 2020. https://www.wsj.com/articles/toyotas-chief-says-electric-vehicles-are-overhyped-11608196665.

"Current business model": Landers, Peter. "Toyota's Chief Says Electric Vehicles Are Overhyped." *Wall Street Journal,* December 17, 2020. https://www.wsj.com/articles/toyotas-chief-says-electric-vehicles-are-overhyped-11608196665.

"Flower on a high summit": Landers, Peter. "Toyota's Chief Says Electric Vehicles Are Overhyped." *Wall Street Journal,* December 17, 2020. https://www.wsj.com/articles/toyotas-chief-says-electric-vehicles-are-overhyped-11608196665.

"The government of Norway": Southwell, Hazel. "Norway Wants People to Park Their EVs and Ride the Bus." *The Drive,* May 5, 2022. https://www.thedrive.com/news/norway-wants-people-to-park-their-evs-and-ride-the-bus.

"Dramatic impacts for investors": BlackRock's Global Executive Committee. "Net Zero: A Fiduciary Approach." BlackRock, January 26, 2021. https://www.blackrock.com/corporate/investor-relations/2021-blackrock-client-letter.

"All in on ESG": Terrett, Eleanor, and Charlie Gasparino. "Larry Fink's BlackRock to benefit from government ESG push." Fox Business, October 28, 2021. https://www.foxbusiness.com/financials/larry-finks-blackrock-benefit-esg.

"Chevron's benefited society": Yahoo! News Transcript. "Buffet: 'I have no compunction about owning Chevron,'" May 1, 2021. https://news.yahoo.com/buffett-no-compunction-owning-chevron-190051565.html.

"That could change": Yahoo! News Transcript. "Buffet: 'I have no compunction about owning Chevron,'" May 1, 2021. https://news.yahoo. com/buffett-no-compunction-owning-chevron-190051565.html.

"Divesting from entire sectors": Fink, Larry. "Larry Fink's 2022 Letter to CEOs: The Power of Capitalism." BlackRock, January 17, 2022. https://www. blackrock.com/corporate/investor-relations/larry-fink-ceo-letter.

"Geothermal sources": Orkustofnun—National Energy Authority of Iceland. "Geothermal." Accessed October 10, 2022. https://nea.is/geothermal/#:~:text=Iceland%20is%20a%20pioneer%20in,the%20country's%20total%20electricity%20production.

"More than triple 1990 levels": Newburger, Emma. "China's greenhouse gas emissions exceed those of U.S. and developed countries combined, report says." CNBC, May 6, 2021. https://www.cnbc.com/2021/05/06/chinas-greenhouse-gas-emissions-exceed-us-developed-world-report.html.

"Between 2010 and 2019": World Bank. "CO2 Emissions (kt) - China, United States." Climate Watch, 2020. GHG Emissions. Washington, D.C.: World Resources Institute. https://data.worldbank.org/indicator/EN.ATM.CO2E.KT?end=2019&locations=CN-US&start=2004.

"By the year 2000": Huggins, Laura E. "Climate Armageddon?" Hoover Institution, January 5, 2011. https://www.hoover.org/research/climate-armageddon.

"Energy demand nearly tripled": Ritchie, Hannah, Max Roser, and Pablo Rosado. "Energy Production and Consumption." Our World in Data, accessed October 23, 2022. https://ourworldindata.org/energy-production-consumption.

"Oil production soared": Organisation for Economic Co-operation and Development (2022). "Crude oil production (indicator)." Accessed December 23, 2022. Doi: 10.1787/4747b431-en.

"Global GDP": Our World in Data. "World GDP." Based on World Bank & Maddison (2017). https://ourworldindata.org/grapher/world-gdp-over-the-last-two-millennia?time=earliest..latest.

"Life expectancy": Macrotrends.net. "U.S. Life Expectancy, 1950–2023." Based on United Nations, World Population Prospects, accessed February 14, 2023. https://www.macrotrends.net/countries/USA/united-states/life-expectancy.

"Climate change will shrink": Ciaccia, Chris. "Climate change will shrink 'virtually all' economies around the globe by 2100, study warns." Fox News,

August 19, 2019. https://www.foxnews.com/science/climate-change-shrink-economies-globe-2100.

"Melting Antarctic ice": Ciaccia, Chris. "Melting Antarctic ice will raise sea levels and might cause humanity to 'give up ... New York.'" Fox News, September 24, 2020. https://www.foxnews.com/science/melting-antarctic-ice-sheet-raise-sea-levels-8-feet-study.

"China built": Vaughan, Adam. "China is building more than half of the world's new coal power." *New Scientist*, April 26, 2022. https://www.newscientist.com/article/2317274-china-is-building-more-than-half-of-the-worlds-new-coal-power-plants/.

"Chinese policymakers recently green-lighted": Collins, Gabriel B. "China's Energy Nationalism Means Coal Is Sticking Around." *Foreign Policy*, June 6, 2022. https://foreignpolicy.com/2022/06/06/china-energy-nationalism-coal/#:~:text=Chinese%20policymakers%20recently%20greenlighted%20a,of%20the%20entire%20European%20Union.

"Our CO_2 emissions": U.S. Environmental Protection Agency. "Climate Change Indicators: U.S. Greenhouse Gas Emissions." Updated July 2022. https://www.epa.gov/climate-indicators/climate-change-indicators-us-greenhouse-gas-emissions.

"In just five years": Yücel, Mine, and Michael D. Plante. "GDP Gain Realized in Shale Boom's First 10 Years." Federal Reserve Bank of Dallas, August 20, 2019. https://www.dallasfed.org/research/economics/2019/0820.

"U.S. economic output": Benson, Tim. "Research & Commentary: New Report Says Fracking Saved Americans $1.1 Trillion over Past Decade." The Heartland Institute, November 21, 2019. https://www.heartland.org/publications-resources/publications/research--commentary-new-report-says-fracking-saved-americans-11-trillion-over-past-decade.

"U.S. Chamber of Commerce Study": Benson, Tim. "Research & Commentary: Fracking Has Turned United States into World's Leading Oil Producer." The Heartland Institute, September 19, 2018. https://www.heartland.org/publications-resources/publications/research--commentary-fracking-has-turned-united-states-into-worlds-leading-oil-producer.

"1.1 trillion in energy savings": Benson, Tim. "Research & Commentary: New Report Says Fracking Saved Americans $1.1 Trillion over Past Decade." The Heartland Institute, November 21, 2019. https://www.heartland.org/publications-resources/publications/research--commentary-new-report-says-fracking-saved-americans-11-trillion-over-past-decade.

328 • **Citations by Chapter**

"Tesla's Supercharger stations": Korosec, Kirsten. "Tesla owners can now see how much solar or coal is powering their EVs." *Tech Crunch,* April 16, 2021. https://techcrunch.com/2021/04/16/tesla-owners-can-now-see-how-much-solar-or-coal-is-powering-their-evs/. https://electrek.co/2021/04/27/tesla-power-all-superchargers-with-renewable-energy-this-year.

"Tesla will eventually disconnect": Lambert, Fred. "Tesla plans to disconnect 'almost all' Superchargers from the grid and go solar+battery, says Elon Musk." ElecTrek, June 9, 2017. https://electrek.co/2017/06/09/tesla-superchargers-solar-battery-grid-elon-musk/.

"Cut discretionary spending": McKinsey & Company. "How current events are shaping German consumer behavior," October 31, 2022. https://www.mckinsey.com/capabilities/growth-marketing-and-sales/our-insights/survey-german-consumer-sentiment-during-the-coronavirus-crisis.

"In California": Mulkern, Anne C. "Surging electric bills threaten Calif. climate goals." E&E News, April 5, 2022. https://www.eenews.net/articles/surging-electric-bills-threaten-calif-climate-goals/.

"Not to charge": CBS Los Angeles. "Flex Alert extended to Saturday; EV owners asked now to charge vehicles during peak hours." September 2, 2022. https://www.cbsnews.com/losangeles/news/flex-alert-extended-to-saturday-ev-owners-asked-to-not-charge-vehicles-during-peak-hours/.

"Electricity in the United States": U.S. Department of Energy. Energy Information Administration. "Frequently Asked Questions (FAQs): What is U.S. electricity generation by energy source?" Updated November 2022. https://www.eia.gov/tools/faqs/faq.php?id=427&t=3.

"Vaclav Smil": Mitchell, Russ. "The energy historian who says rapid decarbonization is a fantasy." *Los Angeles Times*, September 5, 2022. https://www.latimes.com/business/story/2022-09-05/the-energy-historian-who-says-rapid-decarbonization-is-a-fantasy.

"Amin H. Nasser": Saudi Aramco. "Remarks by CEO Amin H. Nasser at Schlumberger Digital Forum 2022." September 20, 2022. https://www.aramco.com/en/news-media/speeches/2022/remarks-by-amin-h-nasser-at-schlumberger-digital-forum.

13 – Presidential Trumpets

"$38 million ": MacPherson, James. "North Dakota can claim pipeline policing costs as damages." AP News, October 20, 2021. https://apnews.com/

article/donald-trump-business-bismarck-north-dakota-wayne-stenehjem-2442da227012c9d2fd1b7b91dfddeb13.

"Cheap gasoline and diesel fuel": U.S. Department of Energy. Energy Information Administration. "Gasoline and Diesel Fuel Update." October 17, 2022. https://www.eia.gov/petroleum/gasdiesel/.

14 – Power Failures: How to Ensure They Don't Happen

"Sensible Bjorn Lomborg": "Sensible alternatives to Russian oil and gas required." *Business Day*, March 17, 2022.

"Energy potential": Layton, Bradley E. "A Comparison of Energy Densities of Prevalent Energy Sources in Units of Joules Per Cubic Meter." *International Journal of Green Energy* 5 (2008): 441. https://drexel.edu/~/media/Files/great-works/pdf_sum10/WK8_Layton_EnergyDensities.ashx.

"Millions went without power": Douglas, Erin. "Gov. Greg Abbott wants power companies to 'winterize.' Texas' track record won't make that easy." *The Texas Tribune*, February 20, 2021. https://www.texastribune.org/2021/02/20/texas-power-grid-winterize/.

"Lost their lives": Svitek, Patrick. "Texas puts final estimate of winter storm death toll at 246." *The Texas Tribune*, January 2, 2022. https://www.texas-tribune.org/2022/01/02/texas-winter-storm-final-death-toll-246/amp/.

"State's power grid": Douglas, Erin. "Texas was 'seconds and minutes' away from catastrophic monthslong blackouts, officials say." *The Texas Tribune*, February 18, 2021. https://www.texastribune.org/2021/02/18/texas-power-outages-ercot/.

"In less than decade": Bullard, Nathaniel. "Predicting the Future of Texas's Grid Is a Texas-Sized Challenge." Bloomberg, May 19, 2022. https://www.bloomberg.com/news/articles/2022-05-19/solar-wind-batteries-will-change-the-texas-power-grid#xj4y7vzkg.

"Fell by ninety-three percent": Editorial Board. "Texas Spins into the Wind." *Wall Street Journal*, February 17, 2021. https://www.wsj.com/articles/texas-spins-into-the-wind-11613605698.

"Not in Texas or Oklahoma": Francis-Smith, Janice. "Commission defers ONG's storm bills." *Journal Record*, March 2, 2021. https://journalrecord.com/2021/03/02/commission-defers-ongs-storm-bills/.

"Will Texas": Solomon, Dan. "Solar Power Is Bailing Texas Out This Summer." *Texas Monthly*, July 12, 2022. https://www.texasmonthly.com/news-politics/renewable-energy-texas-grid-heat-wave/.

"Very next day": Guilfoil, Kyla. "Texas power grid faces limited solar energy supply." ABC News, July 13, 2022. https://abcnews.go.com/US/texas-power-grid-faces-limited-solar-supply-amid/story?id=86755657.

 "Tesla owners": Hawkins, Andrew J. "Tesla asks Texans to avoid charging their EVs during peak times because of the heatwave." The Verge, July 13, 2022. https://www.theverge.com/2022/7/13/23207428/tesla-texas-ev-charging-heatwave-off-peak-grid.

"World War I": Black, Brian C. "How World War I Ushered in the Century of Oil." *The Observer*, April 4, 2017. https://observer.com/2017/04/world-war-i-ushered-in-the-century-of-oil-global-economy-geopolitics-national-security/.

"Dust Bowl years": Mullins, William H. "Okie Migrations." Oklahoma Historical Society. Accessed October 25, 2022. https://www.okhistory.org/publications/enc/entry.php?entry=OK008.

"Raised the IQ": Etter, Jim Marion. "Did you know this about Oklahoma?" *Tampa Bay Times*, December 21, 2003. https://www.tampabay.com/archive/2003/12/21/did-you-know-this-about-oklahoma/.

"California remains": California Department of Food and Agriculture. "California Agricultural Production Statistics." Accessed October 25, 2022. https://www.cdfa.ca.gov/Statistics/.

"Electricity in the Bay Area": U.S. Department of Labor. Bureau of Labor Statistics. "Average energy prices for the United States, regions, census divisions, and selected metropolitan areas." Accessed February 15, 2022. https://www.bls.gov/regions/midwest/data/averageenergyprices_selectedareas_table.htm.

"Lead in energy prices": Connelley, Eileen AJ. "Gas has nearly reached an incredible $10 a gallon." *New York Post*, June 4, 2022. https://nypost.com/2022/06/04/gas-nears-10-a-gallon-at-california-station-tops-5-in-nyc/.

"California's CO$_2$ emissions": Menton, Francis. "California's Zero Carbon Plans: Can Anybody Here Do Basic Arithmetic?" Manhattan Contrarian, May 11, 2021. https://www.manhattancontrarian.com/blog/2021-5-11-californias-zero-carbon-plans-can-anybody-here-do-basic-arithmetic.

"Michael Shellenberger": Justice, Tristan. "California Wildfire Devastation Was Entirely Preventable through Proper Land Management." *The Federalist*, September 3, 2021. https://thefederalist.com/2021/09/03/devastation-from-california-wildfires-was-entirely-preventable-through-proper-land-management/.

"Newsom cut his state's budget": Justice, Tristan. "California Wildfire Devastation Was Entirely Preventable through Proper Land Management." *The Federalist*, September 3, 2021. https://thefederalist.com/2021/09/03/devastation-from-california-wildfires-was-entirely-preventable-through-proper-land-management/.

"Quarter of the electricity": U.S. Department of Energy. Energy Information Administration. "California was the largest net electricity importer of any state in 2019," December 7, 2020. https://www.eia.gov/todayinenergy/detail.php?id=46156.

"California in 2020 imported": California Energy Commission. "Foreign Sources of Crude Oil Imports to California 2020." Updated April 6, 2021. https://www.energy.ca.gov/data-reports/energy-almanac/californias-petroleum-market/foreign-sources-crude-oil-imports.

"Sensible alternatives to Russian oil and gas": Lomborg, Bjorn. "Sensible Alternatives to Russian Oil and Gas Required." *Business Day*, March 17, 2022. https://www.businesslive.co.za/bd/opinion/2022-03-17-bjorn-lomborg-sensible-alternatives-to-russian-oil-and-gas-required/.

"Google searches": Diaz, Clarisa. "Germans are looking to firewood for energy as natural gas prices soar." Quartz, August 26, 2022. https://www.yahoo.com/video/germans-looking-firewood-energy-natural-140600963.html.

15 – Market Changer: How and Why We Fixed Global Oil Markets

"$4 trillion": "Oil and gas industry earned $4 trillion last year, says IEA chief." Reuters, February 14, 2023. https://www.reuters.com/business/energy/oil-gas-industry-earned-4-trillion-last-year-says-iea-chief-2023-02-14/.

"Fundamental supply and demand": McCrank, John. "Oil plunge due to fundamentals, not financial markets: CFTC chairman." Reuters, April 21, 2020. https://www.reuters.com/article/us-usa-oil-cftc/oil-plunge-due-to-fundamentals-not-financial-markets-cftc-chairman-idUSKCN2232QR.

"Nearly $4 million barrels": U.S. Department of Energy. Energy Information Administration. "U.S. Exports of Crude Oil." January 31, 2023. https://www.eia.gov/dnav/pet/hist/LeafHandler.ashx?n=PET&s=CREXUS2&f=M.

"The market worked": Pound, Jesse. "CME boss says his exchange is not for retail investors and it's 'no secret' futures can go negative." CNBC, April 22, 2020. https://www.cnbc.com/2020/04/22/

cme-boss-says-his-exchange-is-not-for-retail-investors-and-its-no-secret-futures-can-go-negative.html.

"Group of traders in London": Vaughan, Liam, Kit Chellel, and Benjamin Bain. "The Essex Boys: How Nine Traders Hit a Gusher with Negative Oil." *Bloomberg*, December 9, 2020. https://www.bloomberg.com/news/features/2020-12-10/stock-market-when-oil-when-negative-these-essex-traders-pounced.

16 – ESG: Horizontal Drilling Delivers Again

"Sub-Saharan Africa": World Bank Global Electrification Database. "Access to Electricity (% of Population)—Sub-Saharan Africa." Accessed October 26, 2022. https://data.worldbank.org/indicator/EG.ELC.ACCS.ZS?locations=ZG.

"Increase tree cover": Kerry, John. "Remarks at World Economic Forum, Davos 2021." Speech, Davos, Switzerland, January 27, 2021. https://www.state.gov/remarks-at-world-economic-forum-davos-2021/.

"Around 2.4 billion people": World Health Organization. "Household air pollution and health," September 22, 2021. https://www.who.int/en/news-room/fact-sheets/detail/household-air-pollution-and-health.

"Tearing down forests": VOA News. "Charcoal Trade Is Destroying Africa's Forest Cover." September 29, 2019. https://learningenglish.voanews.com/a/charcoal-trade-is-destroying-africa-s-forest-cover/5100247.html.

"Burning heavily-polluting fuels": Ogunbunmi, Kayode, and Madalitso Mwando. "Africa's climate policies burned by firewood dependence." Thomas Reuters Foundation, June 2, 2014. https://news.trust.org/item/20140530183509-63ekq.

"Without any access to electricity": International Energy Agency. *SDG7: Data and Projections*. Paris (2022). https://www.iea.org/reports/sdg7-data-and-projections/access-to-electricity.

"Access to clean cooking": International Energy Agency. *SDG7: Data and Projections*. Paris (2022). https://www.iea.org/reports/sdg7-data-and-projections/access-to-clean-cooking#abstract.

"100 million people": World Population Review. "Countries in Africa 2022." Accessed July 25, 2022. https://worldpopulationreview.com/country-rankings/countries-in-africa.

"Nine out of ten people": Bergen, Molly. "A River Lined with Smoke: Charcoal and Forest Loss in the Democratic Republic of Congo." World Resources

Institute, October 24, 2017. https://www.wri.org/insights/river-lined-smoke-charcoal-and-forest-loss-democratic-republic-congo.

"No electricity": Rockefeller Foundation. "End Energy Poverty." Accessed July 26, 2022. https://www.rockefellerfoundation.org/commitment/power/.

"Produce one unit of prosperity": Zitelman, Rainer. "Anyone Who Doesn't Know the Following Facts about Capitalism Should Learn Them." *Forbes*, July 27, 2020. https://www.forbes.com/sites/rainerzitelmann/2020/07/27/anyone-who-doesnt-know-the-following-facts-about-capitalism-should-learn-them/?sh=6117c3dc3dc1.

"Only the last four generations": Burger, Oskar, Annette Baudisch, and James W. Vaupel. "Human mortality improvement in evolutionary context." *Proceedings of the National Academy of Sciences (PNAS)*, 109, no. 44 (October 15, 2012): 18210-14. https://www.pnas.org/doi/10.1073/pnas.1215627109.

"States are pushing back": Catenacci, Thomas. "Republican states are planning an all-out assault on woke banks: 'We won't do business with you.'" Fox News, August 4, 2022. https://www.foxbusiness.com/politics/republican-states-planning-assault-woke-banks-wont-do-business.

"Europe imports megatons": Flach, Bob, and Sophie Bolla. "EU Wood Pellet Annual." U.S. Department of Agriculture. Foreign Agricultural Service, July 13, 2022, 10. https://apps.fas.usda.gov/newgainapi/api/Report/Download-ReportByFileName?fileName=EU%20Wood%20Pellet%20Annual_The%20Hague_European%20Union_E42022-0049.

"Our ESG story": Continental Resources. "What we care about and why." Accessed July 26, 2022. https://www.clr.com/environmental-social-and-governance-esg/.

"Global energy consumption": Ritchie, Hannah. "How have the world's energy sources changed over the last two centuries?" Our World in Data, December 1, 2021. https://ourworldindata.org/global-energy-200-years.

"Fertilizer shortages are real": Parks, Kristine. "Biden official says food shortages will push farmers to green energy: 'Never let a crisis go to waste.'" Fox News, May 1, 2022. https://www.foxnews.com/media/biden-official-says-food-shortages-will-push-farmers-green-energy-never-let-crisis-go-waste.

"Broad-based, market-cap-weighted index": S&P Global. "S&P ESG." Accessed July 26, 2022. https://www.spglobal.com/spdji/en/index-family/esg/core-esg/sp-esg/#overview.

"Two claims alleging racial bias": Jonathan, Robert. "'A clear case of wacktivism': Elon Musk lashes out at 'scam' S&P 500 ESG Index." BizPacReview, May 19, 2022. https://www.bizpacreview. com/2022/05/19/a-clear-case-of-wacktivism-elon-musk-lashes-out-at-scam-sp-500-esg-index-1239695/.

"Few automobiles": Branigan, Tania. "China and cars: a love story." *Guardian*, December 14, 2012. https://www.theguardian.com/world/2012/dec/14/china-worlds-biggest-new-car-market.

"World's largest emitter": "China overtakes U.S. in greenhouse gas emissions." *New York Times*, June 20, 2007. https://www.nytimes. com/2007/06/20/business/worldbusiness/20iht-emit.1.6227564.html.

"Over 30 percent": Ritchie, Hannah, Max Roser, and Pablo Rosado. "China: CO2 Country Profile." Our World in Data, accessed October 26, 2022. https://ourworldindata.org/co2/country/china#what-share-of-global-co2-emissions-are-emitted-by-the-country.

"Even worse in China": Bradsher, Keith, and Clifford Krauss. "China Is Burning More Coal, a Growing Climate Challenge." *New York Times,* November 3, 2022. https://www.nytimes.com/2022/11/03/business/energy-environment/china-coal-natural-gas.html.

"$25 trillion": Ginn, Vance. "We Know What Works in the War on Poverty." Texas Public Policy Foundation, May 6, 2022. https://www.texaspolicy.com/we-know-what-works-in-the-war-on-poverty/#:~:text=Nationally%2C%20about%20%2425%20trillion%20(adjusted,Poverty%20engendered%20the%20Great%20Society.

"Americans living in poverty": U.S. Library of Congress. Congressional Research Service. *Poverty in the United States in 2020*. R47030, February 10, 2022. https://crsreports.congress.gov/product/pdf/R/R47030.

"Chose the wrong path": Bryce, Robert. "Ban Natural Gas! No, Ban Coal!" *National Review*, June 11, 2012. https://www.nationalreview.com/2012/06/ban-natural-gas-no-ban-coal-robert-bryce/.

"My interview with the *Financial Times*": Brower, Derek. "Harold Hamm: 'Republican, Democrat...I'm an Oilcrat.'" *Financial Times*, January 7, 2022. https://www.ft.com/content/93dffdd3-45f3-4628-b3b6-8204f1dd5777.

17 – EQ v. IQ: Which Will Guide Your Energy Future?

"Russia's state revenue": International Energy Agency. *Energy Fact Sheet: Why does Russian oil and gas matter?* Paris (2022). https://www.iea.org/articles/energy-fact-sheet-why-does-russian-oil-and-gas-matter.

"Almost a third of Iran's": Rome, Henry. "Iran's Oil Exports Are Vulnerable to Sanctions." Washington Institute for Near East Policy, November 9, 2022. https://www.washingtoninstitute.org/policy-analysis/irans-oil-exports-are-vulnerable-sanctions.

"Six thousand coal-burning units": Bloomberg Global Coal Countdown. "Tracking Our Progress towards a Coal-Free Future." Accessed July 27, 2022. https://bloombergcoalcountdown.com/.

"China generates": "China generated over half world's coal-fired power in 2020: study." Reuters, March 28, 2021. https://www.reuters.com/article/us-climate-change-china-coal/china-generated-over-half-worlds-coal-fired-power-in-2020-study-idUSKBN2BK0PZ.

"Chinese banks": Colman, Zack. "China's Xi pledges to end funding for overseas coal power plants." *Politico*, September 21, 2021. https://www.politico.com/news/2021/09/21/chinas-xi-pledges-to-end-funding-for-overseas-coal-power-plants-513493.

"Germany dismantled": Harsanyi, David. "Germany's 'Green' Energy Disaster Is a Warning to the United States." *The Federalist*, June 21, 2022. https://thefederalist.com/2022/06/21/germanys-green-energy-disaster-is-a-warning-to-the-united-states/.

"Electricity prices": GlobalPetrolPrices.com. "Electricity Prices, June 2022." Accessed February 15, 2023. https://www.globalpetrolprices.com/electricity_prices/.

"Burning more coal": "Factbox: Germany fires up extra coal power capacity to plug winter supplies." Reuters,November 2, 2022. https://www.reuters.com/business/energy/germany-fires-up-extra-coal-power-capacity-plug-winter-supplies-2022-11-02/.

"I had a call with MbZ": "Macron tells Biden that UAE, Saudi can barely raise oil output." Reuters, June 28, 2022. https://www.reuters.com/article/macron-biden-oil/corrected-macron-tells-biden-that-uae-saudi-can-barely-raise-oil-output-idUSL8N2YE4KE.

"Litigation": Smith, Lem. "Drilling Down on Federal Leasing Facts." American Petroleum Institute, March 24, 2022. https://www.api.org/news-policy-and-issues/blog/2022/03/24/drilling-down-on-federal-leasing-facts.

"Recognized by *Oil and Gas Investor* magazine": Hart Energy. "Continental Resources—Energy ESG Awards." November 29, 2021. https://www.hartenergy.com/energy-esg-awards/Continental-Resources.

"Twelve million tons of carbon": "Billionaire oil driller invests in Ames-based Summit's carbon-capture pipeline." *Des Moines Register*, March 2, 2022. https://www.desmoinesregister.com/story/news/2022/03/02/carbon-capture-pipeline-planned-summit-gets-250-million-harold-hamm/9341140002/.

"40 million tons": Page, Brad. *Global Status of CCS 2020.* Global CCS Institute, December 1, 2020, 5. https://www.globalccsinstitute.com/wp-content/uploads/2021/03/Global-Status-of-CCS-Report-English.pdf.

"Half a billion you invested": Broder, John M. "Energy Department Issues First Renewable-Energy Loan Guarantee." *New York Times*, March 20, 2009. https://archive.nytimes.com/green.blogs.nytimes.com/2009/03/20/energy-department-issues-first-renewable-energy-loan-guarantee/.

18 – Culture of the Possible from a Wildcatter's Mentality

"Largest oil reserves": Nysveen, Per Magnus. "Reserve Estimates." *American Oil and Gas Reporter*, July 2016. https://www.aogr.com/web-exclusives/exclusive-story/u.s.-holds-most-recoverable-oil-reserves.

"Produce more oil and natural gas": Tubb, Katie. "U.S. Is World's Largest Oil and Natural Gas Producer—Despite Biden's Energy-Constraining Policies." Heritage Foundation, March 8, 2022. https://www.heritage.org/coal-oil-natural-gas/commentary/us-worlds-largest-oil-and-natural-gas-producer-despite-bidens.

"GDP growth require cheap energy": Jack, Kelsey. "How much do we know about the development impacts of energy infrastructure?" World Bank Blog, March 29, 2022. https://blogs.worldbank.org/energy/how-much-do-we-know-about-development-impacts-energy-infrastructure.

"Gasoline and electricity bills": United States Congress. Joint Economic Committee. "To Combat Rising Energy Prices, Unleash American Production." February 2, 2022. https://www.jec.senate.gov/public/index.cfm/republicans/2022/2/to-combat-rising-energy-prices-unleash-american-production.

"Anti-fossil fuel policies": Siciliano, John. "CEI warns lawmakers that a 'Green New Deal' would risk a humanitarian crisis." *Washington Examiner*, January 8, 2019. https://www.washingtonexaminer.com/policy/

energy/cei-warns-lawmakers-that-a-green-new-deal-would-risk-a-humanitarian-crisis.

"Lower income families spend": Noor, Dharna. "Poor Households Spend Nearly Four Times as Much on Utilities as Well-Off Ones." Gizmodo, September 10, 2020. https://gizmodo.com/poor-households-spend-nearly-four-times-as-much-on-util-1845010294.

"No access to electricity": International Energy Agency (2022). *SDG7: Data and Projections*, IEA, Paris. https://www.iea.org/reports/sdg7-data-and-projections/access-to-electricity.

Population of South America: World Population Review. "South America Population 2022."Accessed July 28, 2022. https://worldpopulationreview.com/continents/south-america-population.

Population of North America: World Population Review. "North America Population 2022." Accessed July 28, 2022. https://worldpopulationreview.com/continents/north-america-population.

"Chief Justice John Roberts wrote": Stohr, Greg. "Supreme Court Crimps Biden's Climate Agenda with Limits on EPA." Bloomberg Law, June 30, 2022. https://news.bloomberglaw.com/us-law-week/supreme-court-curbs-epas-climate-authority-in-blow-to-biden.

"Float across the Pacific": Bradsher, Keith, and David Barboza. "China's burning of coal casts a global cloud." *New York Times*, June 11, 2006. https://www.nytimes.com/2006/06/11/world/asia/11iht-coal.1947793.html.

"Eighth largest in the world": Bloomberg Global Coal Countdown. "South Korea." Accessed July 28, 2022. https://bloombergcoalcountdown.com/countries/KR.

"Building more and more": Proctor, Darrell. "Coal Generation Reaches New High in South Korea." POWER, April 1, 2018. https://www.powermag.com/coal-generation-reaches-new-high-in-south-korea/.

"We came to an agreement": Continental Resources. "Continental Resources Enters into Joint Venture with SK E&S of South Korea to Develop Northwest Cana Woodford Shale." October 27, 2014. https://www.prnewswire.com/news-releases/continental-resources-enters-into-joint-venture-with-sk-es-of-south-korea-to-develop-northwest-cana-woodford-shale-626548828.html.

"Retiring its two oldest": Lee, Charles. "South Korea retires two oldest coal-fired power plants, to replace with LNG." S&P Global, January 3, 2022. https://www.spglobal.com/commodityinsights/en/market-insights/

latest-news/energy-transition/010322-south-korea-retires-two-oldest-coal-fired-power-plants-to-replace-with-lng.

"They are importing": Lee, Charles. "South Korea to raise domestic natural gas price again to reflect LNG import costs." S&P Global, June 28, 2022. https://www.spglobal.com/commodityinsights/en/market-insights/latest-news/lng/062822-south-korea-to-raise-domestic-natural-gas-price-again-to-reflect-lng-import-costs#:~:text=04%3A15%20UTC-,South%20Korea%20to%20raise%20domestic%20natural%20gas,to%20refle.

19 – *Giving Back*

"Frank and Jane Phillips gave away": Nelson, Mary Jo. "Phillips Book Tells Oil Story Well." *Oklahoman,* July 24, 1988. https://www.oklahoman.com/story/news/1988/07/24/phillips-book-tells-oil-story-well/62644966007/.

"Numbers are devastating": Centers for Disease Control and Prevention. "Diabetes: The Facts, Stats, and Impacts of Disease." Accessed October 27, 2022. https://www.cdc.gov/diabetes/library/spotlights/diabetes-facts-stats.html#:~:text=37.3%20million%20Americans%E2%80%94about%201,t%20know%20they%20have%20it.

"Selling the patent": T1International. "100 Years: From Gift to Greed." Accessed September 22, 2022. https://www.t1international.com/100years/#:~:text=On%20January%2023rd%2C%201923%20Banting,to%20it%20to%20have%20it.

"Donating $50 million": "Hamm donating $50m to Theodore Roosevelt library." Associated Press,January 6, 2023. https://journalrecord.com/2023/01/06/hamm-donating-50m-to-theodore-roosevelt-library/.

20 – *Powering the Future*

"Our energy department": Lenton, Christopher. "Biden Administration's 2023 Budget Doubles Down on Energy Transition." Natural Gas Intel, March 29, 2022. https://www.naturalgasintel.com/biden-administrations-2023-budget-doubles-down-on-energy-transition/.

"Hamm Institute for American Energy": Burke, Mack. "Historic donation establishes Hamm Institute for American Energy at Oklahoma State University." Oklahoma State University, December 15, 2021. https://news.okstate.edu/articles/communications/2021/historic_donation_establishes_hamm_institute_for_american_energy_at_oklahoma_state_university.html.

"Our announcement": Oklahoma State University. "Hamm Institute for American Energy at Oklahoma State University." Accessed July 29, 2022. https://go.okstate.edu/hamm-institute/.

"80 percent of the world's energy": Environmental and Energy Study Institute. "Fossil Fuels." Updated July 22, 2021. https://www.eesi.org/topics/fossil-fuels/description#:~:text=Fossil%20fuels%E2%80%94including%20coal%2C%20oil,percent%20of%20the%20world's%20energ.

"Stanford University canceled summer classes": Lee, Michael. "Stanford cancels summer classes over power outages experts warn may become more common." Fox News, June 22, 2022. https://www.foxnews.com/us/stanford-cancels-summer-classes-over-power-outages-experts-warn-could-become-more-common.

"Failure to act": Carter, Jimmy. "The State of the Union Annual Message to the Congress (January 19, 1978)." The American Presidency Project, UC Santa Barbara. https://www.presidency.ucsb.edu/documents/the-state-the-union-annual-message-the-congress-2.

"Recent Bloomberg headline": "Shale firebrand Harold Hamm's $4.3 billion play to win 'freedom' to drill." *Dallas Morning News*, October 17, 2022. https://www.dallasnews.com/business/energy/2022/10/17/shale-firebrand-harold-hamms-43-billion-play-to-win-freedom-to-drill/.

"What *The Wall Street Journal* said": Morenne, Benoît. "Fracking Pioneer Harold Hamm to Take Continental Resources Private." *Wall Street Journal*, October 17, 2022. https://www.wsj.com/articles/continental-resoures-gets-buyout-from-founder-11666005800.

Drill Deeper into Energy Policy

UNFORTUNATELY, SO MUCH OF WHAT WE ALL HEAR ABOUT energy is either biased, misinformed, or flat-out wrong.

For every chapter in this book, there are many additional resources you may be interested in. Visit our website for more.

To stay informed about important happenings that affect you and your fellow citizens, please subscribe to our email newsletter.

http://www.haroldhammbook.com

Hamm Institute for American Energy

"**S**OLVING HUMANITY'S GREATEST ENERGY NEEDS" IS THE motto of the Hamm Institute for American Energy, and that's exactly what we're doing.

Our vision is to develop the energy leaders of tomorrow by engaging industry and academia in developing practical, global, science-based solutions through collaboration, research, and development.

We promote scholastic excellence in the field of energy development and production to benefit the global environment and serve consumers across the world. We believe everyone should have access to reliable, affordable energy. Ending energy poverty and ensuring energy abundance is the goal.

The Hamm Institute for American Energy is *possibility thinking on a global scale*. Join us and help change the world!

http://www.haroldhammbook.com

A Man and His Dog

'Kota has been by my side and been my hunting partner since
December 2017. I named him in honor of his home state,
and one of my favorite places, North Dakota.